ENGLISH LITERATURE DURING THE LAST HALF-CENTURY

ENGLISH LITERATURE DURING THE LAST HALF-CENTURY

SECOND EDITION REVISED AND ENLARGED

By

JOHN WILLIAM CUNLIFFE

Essay Index Reprint Series

 BOOKS FOR LIBRARIES PRESS
FREEPORT, NEW YORK

PR
461
.C8
1971

First Published 1923
Reprinted 1971

INTERNATIONAL STANDARD BOOK NUMBER:
0-8369-2276-X

LIBRARY OF CONGRESS CATALOG CARD NUMBER:
70-156636

PRINTED IN THE UNITED STATES OF AMERICA

CONTENTS

PREFACE

THE writer of this volume is not unconscious of the difficulties involved in systematic study of the authors of our own time and of the generation immediately preceding ours; but as he has encouraged young people who are preparing themselves for the writer's task to make themselves acquainted with the works of the nearer, as well as of the more remote past, it seems reasonable that he should afford them what help he can. His intention is to provide guidance for firsthand study—assistance in reading the authors themselves, not a substitute for it—and if the reader's own judgment does not fall in with the criticisms here offered, it is hoped that no harm will be done, and no offence taken on either side. The best teaching is that which stimulates and encourages the student to think for himself.

The bibliographies aim not at minute completeness, but at the giving of information likely to be useful.

The call for a new edition has enabled the author to correct a few slips of the pen or the printer, and to add a considerable amount of new material, in particular a discussion of the plays of J. M. Barrie, many of which were not accessible at the time the first edition appeared.

ENGLISH LITERATURE DURING THE LAST HALF-CENTURY

CHAPTER I

INTRODUCTORY

CONTEMPORARY literature presents at first sight a spectacle of multifarious and even bewildering activity. The flood of reading matter produced by cheap printing and quick communication threatens to swamp the student by its own excess. Yet even in this turbulent and ever increasing stream one can discern certain "main currents" —prevalent tendencies which the thoughtful reader may take note of for guidance in his choice of authors and works, and which may help him to appreciate their underlying significance. The writers of the last half-century, like those of other periods, are subject to the conditions under which they lived, and react, each according to his own individuality, to events and influences which are, in the main, common to all of them, although the effect of any particular one varies in each case, and the elusive element of personality must always, in the final analysis, remain unresolved. A review of the general conditions is a necessary preliminary to the study of individual authors.

The prevailing movement of English life during the half-century was that to which Lord Morley has given the loose but convenient name of "Liberalism." The word is here used in its general rather than its restricted meaning, but it will be convenient to take up the political side of the movement first. Even on this side, the liberalising of English political life was not confined to any one party. The Second Reform Act of 1867, which may be taken as the first noteworthy date of our survey, was introduced into the House of Commons by a Conservative leader, Disraeli, afterwards Lord Beaconsfield, though during its passage it was profoundly modified by the Opposition under their great protagonist, Gladstone. It is with the name of the latter that most of the political reforms of the period are associated. The first Gladstone Government (1868–1874) gave the voter the protection of the secret ballot, abolished religious tests in the universities and the purchase of commissions in the army, threw civil service appointments open to competition, and established a system of universal elementary education— important steps in breaking down the barriers of privilege and affording opportunity and encouragement for further advances in the direction of democracy. The second Gladstone administration (1880–1885) by a further extension of the franchise made democratic government a fact. His later cabinets were engaged in fruitless attempts to settle the Irish question; but already the political phase of reform had given way before the need for social legislation, and the only later political measures we need to record are the limitation of the veto of the House of Lords carried under the premiership of Mr. Asquith (1911) and the extension of the parliamentary suffrage to women, carried by the War Ministry of Mr. Lloyd George (1918).

The impulse to social reform goes back a long way and is closely connected with the change of England from an agricultural to a manufacturing country, which had been proceeding with accumulative force for more than a century. The industrial revolution enormously increased the national wealth, but it made the evils of poverty more acute and more obvious by concentrating them in large urban communities. A contemporary observer writes of a Lancashire manufacturing town in 1842: "Anything like the squalid misery, the slow, mouldering, putrefying death by which the weak and feeble of the working classes are perishing here, it never befel my eyes to behold nor my imagination to conceive. And the creatures seem to have no idea of resisting or even repining. They sit down with oriental submission, as if it was God and not the landlord that was laying his hand upon them." Mr. Sidney Webb, contrasting the condition of the same community in the twentieth century, says: "Though there is still individual squalour and personal misery to be found, the population —six times as numerous as in 1842—may, taken as a whole, safely be described as prosperous, healthy, intellectually alert, taking plenty of holidays, and almost aggressive in its independent self-reliance." This change, which was taking place all over England with increasing force and rapidity up to the outbreak of the Great War, Mr. Webb ascribes to "a certain subtle revolution in the ideas of men," finding expression in specific social movements such as municipal organization, co-operative distribution and production, trades unionism, factory legislation, sanitation, education, collective provision for the dependent, the sick, the aged, the unemployed, "and all that vaguely defined social force commonly designated socialism." He sums up the results as the administration on a communal basis of "such services, once entirely a matter for individual self-provision by each household, as paving, lighting, and cleansing the streets; the prevention of assault, theft, and damage by flood or fire; the removal of fæcal matter and garbage; the public supply and distribution on a large scale of the primary needs of existence, such as water, housing, milk, and now, in one place or another, even other food; the communal provision of artificial light, of certain forms of fuel, and of hydraulic or electric power; the provision of the means of transport and of intercommunication; the collective production, in public forests or on drainage farms, or in connexion with other municipal departments or institutions, of all sorts of agricultural products, and of this or that manufacture; the complete and minutely detailed care of the orphans, the sick, the blind, the deaf and dumb, the crippled, the mentally defective, the infirm and the aged; elaborate provision for the special needs connected with maternity, infancy, childhood, and the disposal of the dead; the provision of schools for children and of opportunities of instruction for adolescents and adults, as well as of libraries, museums, and art galleries; the organization of apprenticeship, technical education, artistic production, and scientific research; the public organization of the labour market; the prevention and treatment of destitution and distress caused by unemployment or misfortune; and the provision, for all classes and all ages, of music and other means of recreation, including the regulation of amusement and even its organization."

The invention of the moving picture show (or cinema, as it is usually called in England) gave urban communities cheap and innocent relaxation in the evenings, and helped to reform the entire programmes of the music-halls, so that they became places where the working-man could take his wife and children without fear of offence. Football changed from a sport mainly aristocratic and largely restricted to the public schools and universities to a great popular spectacle, attracting tens of thousands of onlookers. The annual holiday in the country, at the seaside, or on the Continent, was extended from the middle class to the skilled workmen, thanks to the provision of cheap excursions by rail and steamer. An English cabinet minister, joining with an English labour M. P. in a survey of social conditions at the first Victorian Jubilee (1887), could write with a sense of elation: "The people are better paid; they work fewer hours; they are better fed, clothed and housed; they are better educated; their habits and customs are improved; their sports and pastimes are no longer brutal and demoralizing. The children and women are better cared for and better treated. The wheels of progress have gone on and on· with accelerated speed." Even so pessimistic an observer as George Gissing saw in the second Jubilee "a legitimate triumph of the average man. Look back for threescore years, and who shall affect to doubt that the time has been marked by many improvements in the material life of the English people? Often have they been at loggerheads among themselves, but they have never flown at each other's throats, and from every grave dispute has resulted some substantial gain. They are a cleaner people and a more sober; in every class there is a diminution of brutality; education—stand for what it may—has notably extended; certain forms of tyranny have been abolished; certain forms of suffering, due to heedlessness or ignorance, have been abated." This continued to hold true up to the outbreak of the War, and though the process of remedial legislation was arrested by the necessary concentration of the energies of the nation on military measures, the resulting demand for labour, skilled and unskilled, in the manufacture of munitions and other supplies, produced plentiful employment at high wages for women as well as men, and mitigated the lot of the poorest while it diminished the expenditure of the well-to-do. In spite of sporadic extravagance among those to whom the War brought extraordinary profits, and widespread deprivation owing to high prices and restriction of food supplies, the condition of the labouring poor during the War showed continuous improvement.

It is not surprising that as the working people became more independent and more conscious of their opportunities to enjoy life, they should become not less, but more discontented with the limitations of their lot. The more they did for themselves, the more was done for them, the more it became clear that there was much still left undone. Poverty and degradation, though reduced in amount, remained an appalling sore in the commonwealth, and attracted the earnest and sympathetic attention of all classes. Sir Henry Campbell-Bannerman, who became premier in 1905, declared two years before that over twelve millions of the population of Great Britain were "in the grip of perpetual poverty" and on the verge of hunger. Mr. Lloyd George, who was responsible for the National Insurance Act of 1911, and earned his reputation as "the orator of the new social order," speaking at Glasgow on Scottish Land Reform a few months before the outbreak of the War, said:—

"You have hundreds of thousands of men working unceasingly for wages that barely bring them enough bread to keep themselves and their families above privation. Generation after generation they see their children wither before their eyes for lack of air, light, and space, which is denied them by men who have square miles of it for their own use. Take our cities, the great cities of a great Empire. Right in the heart of them everywhere you have ugly quagmires of human misery, seething, rotting, at last fermenting. We pass them by every day on our way to our comfortable homes. We forget that divine justice never passed by a great wrong. You can hear, carried by the breezes from the north, the south, the east, and the west, ominous rumbling. The chariots of retribution are drawing nigh. How long will all these injustices last for myriads of men, women, and children created in the image of God—how long? I believe it is coming to an end."

It was inevitable that this rapid social transformation, accompanied as it was with a growing sense of dissatisfaction and unrest, should react upon the literature of the period and be reflected by it. But the humanitarian impulse which expressed itself in social reforms was not the only "subtle revolution in the ideas of men" which influenced and often distracted the minds of the thinkers and writers of the time. Democracy was not a new idea, and poverty had been familiar to the human race as far back as its history runs. The political and social revolutions were effected gradually, and the underlying conditions which called for remedy had been brought home to the popular conscience by early Victorian writers such as Carlyle, Ruskin, John Stuart Mill, Matthew Arnold, George Eliot, Mrs. Gaskell, and Charles Kingsley, whose influence, in one direction or another, had contributed in no small degree to the impetus for reform. The disturbing element in the intellectual outlook of the writers of the new generation came, not so much from the application of science to means of production and the subsequent organization of industrial communities, as from the effect of scientific theory upon the views of life, of the origin of the universe and man's place in it, which had hitherto met with almost universal acceptance. The establishment of the theory of evolution by natural selection was the great intellectual event of the century; indeed one must go back to the substitution of the Copernican for the Ptolemaic system to find a parallel. The capital importance of the new theory and its implications was emphasized and brought home to the public by an almost dramatic setting of the circumstances of its first publication and the clash of opinion that followed. Darwin's long years of patient investigation came to a sudden climax owing to the simultaneous arrival of A. R. Wallace, after much briefer research, at the same conclusion, and the theory of natural selection received additional weight, not merely from this coincidence, but from the joint publication of the two papers,—in itself an example of the single-minded search after truth which became the watchword of modern science. In the fuller presentation of the evidence in 'The Origin of Species,' published later in the same year (1859), Darwin avoided any insistence on the question of man's place in nature, which was obviously involved in the new theory, but his ecclesiastical opponents at once seized upon this as the main issue, and forced it to the front. Strategically, they were right, if they were to maintain the position of authority the Church had enjoyed for centuries, although their tactics led to an immediate defeat which was prophetic of the ultimate decision. The famous passage at arms between Huxley and Bishop Wilberforce, who undertook "to smash Darwin" at the Oxford meeting of the British Association for the Advancement of Science in 1860, not merely apprised the champions of orthodoxy of the arrival in the arena of a new antagonist, full of intellectual energy and skilled in debate, but brought them face to face with an issue on which the evidence, ever accumulating, left them no chance of holding their original position. The advocates of the new theory had of course to weather a storm of misrepresentation and obloquy. For ten years, says Mr. Leonard Huxley in the biography of his father, which should be consulted for fuller details of the conflict, "he was commonly identified with the championship of the most unpopular view of the time; a fighter, an assailant of long-established fallacies, he was too often considered a mere iconoclast, a subverter of every other well-rooted institution, theological, educational, or moral." But the storm was soon over, and the very violence of the opposition, by attracting universal attention, led to a speedy acceptance of the new theory, which Lord Salisbury, as Chancellor of the University of Oxford, came to acknowledge in Huxley's presence as having received the unanimous assent of the scientific world.

The acceptance was indeed so general, especially among the opposing forces, which made haste to abandon a position proved untenable, that the victory was almost robbed, for the time being, of its full significance, though it was of course not hidden from the leaders of the new movement. Huxley wrote to his wife in 1873: "The part I have to play is not to found a new school of thought or to reconcile the antagonisms of the old schools. We are in the midst of a gigantic movement greater than that which preceded and produced the Reformation, and really only the continuation of that movement. But there is nothing new in the ideas which lie at the bottom of the movement, nor is any reconcilement possible between free thought and traditional authority. One or other will have to succumb after a struggle of unknown duration, which will have as side issues vast political and social troubles. I have no more doubt that free thought will win in the long run than I have that I sit here writing to you, or that this free thought will organise itself into a coherent system, embracing human life and the world as one harmonious whole. But this organization will be the work of generations of men, and those who further it most will be those who teach men to rest in no lie, and to rest in no verbal delusions." Tyndall's presidential address to the British Association at Belfast in 1874 also breathes the atmosphere of battle. "All religious theories, schemes and systems, which embrace notions of cosmogony, or which otherwise reach into the domain of science, must, in so far as they do this, submit to the control of science, and relinquish all thought of controlling it. Acting otherwise proved disastrous in the past, and it is simply fatuous to-day." For "the domain of science" Tyndall made a large claim:—

"Divorced from matter, where is life to be found? Whatever our faith may say, our knowledge shows them to be indissolubly joined. Every meal we eat, and every cup we drink, illustrates the mysterious control of Mind by Matter. . . .

"Believing as I do in the continuity of Nature, I cannot stop abruptly where our microscopes cease to be of use. Here the vision of the mind authoritatively supplements the vision of the eye. By an intellectual necessity I cross the boundary of the experimental evidence, and discern in the Matter which we, in our ignorance of its latent powers, and notwithstanding our professed reverence for its Creator, have hitherto covered with opprobrium, the promise and potency of all terrestrial Life."

The Presbytery of Belfast passed a resolution in which they described Professors Huxley and Tyndall as "ignoring the existence of God, and advocating pure and simple materialism." Tyndall frankly accepted the challenge in his rejoinder: "Had the possessive pronoun 'our' preceded 'God,' and had the words 'what we consider' preceded 'pure,' this statement would have been objectively true."

The note of intense conviction, passionate earnestness, and absolute confidence, which vibrates in the passages from Tyndall and Huxley just quoted, was in part temperamental, but it was also due to the astonishingly rapid triumph of a new theory of far-reaching significance. This produced on the part of some men of science a dogmatism which went far to rival that of the ecclesiastical opponents they had worsted. Professor Henry Fairfield Osborn, of Columbia University, whose eminence in the world of science will not be disputed, says in his 'Origin and Evolution of Life' (1917): "Biology, like theology, has its dogmas. Leaders have their disciples and blind followers. All great truths, like Darwin's law of selection, acquire a momentum which sustains half-truths and pure dogmas." Mr. H. G. Wells, in the amusing sketch of contemporary personalities he has given to the world under the name of 'Boon' (1915), caricatures the dogmatism of agnostic science in the figure of Dodd, "one of those Middle Victorians who go about with a preoccupied, caulking air, as though, after having been at great cost and pains to banish God from the Universe, they were resolved not to permit Him back on any terms whatever. He has constituted himself a sort of alert customs officer of a materialistic age, saying suspiciously, 'Here, now, what's this rapping under the table here?' and examining every proposition to see that the Creator wasn't being smuggled back under some specious new generalization. Boon used to declare that every night Dodd looked under his bed for the Deity, and slept with a large revolver under his pillow for fear of a revelation." On minds of more delicate texture, in which the older faith kept its emotional hold in spite of intellectual difficulties, the necessary adjustment to new and revolutionary views of nature and man's place in the scheme of things was often painfully disconcerting and sometimes, for a time at least, devastating. We have an admirable picture of the gradual and peaceful liberation of a young mind from traditional beliefs in Mr. Edmund Gosse's autobiographical 'Father and Son' (1907), but in many cases there were stages of depression, confusion, and dismay. Messrs. Sidney Low and Lloyd C. Sanders, authors of 'The History of England during the Reign of Victoria,' concluding their survey of the achievements of the period, record the impression: "To some pessimists the orthodoxy of economics, the orthodoxy of science, and the orthodoxy of faith seemed alike 'bankrupt.'" Even so acute a thinker and so detached an observer as Professor Henry Sidgwick, writing at the end of the nineteenth century and looking back over the victory for liberalism he had helped to win, says: "Well, the years pass, the struggle with what Carlyle used to call 'Hebrew old clothes' is over, Freedom is won, and what does Freedom bring us to? It brings us face to face with atheistic science: the faith in God and Immortality, which we had been struggling to clear from superstition, suddenly seems to be *in the air.*" This attitude was characteristic of the more moderate leaders of liberal thought at the turn of the century, and there was no prominent writer of the period who escaped altogether from the quickening and disturbing effects of the evolutionary hypothesis and its implications.

Limitations and modifications of the theory of natural selection came in due course from the scientists themselves. The tone of dogmatic confidence which marked later Victorian science was largely mitigated as further investigation deepened, instead of explaining, the mystery of the origin of life. We may contrast with Tyndall's confident profession of materialism cited above the avowal of Lord Haldane, President of the British Association a generation later (1908): "The physico-chemical theory of life has not worked in the past and never can work." It is true that within four years we find Professor Schaefer quoting with approval, from the same presidential chair, the words of Gley: "The origin and exercise of the highest faculties of man are conditioned by the purely chemical action of the product of a secretion." But the next president, Sir Oliver Lodge, reverted to mysticism, and there are many other indications that the acceptance of the mechanistic theory is no longer a cardinal doctrine of scientific faith.

The opportunities for compromise and mutual understanding were greatly facilitated by the more moderate attitude of the defenders of orthodoxy, who found their citadel undermined from within as well as attacked from without. The methods of scientific investigation were

applied to the documents on which Protestantism based
its claims, and the theory of development was found to
offer new means of defence and explanation for articles
of the Christian faith.   The books of the Old and of the
New Testament, though robbed of some of their ancient
authority by critical examination, were found to possess
new interest and meaning when interpreted as human
documents, and their spiritual significance was based
upon much surer foundations.   The later defenders of
the faith in England welcomed light from whatever source,
and the spheres of religion and science were found not to
overlap so much as the protagonists on both sides of the
conflict in the latter part of the nineteenth century had
supposed.   When the battle was over, it was agreed
that between religion and science there was no necessary
antagonism.

To sum up, the last half-century was a period of extraordinarily rapid transition, political, social, and intellectual.   Men were called upon to adjust their minds,
often with painful suddenness, to new systems of government, new states of society, and new modes of thought.
It is not surprising that while some accepted the changes
with enthusiasm, others made the necessary adjustments
with difficulty.   Many old landmarks had disappeared,
and those left standing were subjected to an ever increasing fire of criticism from all sides.   The general
sweep of thought was revolutionary; there was no political
principle, no religious dogma, no social tradition, no
moral convention that was not called in question.   To
some conservative minds it appeared merely as an era of
destruction, but, powerless to resist the flood of change,
they remained baffled and confused amid the contending

currents, which drove now in one direction, now in another, but ever onward. Future generations will doubtless discern more constructive achievement than is obvious to the contemporary spectator, who is himself merely an atom in the whirl of conflicting tendencies, but even now a study of individual authors will make it clear that the period was rich in accomplishment, both artistic and intellectual.

It is upon the foundations laid by the writers and thinkers of the last half-century that the present generation has built and must continue to build; this generation has been decimated by the War and disorganized by its aftermath, and after such a shattering experience time will be needed for re-adjustment: the older generation has, in many cases, lost confidence in itself; the newer generation, encouraged on all hands to discover new paths, has not yet found them. It becomes increasingly clear that, commercially and spiritually, as well as financially, the War has to be paid for; and though there are still hopeful individuals, especially among the few left in comfortable prosperity, who believe that the more favourable conditions of pre-war British industry and commerce will return, it is evident to the detached observer that changes are taking place in international relations and in the fabric of British society which cannot fail to have permanent results. The internal transition, responding to the disturbed condition of international trade and finance, is causing widespread social friction, distress, and discouragement. The ancient houses of the nobility are passing into the hands of successful profiteers and philanthropic or educational institutions. The middle class, overburdened by taxation and hampered by convention, appears to the

more radical members of its own body to be losing its long
and wisely exercised control of the national destiny for
lack of ideas and leadership, though to the outsider it
seems to have made a magnificent rally at the general
election of 1922. Whether Mr. Bonar Law's programme
of "stability and tranquillity" will prove any more capable
of fulfilment than Mr. Lloyd George's promise to make
Great Britain "a land fit for heroes to live in" remains, at
the time of writing, still to be seen. The Labour party,
which now constitutes the largest minority in the House
of Commons, has been fortunate in escaping for the
present the responsibility of government, for the exchequer
is so depleted and burdened with obligations for the immediate future that no ministry dare undertake remedial
measures which would involve heavier taxation. The fact
remains that with the withdrawal of the Irish peasant
proprietors owing to the establishment of the Irish Free
State, the British electorate has become almost completely
industrialised, and is now composed predominantly of
wage earners and small-salaried workers, their wives and
daughters. Disappointed by the abandonment of the
housing scheme and educational programme of the Lloyd
George Government, they are quietly but sullenly resentful. They know that political power is within their grasp
when they choose to exercise it, and the prophecies of a
Labour Government vary merely in extent of vision, from
five years to fifty. Meanwhile large numbers of the working class are biding their time, and are free enough from
class-consciousness to vote conservative—at any rate in
1922; their patience is exemplary and their courage apparently indomitable. Beggars and loafers haunt the
streets of London and the large manufacturing towns;

the weekly "dole" of Government aid saps the independence of many thousands who cannot get work and demoralises some who prefer to be idle. The gaiety indulged in by those who still have money to spend seems feverish and superficial; and the extravagant addiction of all ages and classes to sport, with its associated vice of betting, is not an encouraging sign.

Such conditions are not favourable to any kind of artistic production or spiritual effort; but it may well be that the wave of depression resulting from the consequences of the War will pass. Considerable advances have already been made toward restoring the normal life of the nation, and though a great deal remains to be done, the dogged tenacity of the race gives ground for hope that it will recover its characteristic virtues of cheerful courage, good-humoured compromise, kindly tolerance and steadfast commonsense. If the external conditions so shape themselves as to give room for these virtues to be successfully exercised, the progress made in the period before the War will be continued, and will include that imaginative literature in which the English genius has so finely expressed itself in the past. In spite of the serious blow struck by the War at the national well-being, one cannot believe that the present plight of England is one from which there is no recovery. An acute and sympathetic observer of the British public, the late Ambassador Walter Hines Page, remarked during the darkest hour of the War, "they *are* the most amusing and confusing and contradictory of all God's creatures, these English"; their actualities, he sadly admitted, "in many ways are pitiful"; but he still confidently held that "their possibilities are infinite."

CHAPTER II

GEORGE MEREDITH (1828-1909)

ONE has only to recall the names of Browning, Tennyson, Arnold and Swinburne in poetry, and of Dickens, Thackeray and George Eliot in fiction to realize that the earlier Victorian period was rich in both these important divisions of literature. Some of these writers continued to publish after the mid-point of Victoria's reign, but their main activity lay behind it; their reputations were established, and though their influence was by no means spent, the public was already acquainted with their characteristic ideas and modes of expression. It was otherwise with George Meredith, for although his first poems were published in 1851 and his first novel in 1856, his books were for the first thirty years of his career little read and their purpose hardly understood. In 1867 he wrote to Swinburne: "'Vittoria' passes to the limbo where the rest of my works repose," and so late as 1881 he described himself as "an unpopular writer." In 1883 Mark Pattison said of him: "Mr. Meredith is well-known, by name, to the widest circle of readers—the novel readers. By name, because his name is a label warning them not to touch." Lord Morley in his 'Recollections' prints under the date 1881 the following story of the publication, apparently of 'The Tragic Comedians,' in the 'Fortnightly Review':

"It was my good fortune, in days when publishers gave him little welcome, to be of use to him by printing two, or was it three, of his

18

novels in the periodical of which I then had charge. Of one of these George Eliot asked me whether we found that it pleased our readers. I answered as best I could. She said she had only discovered one admirer of it, a very eminent man as it happened, and even him she had convicted of missing two whole numbers without noticing a gap."

All his life Meredith bore a grudge against the British public for its lack of appreciation, which not only kept him, as he put it, "always jogging for a shilling," but left him without the stimulating and restraining influence of contact with a wide circle of readers. He was himself conscious of the latter disadvantage, as well as of the former, commenting bitterly: "Who really cares for what I say? The English people know nothing about me. There has always been something antipathetic between them and me. With book after book it was always the same outcry of censure and disapproval. The first time or two I minded it; then I determined to disregard what people said altogether, and since than I have written only to please myself." And again: "I am, I moan to think, disdainful of an English public, and am beset by the devils of satire when I look on it. That is not a good state for composition, although I have pressing matter, many themes to work out before I take the flight" (1888). In 1902 he still wrote of himself as "an unpopular novelist and an unaccepted poet." He was correspondingly grateful for the appreciation of his work in the United States. "I am justly flattered by their praise, if I win it; their censure, if they deal it to me, I meditate on." The admirable letter to Professor G. P. Baker, of Harvard University, written the following year, is conceived in the same spirit of gratitude—and almost humble gratitude. In 1888, he acknowledged the stimulus to composition he had received from American recognition. "The touch of American money has impressed me with concrete ideas of fame." In one of his very last letters, he complained of his lack of acceptance by the British public as a poet, and added: "Indeed, the run of my novels started from American appreciation."

Born at Portsmouth and educated in part at the Moravian school at Neuwied near Cologne, Meredith made futile excursions into law and journalism, though his engagement as a war correspondent for the 'Morning Post' in the summer of 1866 gave additional vividness to the Italian scenes of 'Vittoria,' of which the title was to have been 'Emilia in Italy,' to parallel 'Emilia in England,' the original title of 'Sandra Belloni,' of which 'Vittoria' is the sequel. About the same time he obtained a regular income as reader for the publishing firm of Chapman and Hall and took the editorship of the 'Fortnightly Review,' their most important literary enterprise, in place of his friend John Morley, when the latter was sent on an official mission to the United States in 1867. Meredith's early career was further hampered by his marriage at twenty-one with the daughter of Thomas Love Peacock; they were ill-mated. "No sun warmed my roof-tree" he said to Clodd; "the marriage was a blunder; she was nine years my senior"; and after a few years they separated. After his marriage to Marie Vulliamy in 1864, he lived for a while at Mickleham, near Dorking, Surrey, and a few years later settled down for the rest of his life at Box Hill in the same neighbourhood. Except for an occasional visit to the Continent, his whole life was spent in the South of England, between

Portsmouth and London. He is as much the poet of this district as Wordsworth is of the Northern lakes. It is a rolling, well-wooded country, and its characteristic contour, its prevailing winds, its trees, flowers, and birds make the natural background of Meredith's poems.

It was as a novelist that Meredith first gained any wide recognition, and his success in intellectualising the novel had far-reaching influence, but he considered himself primarily a poet, and it is to the poems and letters that we must look for the more direct statement of his beliefs. If we may judge from a letter written when he was sixteen, he passed through a phase of youthful piety, due, no doubt, to the atmosphere of the school at Neuwied. Of the English church services he attended perforce in his boyhood, the abiding impression he retained was one of intense boredom:—

"'Corinthians' will forever be associated in my mind with rows of wax candles and a holy drone overhead, combined with the sensation that those who did not choose the road to Heaven, enjoyed by far the pleasantest way. I cannot hear of Genesis, or of the sins of amorous David, or of Hezekiah, without fidgetting in my chair, as if it had turned to the utterly unsympathetic Church-wood of yore. In despair, I used to begin a fresh chapter of the adventures of St. George (a serial story, continued from Sunday to Sunday), and carry it on till the preacher's voice fell. Sometimes he deceived me (I hope, not voluntarily) and his voice bade St. George go back into his box, and then ascended in renewed vigour once more; leaving me vacant of my comforting hero; who was not to be revived, after such treatment. I have known subsequent hours of ennui: but nothing to be compared with those early ones."

Except under special provocation, however, his attitude towards the clergy was not aggressive. In a letter in which he warns his friend Maxse against objectless

and unseasonable protests, he makes in 1865 an interesting forecast of the situation during the coming years:

"What we have to anticipate is this: there is, and will further be,
a falling off of the educated young men in seeking an establishment
as Churchmen. These are highly educated, and in their nature
tolerant. They are beginning to think for themselves, and they
give their lives to other matters. The Church will have to be
recruited from a lower, a more illiterate, necessarily a more intolerant
class. These will find themselves at variance with their intellectual
superiors, and in self-defence will attempt to wield the Dogma and
knock us down with a club. In about twenty years' time we may
expect a conflict to come. If in the meantime we alarm such placid
fellows as we see in the clerical robes, we are really doing Truth no
service. . . .

"When the Ministers of Religion press on for an open rupture by
attempts at persecution, it will be time to take rank under colours:
until when I hold myself in reserve. I don't want the day to be
advanced. I think you altogether too impetuous: 500 years too
fast for the human race: I think that where the Christian Ministers
are guilty of little more than boredom, you have got them in a state
of perfection, and at least owe them your tolerance for theirs:—And
so I shall continue to think until next I go to Church."

Ten years later, however (1874), he was stirred by the
protests of the clergy against Tyndall's Belfast address
to write to Maxse: "The man or the country that fights
priestcraft and priests is to my mind striking deeper for
freedom that can be struck anywhere at present. I fore-
see a perilous struggle with them." But he still held
Christian teaching "sound and good," and objected only
to "ecclesiastical dogma," just as he had written a
decade before to Maxse: "You must bear in mind that
Christianity will always be one of the great chapters in
the History of Humanity: that it fought down brutish-
ness: that it has been the mother of our civilization:

that it is tender to the poor, maternal to the suffering, and has supplied for most, still supplies for many, nourishment that in a certain state of the intelligence is instinctively demanded."

No religious difficulties interfered with Meredith's frank acceptance of the theory of evolution. It became indeed his main source of inspiration and the base of his thought. But he combined with it a transcendental view of Nature and an idealistic Theism derived from his great predecessors. In 'The Woods of Westermain' he elaborates with sustained eloquence and passion the doctrine that Ruskin received from Wordsworth, to "go to Nature in all singleness of heart, and walk with her laboriously and trustingly, having no other thoughts but how best to penetrate her meaning and remember her instruction, rejecting nothing, selecting nothing, and scorning nothing, and rejoicing always in the truth." But the teaching of the "vernal woods" of Wordsworth was not in itself sufficient for Meredith; inspiration and enlightenment must be sought also from human society, not only in its present phase but in the course of its development, if we would know 'Earth's Secret':—

> "Not solitarily in fields we find
> Earth's secret open, though one page is there;
> Her plainest, such as children spell, and share
> With bird and beast; raised letters for the blind.
> Not where the troubled passions toss the mind,
> In turbid cities, can the key be bare.
> It hangs for those who hither, thither fare,
> Close interthreading nature with our kind.
> They, hearing History speak, of what men were,
> And have become, are wise.   The gain is great
> In vision and solidity; it lives.

> Yet at a thought of life apart from her,
> Solidity and vision lose their state,
> For earth, that gives the milk, the spirit gives."

Evolution, however, is regarded by Meredith not as a mechanical process dependent on the properties of matter, but as a scheme of progress conducted in accordance with inherent principles.   Men are indeed descended from the lower animals, and have evolved first morality, then reason. "Convenience pricked conscience, that the mind."   If they stray from the onward path, they are doomed to disappear.   "Earth gives the edifice they build no base."

The fullest exposition of Meredith's philosophy is to be found in the series of poems to which he gave the title, 'A Reading of Life.' He was at one with the earlier Victorians in his stout insistence on traditional morality, exemplifying herein a profound observation of Ibsen's that the different spiritual functions do not develop evenly and side by side; the intellect hastens on from conquest to conquest; the moral consciousness, on the other hand, is very conservative.   Meredith found the solution of the problem of conduct in the control by humanity of the two contending forces of sensuous pleasure (typified by Aphrodite, "the Persuader") and asceticism (Artemis, "the Huntress").   If man shuns or too devoutly follows either, he is doomed to destruction.

> "His task to hold them both in breast, and yield
> Their dues to each, and of their war be field."

But the problem cannot be worked out in isolation, not even by aspiration to a higher power, for the assumption of divine favour slays the soul of brotherhood.

"In fellowship religion has its founts:
The solitary his own God reveres:
Ascend no sacred Mounts
Our hungers or our fears.
As only for the numbers Nature's care
Is shown, and she the personal nothing heeds,
So to Divinity the spring of prayer
From brotherhood the one way upward leads."

Man's fear of spectral enemies, which were but the reflex shade of his own mind, and his attitude of distrust and antagonism toward his fellows had to be overcome before the material world had for him any spiritual significance. It is only when the human mind has gained the conception of brotherhood, which turns the world from a warring camp into a fruitful garden, that it is able to discern God, "the Master Mind, the Great Unseen, no wise the Dark Unknown." So, fully developed man comes to be regarded by Meredith as Nature's (or, as he more often says, "Earth's") comrade and helper, rather than her subject or a subordinate part of her kingdom, though he must ever keep in close contact with her if he is to succeed in "the scheme to animate his race" revealed by a study of the past:

"No miracle the sprout of wheat from clod,
She knows, nor growth of man in grisly brute;
But he, the flower at head and soil at root,
Is miracle, guides he the brute to God.
And that way seems he bound; that way the road,
With his dark-lantern mind, unled, alone,
Wearifully through forest-tracks unsown,
He travels, urged by some internal goad."

Resting upon the revelation of the past by historical and scientific investigation as affording sufficient hope and guidance for the future, Meredith, like Huxley, George Eliot, and the other leaders of the new movement, found no need in his philosophy for a belief in personal immortality and saw no evidence to support such a belief.   To the question asked by Tennyson:

"The wages of sin is Death: if the wages of Virtue be dust,
 Would she have heart to endure for the life of the worm and the
     fly?"

Meredith answered:

> "Spirit raves not for a goal.
> Shapes in man's likeness hewn,
> Desires not; neither desires
> The sleep or the glory; it trusts."

In 'A Faith on Trial,' the fine poem from which these lines are quoted, Meredith faced the question of mortality in the emotional crisis which assailed him when his beloved Marie Vulliamy lay on her death-bed—

> "She, my own,
> My good companion, mate,
> Pulse of me."

In his distress he sought from Earth an assurance of a life beyond:

> "I caught,
> With Death in me shrinking from Death,
> As cold from cold, for a sign
> Of the life beyond ashes: I cast,
> Believing the vision divine,
> Wings of that dream of my Youth
> To the spirit beloved: 'twas unglassed
> On her breast, in her depths austere:
> A flash through the mist, mere breath,
> Breath on a buckler of steel. . . .
>
> Not she gives the tear for the tear:
> Harsh wisdom gives Earth, no more."

The religious legends of the past are "good ships of morality" for a partially developed age, but Nature doles barren comfort to "the Questions, the broods that haunt Sensation insurgent;" they are the cry not of faith, but of unfaith—

> "These are our sensual dreams;
> Of the yearning to touch, to feel
> The dark Impalpable sure,
> And have the Unveiled appear."

The vital truth is

> "That from flesh unto spirit man grows
> Even here on the sod under sun."

Reason, "tiptoe at the ultimate bound of her wit," may find

> "The great Over-Reason we name
> Beneficence: mind seeking Mind."

Thus the human intellect discerns God through His handmaiden, Earth. The same conclusion is reached in another beautiful but difficult poem, 'The Hymn to Colour':—

> "This way have men come out of brutishness
> To spell the letters of the sky and read
> A reflex upon earth else meaningless.
> With thee, O fount of the Untimed! to lead;
> Drink they of thee, thee eyeing, they unaged
> Shall on through brave wars waged.
>
> More gardens will they win than any lost;
> The vile plucked out of them, the unlovely slain.
> Not forfeiting the beast with which they are crossed,
> To stature of the Gods will they attain.
> They shall uplift their Earth to meet her Lord,
> Themselves the attuning chord!"

Applied to the political sphere, Meredith's confidence in the power of man to work out his own destiny made him an ardent democrat and apostle of liberty. Of the early Roadside Sketches contributed to 'Once a Week' he speaks too slightingly when he describes them as "flints perhaps and not flowers," for they show genuine sympathy with humble life and real humour; but his most serious political tract in verse—'The Empty Purse' hardly deserves a more exalted description—is flinty enough. The subtitle reads 'A Sermon to our later Prodigal Son,' but one doubts what the later prodigal would make of it, if it ever reached his eyes or ears. He is given wholesome counsel—to follow Moderation and Harmony, not to depend on wealth or privilege—but what will be conveyed to him by such a promise as this?—

> "Then thou with thy furies outgrown,
> Not as Cybele's beast will thy head lash tail
> So præter-determinedly thermonous,
> Nor thy cause be an Attis far fled."

Meredith said that the things he was always trying for in poetry were "concentration and suggestion," and concentration is sometimes overdone, especially where there is no sweep of feeling to help the reader onward. It is precisely when "strong human emotion is not upon him," that Meredith indulges in what he calls "a turn for literary playfulness." He admits that "there is too much of it," and the admission disarms criticism, though one cannot help regretting that the poet put these obstacles in the way of many who were eager to receive what he had to give. He could plead tunefully enough the cause of Italy or Ireland, and he made a gallant effort to convince the United States that the official voice of England during the Civil War was not the real voice of the nation ('Lines to a Friend visiting America'). But his noblest utterance on international issues was his expression of enlightened sympathy with France in the hour of her deepest humiliation (December, 1870)—a message of hope and courage, which was translated for *La Revue des Deux Mondes*, and bore eloquent testimony to his faith in the ultimate triumph of the tortured Prometheus among nations.

Meredith said at that time: "I am neither German nor French, nor, unless the nation is attacked, English. I am European and cosmopolitan—for humanity! The nation which shows most worth is the nation I love and reverence." At heart he was, however, intensely patriotic, and even militantly so. As early as 1878, he wrote to Sir William Hardman of the 'Morning Post': "Press for an army. Ultimately it will come to a conscription, and the sooner the better." Thirty years later he was still of the same opinion, writing to a young French man of letters, M. René Galland, then doing his military service: "I wish this duty to the country were the same over here with our young men." He considered the German menace pressing, and wrote 'The Call' within a few months of his death:—

> "It cannot be declared we are
>   A nation till from end to end
> The land can show such front to war
>   As bids a crouching foe expend
> His ire in air, and preferably be friend.
>
> The grandeur of her deeds recall;
>   Look on her face so kindly fair:
> This Britain! and were she to fall,
>   Mankind would breathe a harsher air,
> The nations miss a light of leading rare."

His imperialism, if such it may be called—he was astonished, at the spectacle of Englishmen's "hugging of
their India, which they are ruining for the sake of giving
a lucrative post to younger sons of their middle class"—
was an imperialism based on freedom.

> "Australian, Canadian,
>   To tone old veins with streams of youth,
>   Our trust be on the best in man
>   Henceforth, and we shall prove that truth.
>   Prove to a world of brows down-bent
>   That in the Britain thus endowed,
>   Imperial means beneficent,
>   And strength to service vowed."

It was inevitable that a writer of independent mind,
possessed with the idea of progress and resentful of
injustice, should interest himself in the position of
women. "Since I began to reflect," he says, "I have
been oppressed by the injustice done to women, the
constraint put upon their natural aptitudes and their
faculties, generally much to the degradation of the race.
I have not studied them more closely than I have men,
but with more affection, a deeper interest in their en-
franchisement and development, being assured that
women of the independent mind are needed for any
sensible degree of progress. They will so educate their
daughters, that these will not be instructed at the start
to think themselves naturally inferior to men, because
less muscular, and need not have recourse to particular
arts, feline chiefly, to make their way in the world."
There is no subject to which Meredith gave more
attention in his writing, and his treatment of it, especially
in his novels, had a marked effect on public opinion.
As will be noticed in the passage above quoted, he rightly

insisted first of all on educational opportunity with a view to economic independence. Later he declared himself in favour of the suffrage, though he condemned the violent manifestations of the suffragettes—"They want the incompatible—Martyrdom with Comfort," he says in one letter, and in another he bids women "Never forget good manners." Probably his most influential treatment of the subject was 'Diana of the Crossways,' which attained considerable popularity, doubtless on account of its somewhat melodramatic plot. The particular incident on which the story turned was proved to have no historical foundation, and it created difficulties in the handling of plot and character which Meredith, in spite of all his efforts, cannot be said to have overcome. When all allowances are made for Diana, her selling of her lover's secret appears inconsistent with her intelligence, her absolute integrity, and her knowledge of the world. But what attracted Meredith to the theme was not the supposed betrayal of the Corn Law secret by Mrs. Norton, who suggested to him the character of his heroine, but her position in other relations of life. Mrs. Norton was a conspicuous victim of the unjust marriage and divorce laws and still more of the conventional ideas by which they were supported, and she had made a gallant fight to earn her living by her pen. Diana says—

"That is the secret of the opinion of us at present—our dependency. Give us the means of independence, and we will gain it, and have a turn at judging you, my lords! You shall behold a world reversed. Whenever I am distracted by existing circumstances, I lay my finger on the material conditions, and I touch the secret. Individually, it *may* be moral with us; collectively, it is material—gross wrongs, gross hungers. I am a married rebel, and thereof comes the social rebel."

Meredith was too much of an artist to set out to write a novel to illustrate any particular principle. He believed that the novel should be "fortified by philosophy." "Close knowledge of our fellows, discernment of the laws of existence, these lead to great civilization. I have supposed that the novel, exposing and illustrating the natural history of man, may help us to such sustaining roadside gifts." But he "never started on a novel to pursue the theory it developed." "The dominant idea in my mind took up the characters and the story midway."

It is in the drawing of characters, especially of women, that he excelled. Diana's personality is worth much more than all her clever sayings and all the wise reflections on the part of the author for which her adventures give occasion. These may gain approval or excite admiration, but it is Diana herself who wins our sympathy. Meredith's array of heroines, endowed with intelligence as well as passion, is the greatest tribute to English womanhood since the time of Shakespeare, and it is also Meredith's greatest service to literature. It enlarged the common vision of what women might be and do, if opportunity were granted them, and was a potent factor in the liberating movement that followed.

The position of woman is an element in 'Modern Love'—a short story told somewhat obscurely in "tragic hints" but including poems of remarkable beauty—and it forms the main theme of 'The Sage Enamoured and the Honest Lady,' and 'A Ballad of Fair Ladies in Revolt,' both carried through with high spirits and great intellectual versatility; but these poems failed to win favour except with the elect. The later novels had a better chance after 'Diana' had opened the way to a larger

public, and they secured a fair share of attention on
both sides of the Atlantic. 'The Amazing Marriage,'
'Lord Ormont and his Aminta,' and 'One of our Conquerors' all enlist our sympathies for women who are
the victims of conventional opinions about marriage
and of tyranny or lack of consideration on the part of
their lords for which the social situation gives occasion.
Aminta breaks her way out of a bad marriage by elopement and is justified of her creator. The lovable Nesta
of 'One of our Conquerors' fights in vain against the
irregularity of her position and has to own herself vanquished. Indeed the latter novel might be interpreted
as a warning to those who are inclined to run counter to
social traditions that they would do well to count the
cost before they venture on the experiment. Meredith's
attitude on the marriage question was by no means so
revolutionary as the public were led to believe by the
prominence given to a newspaper interview, in which
he made a passing allusion to supposed experimental or
"trial marriages" in America ('Daily Mail,' Sept. 24,
1904). "All I have suggested," he wrote later, "is
for the matter to be discussed," and so far as his discussion of it went in the novels and in the poems, the
conservatives of to-day would hardly find anything to
object to. He suggests the advisability of release for
ill-mated couples without incurring social disqualification, and of the pardon of faults for women as for men,
but his ideal of marriage is high, and in his condemnation of self-indulgence he leans rather to the Puritan
than the Epicurean.

> "Sin against immaturity, the sin
> Of ravenous excess, what deed divides

> Man from vitality; these bleed within;
> Bleed in the crippled relic that abides.
> Perpetually they bleed; a limb is lost,
> A piece of life, the very spirit maimed."

Fundamentally marriage must be based upon Nature's Law, but it must also take into account the higher faculties of man, and be a real mating of the spirit.

Meredith was much more than a feminist, though during a large part of his career the woman question was very much to the front, and he helped to put it there. In 'The Ordeal of Richard Feverel' and again in 'The Adventures of Harry Richmond' he deals with the subject of education, and he had a talent for the creation of charming youths. 'Beauchamp's Career' is a political novel suggested by the unsuccessful candidacy of his friend Maxse for Southampton, but in this, as in all his novels, it is the study of character that is of importance rather than the elucidation of any general principle. His greatest achievement in psychological analysis is doubtless 'The Egoist,' in which the central masterpiece is matched by subordinate men and women characters, admirably drawn, including one unforgetable boy.

Meredith's finest characters are mainly taken from the leisured classes, the world which has time to think and discuss, and which has enough cultivation to be interested in self-analysis and the art of conversation. Occasionally he gives us a glimpse into the busier world of politics or commerce, but when he goes below the middle class his delineation inclines to caricature. Subject to this qualification—and the humorous treatment of such characters as Mrs. Berry in 'Feverel,' Danvers in

'Diana,' and Skepsey in 'One of our Conquerors' is in itself a delight—his range is wide and his sympathies all embracing. No novelist of or since his time has come anywhere near him in variety and distinctness of characterization. His women, above all, feel and think and live; and they belong to the modern world he helped to create, while characters in previous fiction always give the impression of belonging to a past more or less removed.

Meredith's novels aimed at a criticism of life, but a criticism conceived in the spirit of comedy. He met to the full Matthew Arnold's demand for high seriousness, but it could not be said of him that

> "He took the suffering human race,
>   He read each wound, each weakness clear;
>   And struck his finger on the place,
>   And said: *'Thou ailest here, and here!'*"

Meredith's conception of his task as a critic of society and of the method to be employed was entirely different. "People are ready to surrender themselves to witty thumps on the back, breast and sides; all except the head: and it is there that he aims. He must be subtle to penetrate." It is for this reason that in 'An Essay on Comedy' he appealed to cultivated women to recognize the Comic Muse as one of their best friends. "They are blind to their interests in swelling the ranks of the sentimentalists. Let them look with their clearest vision abroad and at home. They will see that where they have no social freedom, Comedy is absent: where they are household drudges, the form of Comedy is primitive: where they are tolerably independent, but uncultivated, exciting melodrama takes its place and a sentimental version of them. . . . But where women are on the road to an equal footing with men, in attainments and in liberty—in what they have won for themselves, and what has been granted them by a fair civilization—there, and only waiting to be transplanted from life to the stage, or the novel, or the poem, pure Comedy flourishes, and is, as it would help them to be, the sweetest of diversions, the wisest of delightful companions."

It was in this spirit and with these weapons that he attacked, in men and women alike, sentimentalism, which he defines as "ignoble passion playing with fire." For passion, "noble strength on fire," he evokes our sympathy, and for courage and devotion. Above all he pleads for the use of intelligence, of human reason:

> "Sword of Common Sense!—
> Our surest gift; the sacred chain
> Of man to man."

He sought in his novels, as he does in the 'Ode to the Comic Spirit' from which the above lines are quoted, to make the relations between men and women more rational and more spiritual:

> "More brain, O Lord, more brain! or we shall mar
> Utterly this fair garden we might win."

It was in this spirit that he made egotism in its myriad forms the object of his shafts of wit, and the following passage in 'An Essay on Comedy,' though intended as an exposition of the Comic Spirit, is an excellent survey of his own accomplishment:—

"Whenever men wax out of proportion, overblown, affected, pretentious, bombastical, hypocritical, pedantic, fantastically delicate; whenever it sees them self-deceived or hoodwinked, given to run riot in idolatries, drifting into vanities, congregating in absurdities, planning shortsightedly, plotting dementedly; whenever they are at variance with their professions, and violate the unwritten but perceptible laws binding them in consideration one to another; whenever they offend sound reason, fair justice; are false in humility or mined with conceit, individually, or in the bulk—the Spirit overhead will look humanely malign and cast an oblique light on them, followed by volleys of silvery laughter."

For the enthusiasms of youth he had keen sympathy. "All right use of life, and the one secret of life, is to pave ways for the firmer footing of those who succeed us"; and he thought his works of worth "only when they point and aid to that end." He expresses the same thought more eloquently in 'Youth in Memory':

> "But love we well the young, her road midway
>   The darknesses runs consecrated clay.
> Despite our feeble hold on this green home,
> And the vast outer strangeness void of dome,
> Shall we be with them, of them, taught to feel,
> Up to the moment of our prostrate fall,
> The life they deem voluptuously real
> Is more than empty echo of a call,
> Or shadow of a shade, or swing of tides;
> As brooding upon age, when veins congeal,
> Grey palsy nods to think. With us for guides,
> Another step above the animal,
> To views in Alpine thought are they helped on.
> Good if so far we live in them when gone!"

Without ever imagining himself a hero, Meredith fought a gallant battle against ill health, straitened circumstances, and persistent lack of appreciation on the part of his contemporaries. Fame came to him too late in life to remedy his sense of isolation and failure. This resulted in the cultivation of a habit of intellectual vagary which is sometimes disconcerting and is the more irritating when one realizes that he can write nobly and straightforwardly when he is intent on his main purpose. He protested against this literary playfulness being called his style, and it is certainly not always character·· istic of him. He has many passages, both of poetry and prose, of an admirable simplicity. His extraordinary intellectual energy led him to overestimate the general intelligence to begin with, and in the end to resent the general stupidity. But he succeeded, at any rate for the generation that followed, to a far greater degree than he seemed to realize. He continued, both in poetry and fiction, the intellectual tradition which had been established by Browning and George Eliot, and he avoided some of their errors, lacked some of their shortcomings. He is never heavy-handed, arrogant, or dull. In prose and verse alike he was a cunning craftsman, seeking ever to renew the life of our much-travailed English tongue in word, phrase, and metre. Some of his metrical experiments are more curious than successful, but it was more than a *tour de force* that changed the jingling nursery measure of 'Sing a Song of Sixpence' into the richly flowing music of 'Love in the Valley.' In both matter and form he made notable additions to our literary treasure, and some of the younger men who were inspired by his example found among their contemporaries a sympathy both for ideas and for their effective expression which he sought in vain from the public of his prime.

BIBLIOGRAPHY

PRINCIPAL PROSE WORKS

1856 'The Shaving of Shagpat.'
1857 'Farina.'
1859 'The Ordeal of Richard Feverel.'
1861 'Evan Harrington' ('Once a Week,' 1860).
1864 'Emilia in England' (later called 'Sandra Belloni').
1865 'Rhoda Fleming.'
1867 'Vittoria' ('Fortnightly Review,' 1866)
1871 'The Adventures of Harry Richmond' ('Cornhill,' 1870–1).
1876 'Beauchamp's Career' ('Fortnightly Review,' 1874–5).
1879 'Essay on Comedy' ('New Quarterly Mag.,' 1877).
1879 'The Egoist.'
1881 'The Tragic Comedians' ('Fortnightly,' 1880–1).
1885 'Diana of the Crossways' ('Fortnightly,' 1884).
1891 'One of Our Conquerors' ('Fortnightly,' 'N. Y. Sun,' 'Australasian,' 1890)
1894 'Lord Ormont and his Aminta.'
1895 'The Amazing Marriage' ('Scribner,' 1895).
1910 'Celt and Saxon' ('Fortnightly,' 1910).
1910 'The Sentimentalists' (unfinished Comedy, 'Scribner,' Aug.).

POLITICAL PAPERS AND INTERVIEWS

'A Pause in the Strife,' 'Pall Mall Gazette,' July 9, 1886.
'Concessions to the Celt,' 'Fortnightly Review,' October, 1886.
'Letter to the Working Women's Assn.,' 'Daily News,' May 20, 1904.
'George Meredith's Views,' 'Daily Chronicle,' July 5, 1904.
'The Marriage Handicap,' 'Daily Mail,' Sept. 24, 1904.
'Interviews on the Revolution in Russia,' 'Daily Chronicle,' Jan. 27, and 'Westminster Gazette,' Feb. 9, 1905.
'The Church in Wales,' 'Westminster Gazette,' Oct. 14 and 'Times,' Oct. 24, 1905.
'Letters on General Election of 1906,' 'Times,' Jan. 12, 20.
'The Suffrage for Women,' 'Times,' Nov. 1, 1906.

VOLUMES OF POEMS

(For periodical publication, see Esdaile)

1851 'Poems' (First Version of 'Love in the Valley').
1862 'Modern Love.'
1883 'Poems and Lyrics of Joy of Earth.'
1887 'Ballads and Poems of Tragic Life.'
1888 'A Reading of Earth.'
1892 'Poems (The Empty Purse and Others)'.
1892 'Modern Love, The Sage Enamoured.'
1892 'Jump-to-Glory Jane.'
1898 'Odes in Contribution to the Song of French History.'
1901 'A Reading of Life.'
1909 'Last Poems.'
1910 'Poems Written in Early Youth.'

COLLECTED EDITIONS

1885–7   First collected edition of the novels.
1889–95 New edition.
1896–8   Limited edition (32 vols.—3 of poems).
1897   Selected Poems.
1897–9   Library edition (17 vols.—2 of poems).
1901–5   Pocket edition (18 vols.—2 of poems).
1910–11 Memorial edition (27 vols.).
1912–20 'Standard' edition (17 vols.).
1922   Mickelham edition (17 vols.).

BIOGRAPHY AND CRITICISM

Hannah Lynch, 'George Meredith; a Study,' 1891.
Walter Jerrold, 'George Meredith, An Essay towards Appreciation' (English Writers of To-day Series), 1902.
G. M. Trevelyan, 'The Poetry and Philosophy of George Meredith,' 1906.
M. Sturge Henderson, 'George Meredith: Novelist, Poet, Reformer,' 1907.
    (Chapters XIV to XVII on 'Meredith's Poetry' by Basil de Selincourt.)

A. C. Pigou. 'The Problem of Theism and Other Essays,' 1908. (Essay No. 7, 'Optimism in Browning and Meredith.')

J. A. Hammerton, 'George Meredith in Anecdote and Criticism,' 1909.

Edward Clodd, 'George Meredith: Some Recollections,' 'Fortnightly Review,' July, 1909, republished in 'Memories,' 1916.

Ernst Dick, 'George Meredith, Drei Versuche.' Berlin, 1910.

Constantin Photiades, 'George Meredith, sa Vie, son Imagination, son Art, sa Doctrine.' Paris, 1910, Translation by Arthur Price, 1913.

'The Letters of George Meredith,' 1912.

'The Humanism of George Meredith' in 'Contemporary Literature,' by Stuart P. Sherman, 1917.

J. H. E. Crees, 'George Meredith. A Study of his Works and Personality,' Oxford, 1918.

S. M. Ellis, 'George Meredith. His Life and Friends in Relation to his Work,' 1919, 1920.

Alice Mary, Lady Butcher, 'Memories of George Meredith,' 1919.

There are full bibliographies by John Lane in 'George Meredith: some Characteristics,' (Richard Le Gallienne) 1890 (Fifth edition, revised, 1900), and by A. J. K. Esdaile in 'The Literary Year-Book for 1907.'

CHAPTER III

THOMAS HARDY (1840–   )

HARDY'S fatalistic pessimism offers a strong contrast to Meredith's buoyant optimism and high-spirited insistence on man's power to control his destiny. Their opposite reaction to the same spiritual crisis must be due to temperamental difference, for the circumstances of their birth and early religious associations were not dissimilar, and Hardy had not the excuse Meredith might have pleaded of persistent neglect by the public. Born in the hamlet of Higher Bockhampton in the district to which he later gave the name of Wessex, Hardy received an architect's training in the neighbouring town of Dorchester (the Casterbridge of the novels) and afterwards in London; at twenty-five he had published an article in 'Chambers's Journal' and at thirty-two he had established for himself a recognized place among the writers of fiction. His first attempt at a novel, 'The Poor Man and the Lady,' had the good fortune to fall into the hands of George Meredith, who advised Chapman and Hall against publication, but encouraged the author to try again. Hardy understood Meredith to recommend a sensational plot, and wrote in accordance with this prescription his first published novel, 'Desperate Remedies.' It is a novel of intrigue after the manner of Wilkie Collins, then at the height of his popularity, and gives little promise of its author's peculiar gifts. But 'Under the Greenwood Tree,' though small in scope and slight in texture, caught

42

the charm of the secluded England, as yet untouched
by modern industrialism, which was soon to yield to the
advance of the railway and the elementary school, and
was ultimately to disappear in the melting pot of the
Great War. 'A Pair of Blue Eyes' depended for interest
more on plot than on character, and betrayed the author's
besetting weakness—an excessive extension of the long
arm of coincidence to bring about a striking catastrophe;
but it was a good story and won popular favour. Next
year, in which Hardy married and retired to his beloved
Dorsetshire for the rest of his life, came a really great
novel, 'Far from the Madding Crowd,' and his position
was secure. By the side of rustic humour and pathos,
there was now a firm grasp of character and telling power
of description of natural phenomena. The sensational
element is not absent—the dazzling of Bathsheba by
Sergeant Troy's sword-play is rather stagy, and Troy's
violent death seems as unnecessary as his murderer's
insanity—but apart from these incidents the main
thread of the love of Gabriel Oak for Bathsheba is admirably interwoven with the minor tragedy and comedy
of country life. Gabriel's steadfast devotion meets
with its due reward, and Bathsheba suffers only temporary retribution for her waywardness; they are dismissed to happiness with only the gentle irony of rustic
humour.

Hardy showed wisdom in withholding his dark philosophy from his novels until he had gained public attention, but that he already held it is manifest from its
direct avowal in poems of a much earlier date. He
expressed his constitutional pessimism as early as 1866
in a short lyric significantly named 'Hap.' He asks:

> "How arrives it joy lies slain
> And why unblooms the best hope ever sown?"

His mind would be more at ease if he could find an explanation in the hatred of some malignant Power, but not so—

> "Crass Casualty obstructs the sun and rain,
> And dicing Time for gladness casts a moan."

Nature, instead of giving any answer, seems to him to have her own fruitless questioning—

> "Has some Vast Imbecility,
>   Mighty to build and blend,
>   But impotent to tend,
> Framed us in jest, and left us now to hazardry?

> "Or come we of an Automaton
>   Unconscious of our pains? . . .
>   Or are we live remains
> Of Godhead dying downwards, brain and eye now gone?

> "Or is it that some high Plan betides,
>   As yet not understood,
>   Of Evil stormed by Good,
> We the Forlorn Hope over which Achievement strides?"

If the poet had the ear of the unborn—it is a pauper child he chooses to address, but the poem affords no reason for the distinction—he would counsel non-existence:

> "Breathe not, hid Heart: cease silently,
> And though thy birth-hour beckons thee,
>   Sleep the long sleep:
>   The Doomsters heap
> Travails and teens around us here,
> And Time-wraiths turn our songsingings to fear.

> Hark, how the peoples surge and sigh,
> And laughters fail, and greetings die:
>   Hopes dwindle; yea,
>   Faiths waste away,
> Affections and enthusiasms numb;
> Thou canst not mend these things if thou dost come."

It would have astonished contemporary admirers of the rich humour and rural charm of 'Under the Greenwood Tree' and 'Far from the Madding Crowd' to know that such bitter thoughts were already lodged in the author's mind. He had taken rank as an idyllist, and an idyllist for many readers he remained long after the full scope of his intention as a novelist was revealed.

Passing by 'The Hand of Ethelberta,' which is slight in conception, though carried through with skill and spirit, we come in 'The Return of the Native' to the first and perhaps the most perfect combination of what may be called the tragic and idyllic elements of his genius. The tragic note is struck at the outset in the magnificent description of Egdon Heath, the spirit of which broods over the whole story like an evil fate. The leading character, Eustacia Vye, with her dark beauty, wayward sensuousness, and foolish ambitions is evidently doomed by the author to calamity from our first acquaintance with her. But lest we should hold her responsible for the misfortunes that overtake her, he warns us at the beginning that it is life itself that is at fault:—

"Eustacia Vye was the raw material of a divinity. On Olympus she would have done well with a little preparation. She had the passions and instincts which make a model goddess, that is, those which make not quite a model woman. Had it been possible for the earth and mankind to be entirely in her grasp for a while, had she handled the distaff, the spindle, and the shears at her own free will, few in the world would have noticed the change of government. There would have been the same inequality of lot, the same heaping up of favours here, of contumely there, the same generosity before justice, the same perpetual dilemmas, the same captious alternation of caresses and blows that we endure now."

It is evident that Hardy sympathizes with the final protest of his heroine against the injustice of her fate:

"O, the cruelty of putting me into this ill-conceived world! I was capable of much; but I have been injured and blighted and crushed by things beyond my control! O, how hard it is of Heaven to devise such tortures for me, who have done no harm to Heaven at all!"

It is the force of circumstance—the malignant power of Egdon Heath to dwarf and thwart the aspiring soul—that drives Eustacia Vye to irretrievable disaster. It is circumstance too that involves her husband in the same calamity, for he can hardly be held more fortunate in escaping with his life. His mother falls beneath a stroke of fortune utterly undeserved. All this is, of course, within the author's intention. Indeed, it was his original purpose to deny the final meed of happiness to the gentle Thomasin and her devoted Diggory Venn, condemning the former to perpetual widowhood and the latter to a final disappearance from the heath, "nobody knowing whither." Hardy assures readers with "an austere artistic ccde" that they "can assume the more consistent conclusion to be the true one," and he allows it to be known that it was only "certain circumstances of serial publication" that led to the happy ending. If it is to the editor of 'Belgravia,' in which 'The Return of the Native' was first published, that we are indebted for the author's change of intent, most readers will be grateful for this ray of sunshine in the prevailing gloom, for the union of Diggory and Thomasin, in itself natural enough, can hardly be said to invalidate Hardy's artistic purpose, which is made abundantly clear in the handling of the other characters. Only those of a mind of equal austerity to that of the author would have Diggory's valiant efforts to control the Fates and Thomasin's gentle acquiescence lead only to empty defeat and meaningless renunciation.

The austerity of the plot is happily mitigated by its picturesque setting, in which the peasant figures fall naturally into place. Their superstitions, their fondness for ancient usages, and their homely and often humorous wisdom give the story a warmth and colour which do much to relieve its severity of outline. It is difficult to conceive what the novel would be without the bonfire and the wedding festivities, the play of St. George and the Dragon, the raffle, the village dance, and the burning of the waxen image of Eustacia by Susan Nonsuch, for all these are part of the action, and cannot be conceived in isolation from it. To a degree perhaps unknown outside of Hardy's work, they give a complete representation of the life of an entire community, and not mere glimpses of the lives of a few individual members.

Hardy's declared purpose was to show that in these sequestered spots "dramas of a grandeur and unity truly Sophoclean are enacted in the real, by virtue of the concentrated passions and closely-knit interdependence of the lives therein." His ideal was Greek tragedy, and in 'The Return of the Native,' he may justly be said to have attained it. There is the same great sweep of harmonious design, which in view of Hardy's earlier profession one may without pedantry call architectonic. The novel is magnificently constructed; the story moves easily on the heights of human destiny, without haste or wasted effort, and with a perfection of workmanship in detail of which we are only conscious after careful examination. One scene of impassioned or humorous interest succeeds another, and we follow with ever heightened attention to the appointed end; it is only then that we perceive how every smallest part fits into its place to make the perfect whole. This unity of impression comes mainly from unity of conception, but it is assisted by the subordinate unities of time and place which are in their way no less characteristic of 'The Return of the Native' than of Greek tragedy as it was interpreted by Aristotle and succeeding analysts. The story opens with the Fifth of November bonfires about which the fates of Thomasin and Eustacia centre, and passes to the Christmas Festival which welcomes "the return of the native" and brings as its ultimate consequence the marriage, first of Thomasin and Wildeve, and then of Eustacia and Clym Yeobright. The last hot day of August conducts Clym's mother to her doom, and the unintentional signal fire of the following Fifth of November leads, on the next day, to the fatal flight of Eustacia and Wildeve. Within a year and a day the principal characters have run their appointed courses, and Hardy is so little concerned with what happens to the other characters that he does not much care whether Thomasin and Diggory are married or not.

Compared with 'The Return of the Native,' its successor, 'The Trumpet Major' shows a falling-off in power, though it is a pleasant story and contains some unforgettable scenes. In 'Laodicean' the decline is still further marked—indeed it seems difficult to believe that this superficial work came from the same hand. There is a slight recovery in 'Two on a Tower,' the plot of which is, however, still open to the charge of excessive contrivance, while its *dramatis personœ* take no strong hold on the imagination. But in 'The Mayor of Casterbridge' Hardy's hand won back its old cunning. Michael Henchard is powerfully drawn; his rise is due to his own energy and determination; his fall to the obstinacy which is the defect of these qualities. Farfrae, the Scotchman, defeats him in business because he is within this limited sphere the better man. The loss of Elizabeth-Jane—if a man can be said to lose what was really never his—arises naturally out of the situation. The minor personages—and perhaps we might include Farfrae—lack the vitality and humour of the peasants of the earlier stories, but Henchard himself is one of the most original characters in fiction, and his fate is worked out with overwhelming power. The concentrated bitterness of his "will" is thoroughly in keeping with the author's conception of him and with the desperate view of life that conception was intended to illustrate:—

"That Elizabeth-Jane Farfrae be not told of my death, or made to grieve on account of me.
  & that I be not bury'd in consecrated ground.
  & that no sexton be asked to toll the bell.
  & that nobody is wished to see my dead body.
  & that no murners walk behind me at my funeral.
  & that no flours be planted on my grave.
  & that no man remember me.
  To this I put my name."

There is less bitterness and more charm in 'The Woodlanders,' which kept Hardy to the humble folk and
secluded scenes where his real strength lay. Fitzpiers
is a superficial villain and the mishaps which attend his
amours are too forced to be convincing; but there is
power as well as pathos in the romantic devotion of
Giles Winterborne to Grace Melbury and of Marty
South to Giles Winterborne. Marty's last words at his
grave unite the cry of the heart with the music of exquisite poetry:—

"Now, my own, own love," she whispered, "you are mine, and
on'y mine; for she has forgot 'ee at last, although for her you died!
But I—whenever I get up I'll think of 'ee, and whenever I lie down I'll
think of 'ee. Whenever I plant the young larches I'll think that
none can plant as you planted; and whenever I split a gad, and whenever I turn the cider-wring, I'll say none could do it like you. If
ever I forget your name let me forget home and heaven! . . . But
no, no, my love, I never can forget 'ee; for you was a good man, and
did good things!"

'Tess of the D'Urbervilles,' in spite of its unevenness
and its melodramatic elements, is Hardy's greatest novel.
It lacks the sombre perfection of 'The Return of the
Native,' but it gives fuller voice to the author's passionate indignation at injustice, human and divine. It is
not merely social convention that Hardy rages against
in this picture of "a pure woman faithfully presented,"
but the natural conditions which make such catastrophes
not only possible but inevitable. Take, for instance,
his account of the Durbeyfield family:—

"All these young souls were passengers in the Durbeyfield ship—
entirely dependent on the judgment of the two Durbeyfield adults
for their pleasures, their necessities, their health, even their existence.
If the heads of the Durbeyfield household chose to sail into difficulty,

disaster, starvation, disease, degradation, death, thither were these half-dozen little captives under hatches compelled to sail with them— six helpless creatures, who had never been asked if they wished for life on any terms, much less if they wished for it on such hard conditions as were involved in being of the shiftless house of Durbeyfield. Some people would like to know whence the poet whose philosophy is in these days deemed as profound and trustworthy as his song is breezy and pure, gets his authority for speaking of 'Nature's holy plan.'"

And again his reflection on Tess's first betrayal:—

"Darkness and silence ruled everywhere around. Above them rose the primeval yews and oaks of The Chase, in which were poised gentle roosting birds in their last nap; and about them stole the hopping rabbits and hares. But, might some say, where was Tess's guardian angel? where was the Providence of her simple faith? Perhaps, like that other god of whom the ironical Tishbite spoke, he was talking, or he was pursuing, or he was in a journey, or peradventure he was sleeping and not to be awaked."

The final arraignment is not of social usage or human incapacity or cruelty, but of divine government:—

"'Justice' was done, and the President of the Immortals (in Æschylean phrase) had ended his sport with Tess."

In reply to criticism of this passage, Hardy recalled Gloucester's lines in 'Lear':—

"As flies to wanton boys are we to 'the gods;
They kill us for their sport."

But it is obvious that what Shakespeare said dramatically, Hardy offers in his own person as an interpretation of his own work.

It is a pity that in his anxiety to prove his case against the Immortals, the novelist has at times strained human probabilities. In addition to gratuitous coincidences,

Angel Clare's preternatural coldheartedness, and Alec D'Urberville's conventional villainy, one doubts whether any inducement would have driven the mature Tess back to degradation. Meredith notes the falling-off in the latter part of the book as compared with the beginning:—

"The work is open to criticism, but excellent and very interesting. All of the Dairy Farm held me fast. But from the moment of the meeting again of Tess and Alec, I grew cold, and should say that there is a depression of power, up to the end, save for the short scene on the plain of Stonehenge. If the author's minute method had been sustained, we should have had a finer book. It is marred by the sudden hurry to round the story. And Tess, out of the arms of Alec, into (I suppose) those of the lily-necked Clare, and on to the Black Flag waving over her poor body, is a smudge in vapour—she at one time so real to me."

But when all has been said in the way of objection, 'Tess' remains a notable work of art, springing from deep feeling, nobly planned, and, on the whole, masterfully executed. The author has succeeded, as in 'The Return of the Native' in binding the different "phases" of his narrative (he might have called them acts in the tragedy) to significant scenes. Tess's girlhood is associated with the village of Marlott, her first fall with Trantridge and the neighbouring estate of The Chase. "The Rally" takes place in the beautiful Froom Valley, and the melodramatic incidents following Tess's marriage in the ancient manor-house of Wellbridge. Retribution comes to Tess in the bare and stony surroundings of Flintcomb-Ash farm, and renewed temptation in Kingsbere, the original home of the D'Urbervilles and their last resting place. Tess's second lapse from purity and her terrible vengeance are assigned to a lodging house in the fashionable watering place of Sandbourne (Bournemouth), and the story takes on the unsympathetic colour of its surroundings. But the interest rises again as Tess makes her way with Angel Clare through the steepled Melchester (Salisbury) to Stonehenge, and the climax of her capture is of Hardy's best.

One wishes he had left her there, and not insisted on showing us the hoisting of the black flag at Winchester Gaol and 'Liza-Lu and Angel Clare retiring from the story with joined hands. But in spite of all these shortcomings in details of craftsmanship, Tess remains one of the most vital and impressive figures of modern fiction, and offers a convincing plea for sympathetic consideration of the social problem the author wished to present. The art and power of the picture, with its wealth of description of country life, its frequent pathos and occasional humour, will remain a delight to readers who have no sympathy with Hardy's angry rebellion against the Fates and pay no attention to it.

If in 'Tess of the D'Urbervilles' the author's sympathies sometimes outrun his judgment, in 'Jude the Obscure' his pessimistic philosophy submerges his art. The sex-obsession from which Hardy and some other writers of fiction suffered at the time—perhaps as a reaction from the severe repression of this element in the English novel of the previous generation—is unpleasantly obtrusive, and the figure of the triple fratricide, Father Time, with his "Done because we are too menny" is too grotesque to be effective. One can imagine no state of human society in which Jude's weakness and shiftlessness would bring anything but misfortune to himself and those who had the ill-luck to be dependent on him; but wholesale childmurder is not one of the usual results of domestic mismanagement.

'The Well Beloved,' Hardy's last published novel, is an earlier work betraying all his characteristic weaknesses, and it would have been better for his fame if it had been left unprinted. He was a curiously uneven writer, interspersing masterpieces with failures or conventional successes of which the most probable explanation is fatigue; but his best work reaches to the highest mark of attainment of the English novel, and his weaker stories are already being buried in a kindly oblivion. Hardy seems to have been himself not unaware that his fame would rest upon the Wessex novels, which he lists under the general title "Novels of Character and Environment." He describes 'A Pair of Blue Eyes,' 'The Trumpet Major,' 'Two on a Tower' and 'The Well Beloved' as "Romances and Fantasies," and classes 'Desperate Remedies,' 'The Hand of Ethelberta' and 'A Laodicean' as "Novels of Ingenuity." Two collections of Hardy's short stories, 'Life's Little Ironies' and 'Wessex Tales', are rightly included by him under the first classification, for they present in miniature the method and point of view of the Wessex novels. 'A Group of Noble Dames' falls into the second category and hardly calls for further notice. Hardy's analysis of feminine character has nothing like the range and balance of Meredith's. His women are too passive victims of "character and environment." A recent critic, Professor Stuart P. Sherman, in his 'Contemporary Literature' (1917), notes "what pitiful antagonists of destiny these rural people of Mr. Hardy make. The intelligence of mortals is wholly inactive in the combat." He endows his women richly on the passionate side, but he rarely gives them credit for good judgment. His estimate of their intelligence was not high. He speaks in 'A Pair of Blue Eyes' of "those stealthy movements by which women let their hearts juggle with their brains," and again of "woman's ruling passion—to fascinate and influence those more powerful then she." "Decision, however suicidal, has more charm for a woman than the most equivocal Fabian success." The habit of self-dispraise, he says in the same novel, is "a peculiarity which, exercised towards sensible men, stirs a kindly chord of attachment that a marked assertiveness would leave untouched, but inevitably leads the most sensible woman in the world to undervalue him who practises it. Directly domineering ceases in the man, snubbing begins in the woman; the trite but no less unfortunate fact being that the gentler creature rarely has the capacity to appreciate fair treatment from her natural complement." Indeed the significance of the whole novel, so far as it has any general significance, is the evil influence of "a pair of blue eyes"—mere feminine attractiveness—on the fates of men of much greater value in heart and mind. The same conclusion is suggested by 'Far from the Madding Crowd,' 'The Return of the Native,' and 'Jude the Obscure.'

Hardy's poems have perhaps been unduly neglected, but on the whole the general preference for his works of prose fiction is justified. In some cases he has taken characters and situations in the novels as the subjects of poems, and it is curious to note how much more concentrated power he gets in the prose medium. 'Tess's Lament,' for instance, is surpassed in emotional intensity by many a scene in the novel; for pathos and sheer beauty 'Marty South's Reverie, The Pine Planters' will not compare with her last words over Giles Winter-

borne's grave, quoted above, and the various poems in
which the Mellstock Quire appears are surpassed in
charm by 'Under the Greenwood Tree.' What we do
get, in the later poems, as in the earlier ones, is a more
direct statement of Hardy's philosophy. He still holds,
with the ancient Greek poet, that the best lot of all is
not to be. Before the birth of consciousness "all went
well":

> "But the disease of feeling germed,
> And primal rightness took the tinct of wrong,
> Ere nescience shall be reaffirmed
> How long, how long?"

As not-being is his ideal for the race, it is his best wish
for the individual. 'In Childbed' and 'The Unborn'
regard the beginning of life with dismay; 'Regret not
Me' and 'After the Last Breath' look on the end with
satisfaction:

> "We see by littles now the deft achievement
> Whereby she has escaped the Wrongers all,
> In view of which our momentary bereavement
> Outshapes but small."

The one thing that moves the poet to a kind of cheerfulness is triumphant indulgence in sexual desire. Julie-
June is a "girl of joy" in the literal, as well as the conventional sense of the word, and "bubbling and bright-
some eyed" on her death-bed chooses her bearers "from
her fancymen." The girl who allows "the dark-eyed
gentleman" to tie up her garter, with consequences
generally regarded as untoward, takes entire satisfaction
in the outcome. Ralph Blossom, by whose fornications
"seven women who were maids before he knew them

have been brought upon the town" soliloquizes with grim humour upon their probable reflections—but only two out of the seven offer any reproval; the other five run the gamut from resignation to triumphant thankfulness.

In his sixth and seventh decades Hardy launched and completed a vast dramatic study, 'The Dynasts,' partly in prose, partly in verse, dealing with the Napoleonic wars, in which he had been led to interest himself while writing 'The Trumpet Major.' It is a huge spectacle in nineteen acts and one hundred and thirty scenes, intended for "mental performance alone" (though part of it has been successfully staged). The list of characters for each of the three parts covers two or three pages, beginning with "certain impersonated abstractions, or Intelligences, called Spirits" and ending with Wessex peasants enlisted as soldiers against Napoleon and still lowlier camp followers. The "forescene in the Overworld" represents the Immanent Will as working "with an absent heed,"

"like a knitter drowsed,
Whose fingers play in skilled unmindfulness."

The Will winds up Napoleon and other "flesh-hinged manikins" "to click-clack off Its preadjusted laws," but all are merely puppets, pulled by invisible strings. Then follows in ever changing procession a panorama of the successive events of the epoch and the actors in it, great and small; we see Nelson on the deck of his ship, Pitt taking counsel with George III, Napoleon in every conceivable relation, the English House of Commons in debate, the common soldiers of both sides on the battlefield, on the march, and in their cups. It is a combination of the method of Shakespeare's historical plays, with that of Goethe's 'Faust,' but with less humour than is afforded by either, and the Wessex scenes hardly give sufficient relief for the intolerable length of the parliamentary speeches and diplomatic discussions. The philosophy is that of the Wessex novels and of the poems, though in the closing lines the Chorus of the Pities breathes a hope that the Immanent Will, "That neither good nor evil knows" may "wake and understand." If "God's Education" is to come about at all, Hardy sets forth in a poem published contemporaneously with 'The Dynasts,' it must be brought about by men. "Theirs is the teaching mind." God is without pity, as he is without plan or purpose.

> "My labours—logicless—
> You may explain; not I:
> Sense-sealed I have wrought, without a guess
> That I evolved a Consciousness
> To ask for reasons why.
>
> "Strange that ephemeral creatures who
> By my own ordering are,
> Should see the shortness of my view,
> Use ethic tests I never knew,
> Or made provision for!"

It is strange that Hardy should not see the inconsistency of ascribing to the "First or Fundamental Energy" (to use his own phrase) on the one hand absolute control of its own designs, on the other the production of unknown and unforeseen elements of life and consciousness. But in the preface to the volume of his poems which he regards as "perhaps the last" (1922), he protests against the acceptance, as his "view," of "a series of fugitive impressions which I have never tried to coordinate." He protests too against the description of this view as "pessimism" and defines his intention as "the exploration of reality, and its frank recognition stage by stage along the survey, with an eye to the best consummation possible: briefly, evolutionary meliorism." He holds fast to the conviction that pain to all upon earth, "tongued or dumb, shall be kept down to a minimum by loving-kindness, operating through scientific knowledge and actuated by the modicum of free-will conjecturally possessed by organic life when the mighty necessitating forces—unconscious or other—that have 'the balancing of the clouds,' happen to be in equilibrium, which may or may not be often."

Hardy's admission of this small avenue of escape from evolutionary determinism is worth noting; but the poet has no right to complain if certain tendencies of thought, recurring in his novels and poems, have been interpreted as arising from a general attitude towards life. His tone in the later poems is rather one of gentle resignation than of fierce indignation, but his main themes are still the ironies and illusions of life, the inconstancy of man and woman, the disappointment and frustration of human hopes and desires. That his persistent choice of these themes and his occasional comment on them should be described as pessimistic is not surprising, and should not be regarded as a reproach. His attitude towards human suffering is intensely sympathetic, and very far from cynical; his keen sensibility is matched with kindness. His imaginative power and artistic skill have met with increasing recognition in his later years, and his position as the last great survivor of the Victorian age has been one of unique honour and almost universal appreciation. As

he sank to rest, he recalled the fame of the great gentlemen of the past who "burnt brightlier towards their
setting-day," and wrote his own modest 'Epitaph':—

"I never cared for Life: Life cared for me,
And hence I owed it some fidelity.
It now says, 'Cease; at length thou hast learnt to grind
Sufficient toll for an unwilling mind,
And I dismiss thee—not without regard
That thou didst ask no ill-advised reward,
Nor sought in me much more than thou couldst find.'"

BIBLIOGRAPHY

NOVELS

1871 'Desperate Remedies.'
1872 'Under the Greenwood Tree.'
1873 'A Pair of Blue Eyes.'
1874 'Far from the Madding Crowd' ('Cornhill Magazine').
1876 'The Hand of Ethelberta.'
1878 'The Return of the Native.'
1880 'The Trumpet Major.'
1881 'Laodicean.'
1882 'Two on a Tower.'
1886 'The Mayor of Casterbridge.'
1887 'The Woodlanders.'
1891 'Tess of the D'Urbervilles.'
1895 'Jude the Obscure.'
1897 'The Well Beloved.'

SHORT STORIES

1888 'Wessex Tales.'
1891 'A Group of Noble Dames.'
1894 'Life's Little Ironies.'
1913 'A Changed Man, The Waiting Supper and Other Tales'

POEMS

1898 'Wessex Poems' (wr. 1865–70).
1901 'Poems of the Past and Present.'
1904 'The Dynasts' Pt. 1.
1906 "   "   " 2.
1908 "   "   " 3.
1910 'Time's Laughing Stocks.'
1916 'Satires of Circumstance.'
1917 'Moments of Vision and Miscellaneous Verses.'
1922 'Late Lyrics and Earlier.'

MAGAZINE ARTICLES

'The Dorsetshire Labourer,' 'Longmans,' July, 1879.
'The Profitable Reading of Fiction,' 'New Review,' March, 1888.
'Candour in English Fiction,' 'New Review,' January, 1890.
'The Science of Fiction,' 'New Review,' April, 1891.
'Hodge, as I Know Him,' 'Pall Mall Gazette,' Jan. 2, 1892.

BOOKS ABOUT HARDY

Lionel Johnson, 'The Art of Thomas Hardy,' 1895.
F. A. Hedgcock, 'Thomas Hardy, Penseur et Artiste,' 1911.
Lascelles Abercrombie, 'Thomas Hardy' (Contemporary Writers Series), 1912.
H. C. Duffin, 'Thomas Hardy; A Study of the Wessex Novels,' (Publications of the University of Manchester, England), 1916.
Samuel C. Chew, 'Thomas Hardy, Poet and Novelist,' (Bryn Mawr Notes and Monographs), 1921.
Joseph Warren Beach, 'The Technique of Thomas Hardy,' 1922.
Bibliography (1865–1915) by A. P. Webb.

BOOKS ABOUT THE HARDY COUNTRY

Wilkinson Sherren, 'The Wessex of Romance,' 1903.
Charles George Harper, 'The Hardy Country,' 1904.
Clive Holland, 'Wessex,' 1906.
Bertram Windle, 'The Wessex of Thomas Hardy,' 1906.
C. G. Harper, 'Wessex,' 1911.
S. H. Heath, 'The Heart of Wessex,' 1911.
Herman Lea, 'Thomas Hardy's Wessex,' 1913.
R. Thurston Hopkins, 'Thomas Hardy's Dorset,' 1922.
A useful little 'Handbook of the Wessex Country of Thomas Hardy's Novels and Tales' is published by Kegan Paul (London).

CHAPTER IV

SAMUEL BUTLER (1835-1902)

BY JEFFERSON B. FLETCHER

"If I die prematurely, at any rate I shall be saved from being bored by my own success." Perhaps death at sixty-seven years of age can hardly be called premature; but Samuel Butler died none too soon. In the decade and a half since his death, the success denied him—or spared him—has been piling up. His ideas, which shocked his own generation, are no longer shocking. They seem even tame as compared with the audacities of his own disciple, Mr. Bernard Shaw, with whom, by the way, he may be said to compare as light with its own reflection in polished brass.

Butler liked to regard himself as an amateur in whatever he did. He did for a while try to paint for a living, but good-humouredly admitted failure. But to be an amateur did not mean for him to be irresponsible. On the contrary, "there is no excuse," he said, "for amateur work being bad." The professional works under compulsions, the amateur at his own sweet will. More than all but a very few writers, Butler throughout his life worked at his own sweet will. "Butler used to declare," notes his friend Mr. R. A. Streatfeild, "that he wrote his books so that he might have something to read in his old age, knowing what he liked better than anyone else could do."

Butler believed not only in the amateur spirit, but also

in a reticence that refuses to break silence except under inner compulsion. He says in a note on his books:

"I never make them: they grow; they come to me and insist on being written, and on being such and such. I did not want to write 'Erewhon,' I wanted to go on painting and found it an abominable nuisance being dragged willy-nilly into writing it. So with all my books—the subjects were never of my own choosing; they pressed themselves upon me with more force than I could resist. If I had not liked the subjects, I should have kicked, and nothing would have got me to do them at all. As I did like the subjects and the books came and said they were to be written, I grumbled a little and wrote them."

This may be playfully put, but it is not pose. Butler meant to say that live ideas strive to get themselves expressed very much as live germs strive to get themselves born. As he put it, "a hen is only an egg's way of making another egg." And again he writes that the "base" of reproduction "must be looked for not in the desire of the parents to reproduce but in the discontent of the germs with their surroundings inside their parents, and a desire on their part to have a separate existence."

As Butler's ideas preëminently germinated spontaneously out of his experience, it is more than usually necessary to know his life and personality if we are to understand his books.

Samuel Butler was born December 4th, 1835, at Langar Rectory, Nottingham. His father, the Rev. Thomas Butler, was the son of Dr. Samuel Butler, Headmaster of Shrewsbury School from 1798 to 1836, and afterwards Bishop of Lichfield. It was to Shrewsbury School that the younger Samuel went at thirteen. The Headmaster at that time was the grammarian Benjamin Hall Kennedy, who was the original of Dr. Skinner in 'The Way

of All Flesh.' It is only fair to add, however, that Butler's references to Dr. Kennedy in his memoir of his
grandfather would suggest a far less repellent person-
age, and that Butler's own school days were by no means
unhappy. In 1854 he went to St. John's College, Cambridge, where, beginning with a mathematical course, he
later changed to the classics, and graduated creditably
enough, but not brilliantly.

While still at college, he already showed his satiric
bent. There has been recovered a skit in verse at the
expense of the Deans of St. John's which is already in
Butler's characteristic manner. The two Deans are
on their way to morning chapel.

> "*Junior Dean:* Brother, I am much pleased with Samuel Butler,
> I have observed him mightily of late;
> Methinks that in his melancholy walk
> And air subdued when'er he meeteth me
> Lurks something more than in most other men.

> "*Senior Dean:* It is a good young man. I do bethink me
> That once I walked behind him in the cloister,
> He saw me not, but whispered to his fellow:
> 'Of all men who do dwell beneath the moon
> I love and reverence most the senior Dean.'"

It is unnecessary to quote the ironic catastrophe. The
tone is set; the satiric point made. He also parodied
the tracts of the Simeonites, evangelical agitators, who
nevertheless powerfully moved him for a time even
like his ectype Ernest Pontifex in 'The Way of All Flesh.'

After graduation Butler prepared for ordination in a
poor London parish. He was rather expected, than
called, to enter the ministry. It was the family tradition. The particular doubt that deterred him may well

have been therefore but the last straw. He says, however, that it occurred to him that the unbaptized boys in his night-school were on the whole as well disposed as those that had been sacramentally purified in infancy. His faith too much shaken for further thought of taking orders, Butler desired to become an artist, but as his family would not hear of that, he compromised on sheep-farming in New Zealand.

For five years, 1859–64, he led a healthy outdoor life among downright and virile pioneer folk. The impressions gained powerfully affected him, especially on his return to the over-sophisticated and conventional life of Victorian London. Meanwhile, in New Zealand itself he had far from rusticated mentally. Especially, the just published 'Origin of Species' gripped his imagination, and gave a new turn to his thinking. He laid aside a pamphlet he had begun on "the evidence for the Resurrection," and wrote the brilliant skit entitled 'Darwin Among the Machines.' This was published in the 'Press' of Christchurch, 1863. The idea is the gradual evolution of super-machines that with ever-increasing complexity of organism have, like the higher animals, developed a consciousness, and with their irresistible might dominate their creator man. The biological analogies are ingeniously worked out. Besides the cleverness of the skit, it can also be taken as a sermon on the industrial age when men and women are literally slaves of the machine.

On his return to England in 1864 with the proceeds of his sheep-run in his pocket, Butler settled himself in modest quarters at 15 Clifford's Inn, London. Apart from vacation-journeys to Italy, he stayed in Clifford's

Inn the rest of his life. At first he seems not to have taken up writing in any serious way. "My study is art," he wrote Darwin, "and anything else I may indulge in is only by-play." In fact, however, until the death of his father in 1886, his financial support came from the profits of his sheep and a small reversionary bequest from his grandfather.

In spite of himself, however, he could not, as he says, help writing. In 1865 he contributed, again to the Christchurch 'Press,' a pendant and corrective of 'Darwin Among the Machines' entitled 'Lucubratio Ebria.' Machines are now considered as "extra-corporaneous limbs" and so "extensions of the personality of him who uses them," and who may thus be said to have "become not only a vertebrate mammal, but a vertebrate machinate mammal into the bargain." Machines are not enemies of mankind, but "are to be regarded as the mode of development by which the human organism is most especially advancing, and every fresh invention is to be considered as an additional member of the resources of the human body." These new "machinate" extensions of personality are likely to be costly; accordingly, the right differentiation of civilized man is not by race but by purse. Mankind has two essential categories—the rich and the poor. "He who can tack a portion of one of the P. and O. boats on to his identity is a much more highly organized being than one who cannot."

Those two essays, half playful, half serious, but shrewdly reasoned, were, as Butler himself declared, the germs of 'Erewhon,' his first, and in the opinion of his contemporaries, his only important book. In the Erewhonians Butler discovered a people wise enough to realize the peril latent in machines, and so to make the possession of even an innocent watch a criminal offense. On the other hand, the Erewhonians frankly admitted the real superiority conferred by the possession of the greatest of tools—wealth. They exempted from taxation anyone with an income of over £20,000 a year.

'Erewhon, or Over the Range' (1872) is partly, but only partly, a Utopia in More's sense. The title implies the same idea: Utopia means nowhere, and 'Erewhon' is "nowhere" written backwards. But Utopia for More meant very nearly an ideal commonwealth,—a place in which "there are many things that I rather wish, than hope, to see followed out in our governments." 'Erewhon' is a far more subtle conception. Butler approved the Erewhonian manners and customs in a sense, but only in a sense, and not always. Often his sympathy is ironical. He might himself at times have been puzzled to say whether he approved or not. He probably would have said it did not very much matter. He thought it "a bad sign for a man's peace in his own convictions when he cannot stand turning the canvas cf his life occasionally upside down, or reversing it in a mirror, as painters do with their pictures that they may judge the better concerning them." Such "spiritual outings" give relish to one's "normal opinions." It is the same notion as that which William James was to express later in his "moral holidays." All of Butler's works are full of "spiritual outings," and he never tells us when they are going to happen. His mood is protean, and his reader must be at once sympathetic and quick-witted to keep up with its changes. So anyone who ventures to expound his views must beware of too downright statements. He must be ready to point out that the opposite opinion has weight with Butler also. For perhaps the most nearly positive of Butler's opinions may be expressed in the word moderation, the gospel of the mean. He abhorred the zealot, and one of his principal counts against his countrymen was their excess of zeal. "God," he said, "does not intend people, and does not like people, to be too good. He likes them neither too good nor too bad, but a little too bad is more venial with him than a little too good." And so it is, Butler thought, with truth. "Whenever we push truth hard, she runs to earth in contradiction in terms, that is to say, in falsehood."

This moderation in conduct and belief the Erewhonians certainly showed. In practical terms moderation comes close to the spirit of compromise. The Erewhonians unashamedly preached and practised compromise. "A man must be a mere tyro in the arts of Erewhonian polite society, unless he instinctively suspects a hidden 'yea' in every 'nay' that meets him." The obvious business of any society is to "get on" with itself. Conformity, conventionality, respectability—all within reason—are principles in accord with which sensible people find they "get on" best. So the most substantial citizens of "Erewhon" were worshippers—more or less on the side—of the goddess Ydgrun. And although Butler is here of course hitting at British deference to Mrs. Grundy, he was himself not altogether averse to her limited sovereignty. For after all, her court is very largely made up of "nice people," and Butler believed in "nice people,"—people, that is, with "good health, good looks, good sense, experience, a kindly nature, and a fair balance of cash in hand." Yram in 'Erewhon Revisited' was that kind of person, and every reader will agree that she was thoroughly nice. We are reminded of Rabelais's recipe of "Pantagruelisme": "*c'est à dire vivre en paix, joye, santé, faisants tousjours grand chere.*"

The Erewhonians set particular store by physical well-being—"good health, good looks." They regarded sickness as a crime against society, and punished it as such. One of their judges, in summing up the case in a trial of a man for pulmonary consumption, says:

"You may say that it is not your fault. The answer is ready enough to hand, and it amounts to this—that if you had been born of healthy and well-to-do parents, and been well taken care of when you were a child, you would never have offended against the laws of your country, nor found yourself in your present disgraceful position. If you tell me that you had no hand in your parentage and education, and that it is therefore unjust to lay these things to your charge, I answer that whether your being in a consumption is your fault or no, it is a fault in you, and it is my duty to see that against such faults as this the commonwealth shall be protected. You may say that it is your misfortune to be criminal; I answer that it is your crime to be unfortunate."

If Butler may not intend this decision with absolute literalness, yet he would certainly assert that there was something in that point of view. A poisonous snake might urge that it could not help being poisonous, but we kill it nevertheless—for being a snake.

What is usually called crime, on the other hand,— the deliberate breaking of laws made for the general good,—is so atrocious a proceeding that it can only be explained as a kind of mental obliquity, an astigmatism of the mind's eye. And that is a case calling not for punishment but correction. For criminals, accordingly, the Erewhonians provide "moral straighteners," whose procedure is substantially like that of our physicians.

The social importance of individual health is recognized by the Erewhonians especially from a eugenic point of view. They hold to a kind of mythology of birth, according to which the Unborn, already existing in an organized and conscious world of their own, get themselves born out of a certain unrest and curiosity about the temporal world. They are indeed told of the risks they run,—how it is a matter of lot what dispositions, parents, prospects may be assigned to them. Furthermore, each must sign an affidavit assuming entire responsibility. Naturally, only the more foolish insist. These then become a kind of blind impulse harassing two married people until they get themselves born. Apparently, indeed, they sometimes harass even unmarried people. Thus Butler has a note on the importunities of his unborn son.

"I have often told my son that he must begin by finding me a wife to become his mother who shall satisfy both himself and me. But this is only one of the many rocks on which we have hitherto split. We should never have got on together; I should have had to cut him off with a shilling either for laughing at Homer, or for refusing to laugh at him, or both, or neither, but still cut him off. So I settled the matter long ago by turning a deaf ear to his importunities and sticking to it that I would not get him at all. Yet his thin ghost visits me at times, and, though he knows that it is no use pestering me further, he looks at me so wistfully and reproachfully that I am half-inclined to turn tail, take my chance about his mother and ask him to let me get him after all. But I should show a clean pair of heels if he said 'Yes.'—Besides, he would probably be a girl."

(This is certainly a fit *scherzo* to go with the *andante* of Elia's 'Dream-Children.') In truth, children are bound to be more or less a nuisance to their parents, as parents to their children, but either less so in proportion if they are well and strong. And this is another reason for the Erewhonian insistence on physical well-being.

It was ideas like these, may be quizzically phrased but at bottom serious, that "got themselves born" in 'Erewhon.' The romantic setting and action were mostly afterthought, imperfectly worked out. Indeed, when George Meredith reported to the publishers, Chapman and Hall, that 'Erewhon,' was overphilosophical and unlikely to interest the public, he was wrong only in the second clause. The first half of the book, in which is told how Higgs got "over the range" and what happened to him in 'Erewhon,' is a narrative as stirring and graphic and real as Defoe could have written. But later the story grows perfunctory; long essays are patched in, interesting in themselves, but artistically quite out of scale. In this respect, 'Erewhon Revisited,' the sequel appearing thirty years later, is far more of an artistic piece, if it lacks in variety and audacity compared with the original.

'Erewhon' succeeded. A year after publication, it was translated into Dutch; in 1879 into German. The British public clamoured for more—of the same kind. Butler characteristically baulked. Another idea in his brain was pestering him for expression, and prevailed. This idea, which had to do with the evidence for the Resurrection, he had already begun to treat in New Zealand, but had laid aside the unfinished essay. He now took up the matter afresh, and produced 'The Fair Haven' (1873) anonymously.

If 'Erewhon' had puzzled, 'The Fair Haven' bewildered and angered. If the ideas in 'Erewhon' sometimes seemed unorthodox, even revolutionary, they might be excused as witty fooling. But 'The Fair Haven' trifled with sacred subjects. Moreover irony is more offensive to most people than a direct attack. Ostensibly the book was a serious defence for the Resurrection, but in making that defence covertly absurd Butler, in the eyes of pious people, showed himself not merely a sceptic, but worse—a blasphemer. For he revealed his authorship in a second edition.

Indeed, there was still another count against the book. To give verisimilitude to the ironically conceived defence of the faith, Butler created for its author a certain John Pickard Owen, a literal-minded evangelical religionist, whose life and character are discussed in a prefatory memoir by his brother, William Bickersteth Owen. From a disinterested point of view of art the full-length portrait of an authentic prig is delightful. The brother William is hardly less real, if intensely disagreeable. But to the pious it was all an outrageous parody of piety. Almost the only exceptions to the chorus of disapproval were the act of a prominent clergyman, who sent the book to a friend whom he wished to convert, and the reviews of several evangelical journals that mistook 'The Fair Haven' for a genuine piece of Christian apologetics, and were greatly impressed by the edifying life of the supposed author. Naturally, when these people discovered their mistake, they more than most held the name of Butler in anathema.

Having so arraigned the clergy against him, Butler now proceeded to invite the hostility of the British scientific world by attacking its idol, Charles Darwin.

Such an attack by an amateur was audacious but not
necessarily impious, until unfortunately Butler injected
personal charges into it. He accused Darwin not only of
bad science but also of dishonourable conduct in failing to
give due recognition of precursors, including his own
grandfather, Erasmus Darwin. The quarrel was never
made up, but Darwin's son, Sir Francis, has taken the
opportunity to express before the British Association
generous recognition of Butler's important contributions
to the theory of Evolution.

Certainly, recognition was conspicuous by its absence
during his lifetime. Professional men of science refused
to take seriously this amateur who made biological heresy
amusing. His first foray was in the work called 'Life
and Habit' (1877). This was followed up by 'Evolution Old and New' (1879; second edition, 1882); 'Unconscious Memory' (1880), and 'Luck or Cunning'
(1887).

The essence of Butler's amendment to Darwin's
theory is implied in the last named title. Luck? or
Cunning?—Is development, as Darwin thought, by the
perpetuation of "small fortuitous variations," and so at
bottom blindly mechanical? Or is there foresight in
development? Are changes brought about by response
to need? Butler vehemently urged the latter, vitalistic,
conception as against Darwin's mechanistic. Successful
organs, effective habits, produced in response to need, are
propagated by what he called "unconscious memory,"
that is, the impulse of an organism, which is substantially a prolongation in life of its ancestors, to react as
they reacted to similar conditions.

The germ of this view in Butler's mind was the fanci-

ful 'Elucubratio Ebria' and its echo in 'Erewhon.'   "I
proposed, to myself," wrote Butler, "to see not only
machines as limbs, but also limbs as machines."   A
machine is a contrivance consciously contrived to meet
a need: why may not a limb be?   No reason, replied
Butler; and science to-day appears to be making the
same reply.

Butler was continually revolving, recombining, rephras-
ing his notions.   That is one reason why it is never safe
to dismiss as mere fantasy his most fancifully expressed
ideas.   Thus the mythology of the Unborn in 'Erewhon,'
which reads like a Swiftian satirical allegory, really hangs
together in principle with the sober biological theories
of 'Life and Habit' and 'Unconscious Memory.'   Butler,
like Weissmann, held to the view that the germ has an
existence independent of the organism in which it inheres
and continuous from generation to generation.   The
organism, then, is the germ's means of subsistence, and
of getting itself propagated.

In close analogy with the same biological tenet is
Butler's notion of "vicarious immortality," a very precious notion with him.   He elaborated it fully in chapter
eleven of 'Erewhon Revisited,' but also epitomized it in
many notes and some poems.

Life does not consist in the mere possession of organs
or tools, but in the use of them.   The more tools or organs we have, the more complex and extended is our personality.   But the more we master our tools the more our
use of them is spontaneous or "unconscious."   The
fingers of a master-pianist play for him, leaving his mind
free to meditate the effects produced by them.   The
healthy stomach digests for its owner without his being

aware of what is going on. Similarly, other people work for us, carry out the ideas they have got from us, even in our absence, even—if we have made our lives count—after we are dead. So far as we live by a great man's ideas, he may be said to live in us. Butler's most perfect expressions of this noble, if not wholly satisfying, conception are in the epitaph to the nameless old lady in 'Erewhon Revisited' and in the sonnet Μέλλοντα ταῦτα They may be quoted as good specimens of Butler's graver manner and mood.

> "I fall asleep in the full and certain hope
>   That my slumber shall not be broken;
> And that though I be all-forgetting,
>   Yet shall I not be all-forgotten,
> But continue that life in the thoughts and deeds
>   Of those I loved,
> Into which, while the power to strive was yet vouchsafed me,
>   I fondly strove to enter."

> "Not on sad Stygian shore, nor in clear sheen
> Of far Elysian plain, shall we meet those
> Among the dead whose pupils we have been,
> Nor those great shades whom we have held as foes;
> No meadow of asphodel our feet shall tread,
> Nor shall we look each other in the face
> To love or hate each other being dead,
> Hoping some praise, or fearing some disgrace.
> We shall not argue saying ''Twas thus' or 'Thus.'
> Our argument's whole drift we shall forget;
> Who's right, who's wrong, 'twill be all one to us;
> We shall not even know that we have met.
> Yet meet we shall, and part, and meet again,
> Where dead men meet, on lips of living men."

A further extension of the idea leads Butler to his conception of God. As others may function for us, entering

thus into our personality, as it were, to constitute it in
its fullness, so we and they and all living things function
together to form a total personality that may be called
God. This conception Butler developed in an essay for
the 'Examiner' (1879) entitled 'God the Known and God
the Unknown.'

In 1881 appeared 'Alps and Sanctuaries of Piedmont
and the Canton Ticino,' quizzically labelled on the title-
page 'Op. 6.' This was an account of Butler's holidays
in Italy with digressive meditations on many things.
The volume was illustrated by himself, with some collaboration by his friends, Charles Gogin and H. F. Jones.

It is a fascinating book for anyone who already cares
for Samuel Butler. He is in it at his kindliest. His
humour is, for the most part, without its usual mordant
edge. In his beloved "second country," in the Italy
not of art and antiquity but of homely hamlet and rugged
alp, out of sight of "the science-ridden, art-ridden, cul-
ture-ridden, afternoon-tea-ridden cliffs of old England,"
his mood was holiday. Indeed his Italians were to him
altogether a holiday people. He saw them as gracious
children, without consciousness or priggishness,—perhaps "sometimes one comes upon a young Italian who
wants to learn German, but not often." They seemed
to him to be forever clapping their hands, and crying
out *"Oh bel!"* The genius of their language even con-
firmed the Erewhonian association of ill-being with guilt.
Italians say of a person who has met with an accident or a
misfortune, *"è stato disgraziato."* Take it all in all,
Italians realized for Butler more nearly than any other
people his own gracious gospel of grace, true spirit and
reward of human redemption, although not as Paul

understood grace.   Butler defines the gospel of grace in
'Life and Habit,' and with a lyric fervour unusual for his
habitually rather plain style:

"And grace is best, for where grace is, love is not distant.   Grace!
the old Pagan ideal whose charm even unlovely Paul could not withstand, but, as the legend tells us, his soul fainted within him, his
heart misgave him, and, standing alone on the seashore at dusk, he
'troubled deaf heaven with his bootless cries,' his thin voice pleading
for grace after the flesh.   The waves came in one after another, the
sea-gulls cried together after their kind, the wind rustled among the
dried canes upon the sandbanks, and there came a voice from heaven
saying, 'Let My grace be sufficient for thee.'   Whereon, failing of
the thing itself, he stole the word and strove to crush its meaning
to the measure of his own limitations.   But the true grace, with her
groves and high places, and troops of young men and maidens
crowned with flowers, and singing of love and youth and wine—the
true grace he drove out into the wilderness—high up, it may be, into
Piora, and into such-like places."

Piora is an Italian alpine hamlet described in 'Alps and
Sanctuaries.'

'Alps and Sanctuaries' is a "sentimental journey" by
a philosophic traveller as sensitively responsive as Sterne,
and more clean-minded.   But there was no hope for it,
or for any book by Butler, in England in the last two
decades of the century.   "The clerical and scientific
people rule the roost between them," he said; and he
was anathema to both.   "What is the good," he wrote
in 1883, "of addressing people who will not listen?   I
have addressed the next generation and have therefore
said many things which want time before they become
palatable."   Such a declaration on the part of an unsuccessful autnor is rather commonly an expression of hurt
pride, and means little.   In Butler's case, it was apparently quite sincere, and certainly "the next generation"

is justifying him to an extraordinary extent. But even
this admiring "next generation" boggles at Butler's next
pronouncement. In 1897 appeared 'The Authoress of
the Odyssey, where and when she wrote, who she was,
the use she made of the Iliad, and how the poem grew
under her hands.' The clairvoyant promise is fully
redeemed. We learn with stupefaction that young
Nausicaa really wrote the great epic,—Nausicaa, the
sweet and sportive maiden who was so discreetly hospi-
table to the shipwrecked Ulysses. And we learn also
precisely where she lived and wrote, to wit, at Trapani
on the Sicilian coast. It is a charming fancy but too
strong for even the generation of Shaw and Chesterton.
At the same time, if Butler's discovery seems as fabulous
as that other "fountain of youth," at least he, like
Ponce de Leon, opens up new prospects almost as valu-
able. He reintroduces us to the Iliad and the Odyssey
almost as if they were published yesterday. He does
this both by keen and humour-full criticism and by racy
colloquial translation. For as by-work, he translated
both poems. Perhaps at times he leans too far away from
the stilted solemnity of such translations as Butcher and
Lang's, as when he makes Nausicaa say: "Papa, dear,"
said she, "could you manage to let me have a good big
wagon? I want to take all our dirty clothes to the river
and wash them. You are the chief man here, so it is
only proper that you should have a clean shirt when you
attend meetings of the council." But this is an extreme
instance. In general, Butler's versions are at least
prophylactic to the sense of frigid remoteness given by
most renderings of established classics.

As fanciful as the feminine authorship of the Odyssey

was the identification of "W. H." which Butler proposed in 'Shakespeare's Sonnets reconsidered and in part rearranged' (1899). "W. H." is found to be a certain William Hughes, who, being in want of money, sold the sonnets addressed to him to a bookseller. The idea has not so far been taken seriously. Butler himself at any rate took his investigation seriously enough to learn the sonnets by heart in the process.

In 1901, a year before his death, he published 'Erewhon Revisited.' As has been said, the sequel is, in point of artistic unity, an advance on the original. Its plot is interesting and well-handled; its characters are clearcut and original; it has striking situations; it contains piquant ideas; yet it lacks somehow the vision, the surprise, of 'Erewhon.' Possibly, Butler for once was pushing his idea, instead of his idea pushing him. In any case, 'Erewhon Revisited' is to some slight degree what Butler calls an "academy piece."

Its plot ingeniously hinges on to that of 'Erewhon.' At the end of 'Erewhon' Higgs, the intruder, had escaped with an Erewhonian maiden in an improvised balloon. At the beginning of 'Erewhon Revisited' we find him in England in possession of a large inheritance. Arowhena is dead; their son is a young man. Possessed with a desire to revisit Erewhon, he returns there. But it is no longer the same, and he himself is responsible for the change. His ascent in the balloon had been taken as an ascension into heaven, and himself deified. A religious cult had developed around his legendary person as the Sunchild, and most of the old institutions had been superseded—for the worse. Higgs's brain reels under the shock. Aided by Yram, his former love in

'Erewhon,' and their son, he escapes a second time, but only to die presently of softening of the brain.

The characters in 'Erewhon Revisited' are interesting, but the highest triumphs of Butler in pure art are the characters in his posthumous novel, 'The Way of All Flesh' (1903). In a way they are Dickens-like, yet, though satirically emphasized, not so much caricatured out of reality. Their creator had lived with them a long time—from early in the seventies, when he conceived also John Pickard Owen. Indeed, Butler may be said to have lived with most of them longer still, for these are drawn from his own family and youthful acquaintance. 'The Way of All Flesh' is largely autobiographical, though its author breaks away from fact when and as much as he likes.

The commandment "Thou shalt honour thy father and thy mother" ranked in Victorian England high among the established respectabilities. But the family tie, institutionalized, proved, Butler thought, a source often of the most refined tyranny and cruelty. And this might be, even when all parties concerned are actuated, like Christina in 'The Way of All Flesh,' by high and unselfish motives. Christina is a spiritual vampire with her little son, even while she is striving devotedly towards sainthood, and is really good-hearted. The Rev. Theobald is a moral clam, to be sure, always, but he becomes still worse trying to live up to what he conceives to be the duties of a father. Butler would indict the institution, not the individual. "I believe," he writes in a Note, "that more unhappiness comes from this source [the Family] than from any other—I mean from the attempt to make people hang together artifi-

cially who would never naturally do so. The mischief
among the lower classes is not so great, but among the
middle and upper classes it is killing a large number
daily. And the old people do not really like it much
better than the young." The youth of Ernest Pontifex
is an elaborated illustration of this reflection.

On the other hand, Butler fully accepted the saying
that "blood is thicker than water." In so far, 'The Way
of All Flesh' itself is an illustration of this. Ernest does
not merely take after his ancestors, he is literally a prolongation of them, as Butler had explained in 'Life and
Habit.' That is why the novel begins with the fourth
generation back. Old John Pontifex, the village carpenter who married a "Gothic woman" and built himself
an organ, as passed through travelled and worldly George
and parochial and hypocritical Theobald, with suitable
modifications from their women, is Ernest. Ernest is
purged of the vices of the stock only by moral overthrow,
by enforced revolt against all the sanctities of his house.
Incidentally, he is aided by his Aunt Alethea, arch-
enemy of all humbug and provider of his necessary financial independence.

What escaped the blighting institution of the Victorian
pious family in Ernest was nearly spoiled by those other
institutions of school, of university, of church. Rough-
borough is no hall of physical torture like Dotheboys
Hall. Its rack was subtle and spiritual. Dr. Skinner,
the headmaster, was not a bad man. He was merely an
institutionalized egotist. His manner of accepting a
summons to supper reveals him—and Butler's art. The
great man is playing chess with Overton, the supposed
narrator of the story, and Ernest's later guardian.

"The game had been a long one, and at half-past nine, when supper came in, we had each of us a few pieces remaining. 'What will you take for supper, Dr. Skinner?' said Mrs. Skinner in a silvery voice.

"He made no answer for some time, but at last in a tone of almost superhuman solemnity, he said, first, 'Nothing,' and then, 'Nothing whatever.'

"By and by, however, I had a sense come over me as though I were nearer the consummation of all things than I had ever yet been. The room seemed to grow dark, as an expression came over Dr. Skinner's face, which showed that he was about to speak. The expression gathered force, the room grew darker and darker. 'Stay,' he at length added, and I felt that here at any rate was an end to a suspense which was rapidly becoming unbearable. 'Stay—I may presently take a glass of cold water—and a small piece of bread and butter.'

"As he said the word 'butter' his voice sank to a hardly audible whisper; then there was a sigh as though of relief when the sentence was concluded, and the universe this time was safe.

"Another ten minutes of solemn silence finished the game. The Doctor rose briskly from his seat and placed himself at the supper-table. 'Mrs. Skinner,' he exclaimed jauntily, 'what are those mysterious-looking objects surrounded by potatoes?'

"'Those are oysters, Dr. Skinner.'

"'Give me some, and give Overton some.'

"And so on till he had eaten a good plate of oysters, a scallop shell of minced veal nicely browned, some apple tart, and a hunk of bread and cheese. This was the small piece of bread and butter.

"The cloth was now removed and tumblers with teaspoons in them, a lemon or two, and a jug of boiling water were placed upon the table. Then the great man unbent. His face beamed.

"'And what shall it be to drink?' he exclaimed persuasively. 'Shall it be brandy and water? No. It shall be gin and water. Gin is the more wholesome liquor.'

"So gin it was, hot and stiff too."

Influences at Cambridge are shown as rather lateral than vertical. We see Ernest moulded less by tutors and professors than by associates. Full-drawn are Gideon

Hawke, the Simeonite, and the machiavellian **Pryer**, and the "nice chap" Towneley. For Ernest, however, foreordained by father and mother to ordination, not academicism but clericism is the bogey. Of what gradually overthrew that bogey, of his extraordinary "break" with Miss Maitland and the disgrace which followed, of his still more extraordinary evangelical marriage with the drunken prostitute Ellen, of his awakening sense of fact, of Aunt Alethea's timely bequest, of his triumphant home-coming, well-dressed, calm, and prosperous,—a prodigal against all precedent and to the secret scandal of his family,—of these climactic steps in the story I have not space to speak in detail. The very last of the novel is somewhat doctrinaire rather than dramatic.

'The Way of All Flesh' is an interesting story about interesting people, though hardly for the most part people one would care to meet; it is a masterly arraignment of the defects of the Victorian qualities, and a mordant commentary on the perennial frailties of human nature; but, as usual with Butler's work, far from perfect as a work of art. It goes on after it is properly ended; it is too often disquisitional; it has an annoying way of continuing to lead up to the point for some time after the reader has arrived there. Although it is the one of Butler's writings that has since his death been most talked of, and is no doubt the weightiest, there may be question whether his quality is not more transparently discernible in 'Erewhon,' 'Alps and Sanctuaries,' and the 'Notebooks' taken collectively. Christina, Dr. Skinner, Mrs. Jupp, even disagreeable Theobald are real additions to the world of the best fictitious characters, but in general the lasting things about Butler are his flashes of intellectual wit and quizzical humour. And most of all the authentic Butlerian—for there is a growing tribe of such—will turn to the 'Notebooks,' as published in selection by the author's friend, Henry Festing Jones (1912). Here Butler does not betray his imperfect powers of construction. His genius is happiest in the "happy thought," the pithy epigram, that paradox that is not merely paradoxical, the graphic thumbnail sketch, sudden illuminations of dark places in men and things. It is a book for the understanding, but only the understanding, to live by.

This is a sketch of Samuel Butler's literary work. He was also painter and composer. And doubtless a more thorough analysis might reveal important interaction between his several arts. But he himself has said the the best things about himself,—for instance, this: "I had to steal my own birthright. I stole and was bitterly punished. But I saved my soul alive."

BIBLIOGRAPHY

1862 'Dialogue on the Origin of Species.'
1863 'Darwin among the Machines.'
       'A First Year in Canterbury Settlement.'
1865 'The Evidence for the Resurrection' ('The Fair Haven,'
       1873).
1872 'Erewhon.'
1877 'Life and Habit.'
1878 'A Psalm of Montreal' ('Spectator').
1880 'Unconscious Memory.'
1887 'Luck or Cunning as the Main Means of Organic Modifica-
       tion?'
1897 'The Authoress of the Odyssey.'
1901 'Erewhon Revisited.'
1903 'The Way of All Flesh' (wr. 1872–84).
1906 'Essays.'
1912 'Note-Books.'
1913 'The Humour of Homer and Other Essays with Biographical
       Note.'

In addition to the biographical note by Henry Festing Jones
mentioned above, there are two volumes of an authoritative biography, 'Samuel Butler' (1919), by the same author and critical
books on Butler by Gilbert Cannan (1915), and John F. Harris
(1916).

CHAPTER V

ROBERT LOUIS STEVENSON (1850-1894)

STEVENSON was not unaffected by the spiritual disturbances which assailed his immediate predecessors and contemporaries, but he succeeded in keeping the indications of them out of his published work. What he had to say met with almost universal acceptance in his own generation, and he said it with a verbal felicity and an engaging personal touch which won him immediate popularity. The next generation was inclined to deem contemporary eulogy of his work excessive, and perhaps to depreciate him unduly. His latest critic, Mr. Frank Swinnerton ('R. L. Stevenson, A Critical Study,' 1914) describes him as a poseur who exploited his charm. Well, if he were a poseur, he was a most ingenuous one, and if he exploited his charm, he must have had it. In an age of science and of realism, he revived the romantic manner of Scott in the novel and the personal manner of Lamb in the essay; and it is agreed that those who have continued the traditions since have run them into the ground. Mr. Swinnerton says that if romance is dead, "Stevenson killed it." It seems truer to say that he brought it, temporarily at least, to life again; and it is unjust to blame him for the lack of vitality in the work of his successors. Whether his own work is really alive, or merely imposed on his contemporaries by an appearance of vitality is another question which Mr. Swinnerton, in the evidently congenial rôle of devil's advocate, pleads against

87

Stevenson. It is certain that the growing fondness for realism has greatly restricted the extent of the once powerful appeal of Stevenson's romances; and the new generation often demands stronger meat than the somewhat delicate fare of the essays. But the charm of Stevenson's personality remains, and it seems likely always to win him readers. His invariable lucidity makes the approach to his work easy, his ideas move within a limited range and are often familiar except for a felicitous novelty of phrase. All this makes his work quite as likely to endure as that of more original authors less concerned with beauty of expression than with impressing their views upon their own generation. The attempt of some fervent admirers to count Stevenson among the masters of our literature is steadily losing ground; but his place as a minor classic seems secure.

A writer so lucid as Stevenson stands in no need of an interpreter: it is enough to let him tell his own story,— not a difficult thing to do, as much of his writing—and that the most permanent in interest—was directly or indirectly autobiographical. The only son of well-to-do and indulgent parents—his father was an eminent engineer and President of the Royal Society of Edinburgh— Louis (or Lewis as he was then called) was nursed through a delicate childhood by his devoted "Cummie," of whom he has left us so admirable a picture, and educated at Edinburgh University for the family profession. He accompanied his father on engineering expeditions until, as he says, "I had worn him out with my invincible triviality. The river was to me a pretty and various spectacle; I could not be made to see it otherwise. To my father it was a chequer-board of lively forces, which

he traced from pool to shallow with enduring interest."
Stevenson had, as a matter of fact, decided from his
childhood to be a writer, and at the age of sixteen had the
good luck to see his historical sketch of the Cove-
nanters, 'The Pentland Rising,' printed privately. He
wrote essays, plays and stories, and edited the 'Edinburgh University Magazine' which "ran four months
in undisturbed obscurity and died without a gasp."
His father was prudently averse to his adoption of literature as a profession, and when engineering was rejected
suggested the law. The son dutifully submitted and
learnt that "Emphyteusis was not a disease, nor Stilli-
cide a crime," but the legal lore he acquired served only
to turn a phrase; he was still set on being a writer, and
sought his way to that end, notebook in hand, in a mild
Bohemianism:—

"I was always kept poor in my youth, to my great indignation at
the time, but since then with my complete approval. Twelve
pounds a year was my allowance up to twenty-three and though I
amplified it by very consistent embezzlement from my mother, I
never had enough to be lavish. My monthly pound was usually
spent before the evening of the day on which I received it; as often
as not, it was forstalled; and for the rest of the time I was in rare
fortune if I had five shillings at once in my possession. Hence my
acquaintance was of what would be called a very low order. Looking back upon it, I am surprised at the courage with which l first ventured alone into the societies in which I moved; I was the com-
panion of seamen, chimney sweeps and thieves; my circle was being
continually changed by the action of the police magistrate. I see
now the little sanded kitchen where Velvet Coat (for such was the
name I went by) has spent days together in silence and making sonnets in a penny version book; and rough as the material may appear, I do not believe these days were among the least happy I have
spent."

Stevenson's mother was the daughter of a Presbyterian minister, and his father held strong religious convictions, so that it is not surprising that the youthful vagaries of their only child caused distress and misunderstanding. Fundamentally, however, the son was at one with his Puritan ancestors in his view of life, and his Bohemianism was merely superficial. The Puritan conscience had shifted its emphasis from doctrinal to social issues, and Stevenson felt the stress of the new time. He retained throughout his life the moral earnestness of the Puritan and his passion for exhortation. His account of the spiritual crisis he passed through, given in 'Lay Morals' (written in 1879, though not published till after his death), is characteristic:—

"At college he met other lads more diligent than himself, who followed the plough in summer-time to pay their college fees in winter; and this inequality struck him with some force. He was at that age of a conversable temper, and insatiably curious in the aspects of life; and he spent much of his time scraping acquaintance with all classes of man- and womankind. In this way he came upon many depressed ambitions, and many intelligences stunted for want of opportunity; and this also struck him. He began to perceive that life was a handicap upon strange, wrong-sided principles; and not, as he had been told, a fair and equal race. He began to tremble that he himself had been unjustly favoured, when he saw all the avenues of wealth and power and comfort closed against so many of his superiors and equals, and held unwearyingly open before so idle, so desultory, and so dissolute a being as himself. There sat a youth beside him on the college benches, who had only one shirt to his back, and, at intervals sufficiently far apart, must stay at home to have it washed. It was my friend's principle to stay away as often as he dared; for I fear he was no friend to learning. But there was something that came home to him sharply, in this fellow who had to give over study till his shirt was washed, and the scores of others who had never an opportunity at all. If one of these could take his place, he thought; and the thought tore away a bandage from his eyes. He was eaten by the shame of his discoveries, and despised himself as an unworthy favourite and a creature of the backstairs of Fortune. He could no longer see without confusion one of these brave young fellows battling up hill against adversity. Had he not filched that fellow's birthright? At best was he not coldly profiting by the injustice of society, and greedily devouring stolen goods? The money, indeed, belonged to his father, who had worked, and thought, and given up his liberty to earn it; but by what justice could the money belong to my friend, who had, as yet, done nothing but help to squander it? A more sturdy honesty, joined to a more even and impartial temperament, would have drawn from these considerations a new force of industry, that this equivocal position might be brought as swiftly as possible to an end, and some good services to mankind justify the appropriation of expense. It was not so with my friend, who was only unsettled and discouraged, and filled full of that trumpeting anger with which young men regard injustices in the first blush of youth; although in a few years they will tamely acquiesce in their existence, and knowingly profit by their complications. Yet all this while he suffered many indignant pangs. And once, when he put on his boots, like any other unripe donkey, to run away from home, it was his best consolation that he was now, at a single plunge, to free himself from the responsibility of this wealth that was not his, and do battle equally against his fellows in the warfare of life.

"Some time after this, falling into ill health, he was sent at great expense to a more favourable climate; and then I think his perplexities were thickest. When he thought of all the other young men of singular promise, upright, good, the prop of families, who must remain at home to die, and with all their possibilities be lost to life and mankind; and how he, by one more unmerited favour, was chosen out from all these others to survive; he felt as if there were no life, no labour, no devotion of soul and body, that could repay and justify these partialities. A religious lady, to whom he communicated these reflections, could see no force in them whatever. 'It was God's will,' said she. But he knew it was by God's will that Joan of Arc was burnt at Rouen, which cleared neither Bedford nor Bishop Cauchon; and again, by God's will that Christ was crucified outside Jerusalem, which excused neither the rancour of the priests nor the timidity of Pilate. He knew, moreover, that although the possibility of this favour he was now enjoying issued from his circumstances, its acceptance was the act of his own will; and he had accepted it greedily, longing for rest and sunshine. And hence this allegation of God's providence did little to relieve his scruples. I promise you he had a very troubled mind. And I would not laugh if I were you, though while he was thus making mountains out of what you think mole-hills, he were still (as perhaps he was) contentedly practising many other things that to you seem black as hell. Every man is his own judge and mountain-guide through life. There is an old story of a mote and a beam, apparently not true, but worthy perhaps of some consideration. I should, if I were you, give some consideration to these scruples of his, and if I were he, I should do the like by yours; for it is not unlikely that there may be something under both. In the meantime you must hear how my friend acted. Like many invalids, he supposed that he would die. Now should he die, he saw no means of repaying this huge loan which, by the hands of his father, mankind had advanced him for his sickness. In that case it would be lost money. So he determined that the advance should be as small as possible, and, so long as he continued to doubt his recovery, lived in an upper room, and grudged himself all but necessaries. But so soon as he began to perceive a change for the better, he felt justified in spending more freely, to speed and brighten his return to health, and trusted in the future to lend a help to mankind, as mankind, out of its treasury, had lent a help to him."

Stevenson's precarious health ensured a considerable degree of parental consideration, and necessitated visits to the Riviera and Fontainebleau which afforded literary material. His devotion to his chosen profession was beyond praise and won speedy acknowledgment. He wrote in 1887 "I imagine nobody had ever such pains to learn a trade as I had; but I slogged at it day in and day out; and I frankly believe (thanks to my dire industry) I have done more with smaller gifts than almost any man of letters in the world."

At twenty-four he had published half a dozen articles, in different magazines, and "found himself able to

say several things in the way in which he felt they
should be said." He was elected a member of the Savile
Club, and became acquainted with Sidney Colvin, Leslie
Stephen, W. E. Henley, Andrew Lang, and Edmund
Gosse. From every point of view except that of financial return, he was making satisfactory progress in his
literary career.

The financial side of the matter became important
when Stevenson fell in love with Mrs. Fanny Osbourne,
an American lady who had come to Barbizon with her
two children to study art. In 1878 she returned to
California to secure a divorce from her husband, and
thither in 1879 Stevenson followed her. He had already
published an account of a canoe trip in Belgium and
France, 'An Inland Voyage' (1878), which contains
amusing and well written passages, and 'Travels with a
Donkey in the Cevennes' (1879), in which he recaptured
the sentimental charm of Sterne. His experiences in
crossing first the Atlantic and afterwards the American
Continent afforded material later for 'The Amateur
Emigrant' and 'Crossing the Plains'; but these experiences are more important from the biographical
than from the literary point of view. Stevenson felt
that his American expedition would not meet with the
approval of his parents, and he accordingly relied on his
own resources, which were slight, his earnings at that
time amounting to some fifty pounds a year. He
shared the hardships of the ordinary emigrant in what
was then called "intermediate" on the steamer and in the
long railway journey across the Continent. To a robust
enterprising youth it would have been merely a disagreeable adventure, but to Stevenson with his delicate

health and gentle nurture it was a wellnigh fatal experience. He arrived in San Francisco without resources of strength or pocket, and only Mrs. Osbourne's devoted nursing saved him from immediate death from consumption. His father came to the rescue with a telegram assuring him of a permanent income of £250 a year, and he was able to marry. The honeymoon, spent in the mountains north of San Francisco, gave occasion for perhaps the most delightful of his books of description, 'The Silverado Squatters.' With his wife, always a congenial and stimulating comrade and a devoted nurse, Stevenson returned to Europe, and spent the next two years mainly in the Austrian Alps at Davos. There he prepared for the press two collections of essays, 'Virginibus Puerisque' and 'Familiar Studies of Men and Books,' and a collection of short stories, 'New Arabian Nights.' His first romance, 'Treasure Island,' was completed and ran an obscure career in 'Young Folks.' But it was not until the publication of 'Treasure Island' in book form in 1883 that he gained any considerable share of attention. Its success, both with the public and the critics, was phenomenal, and it has enjoyed widespread popularity ever since.

Stevenson was enormously encouraged and stimulated: he was able to settle down to steady work at Bournemouth, and produced in rapid succession 'Prince Otto,' 'More New Arabian Nights,' and 'A Child's Garden of Verses' (1885)—the last a really notable achievement and in its way a classic. Next year followed 'The Strange Case of Dr. Jekyll and Mr. Hyde,' —the idea of which came to him in a dream, but was very carefully elaborated—and 'Kidnapped,' which he began with great enthusiasm, but broke off abruptly, inspiration having failed, doubtless owing to fatigue.

The illness and death of his father took Stevenson in 1887 to Edinburgh for what proved to be his last visit. His health failed, and he sought refuge at Saranac in the Adirondacks. 'Dr. Jekyll and Mr. Hyde' had had an immense success in the United States, both in its original form and in dramatized versions, and Stevenson found himself a literary celebrity. He was able to make advantageous arrangements with New York publishers, and began in 'In the Wrong Box' the collaboration with his stepson, Lloyd Osbourne, which was continued in 'The Wrecker' and 'The Ebb Tide.' In spite of Stevenson's better acquaintance with sea-life— he spent three years cruising in the yacht 'Casco' on the Pacific—the two latter are inferior in interest and power to 'Treasure Island,' and rather took away from than added to his reputation. A series of descriptive letters he wrote on the South Seas had the same effect; but a visit to the leper island Molokai gave him the opportunity for refuting an unworthy attack on the devoted missionary-martyr, Father Damien, in one of his most effective pieces of prose. It is full of feeling, tense and vigorous, and has not a trace of the conscious effort which may be sometimes discerned, even in Stevenson's finest work.

In 1891 Stevenson bought an estate near Apia in Samoa, and named it Vailima, "the five waters." He interested himself in the natives, and in the management of a large household cunningly combined the traditions of a Samoan chief with those of the head of a Highland clan. His Pacific experiences gave material for a new volume of short stories, 'The Island Nights

Entertainments,' and for charming accounts of his life at Samoa sent to Sir Sidney Colvin and afterwards published as 'The Vailima Letters.' His health seemed to improve and he worked steadily, bringing 'Kidnapped' to a successful conclusion in a sequel 'Catriona,' and making considerable progress with two other stories, 'St. Ives' (finished by Sir Arthur Quiller Couch), and 'Weir of Hermiston,' which remained a fragment at his death. He was buried on Vaea Mountain near the home he had made for himself, and his tomb, which overlooks a wide stretch on the Pacific, is inscribed with the 'Requiem' which is among his best poems:—

> "Under the wide and starry sky,
> Dig the grave and let me lie.
> Glad did I live and gladly die,
> 　　And I laid me down with a will.
> This be the verse you grave for me:
> *Here he lies where he longed to be;*
> *Home is the sailor, home from sea,*
> *And the hunter home from the hill.*"

Stevenson's poetry and the plays he wrote with W. E. Henley hardly call for serious discussion. He will be remembered as an essayist and romance writer, and above all as a literary personality which succeeded in conveying itself in imperishable prose. His life was one of almost continuous invalidism, and he succeeded, not merely in triumphing over this infirmity, but in making it a source of interest to his readers. He wrote to Meredith the year before his death:—

"For fourteen years I have not had a day's real health; I have wakened sick and gone to bed weary; and I have done my work un-flinchingly. I have written in bed, and written out of it, written in hemorrhages, written in sickness, written torn by coughing, written when my head swam for weakness; and for so long, it seems to me I have won my wager and recovered my glove. I am better now, have been, rightly speaking, since first I came to the Pacific; and still few are the days when I am not in some physical distress. And the battle goes on—ill or well is a trifle: so as it goes. I was made for a contest, and the powers have so willed that my battlefield should be this dingy inglorious one of the bed and the physic bottle."

This is a very good example of what some critics of Stevenson object to as a pose. There would be some ground for complaint if there were any insincerity involved; but there is not. What Stevenson says is true, and the fact that he uses telling phrases cannot be urged against him, for he had practised the art of writing until phrase-making became habitual to him. There is self-consciousness, no doubt, but the personality revealed is an entirely sympathetic one. The virtues which Stevenson extolled in his essays and exemplified in his romances are the ordinary virtues of courage and loyalty and devotion to duty; but they are the virtues men live by. To invest them with freshness and charm is no easy task, as the multitude of Stevenson's imitators have proved. He lacks the originality of genius, for his mind was not either a powerful or a subtle one. He is at his best in writing for and about young people, whose emotions are simple and whose intellectual insight is not profound. Though his unfinished 'Weir of Hermiston' shows a greater grasp on character than he had yet achieved, it is probable that he had not either the inclination or the strength to grapple with the complex problems of modern life. But to be the delight and inspiration of youth is a sufficient meed of praise for one whose powers were always limited by physical weakness, and so long as Stevenson wins the regard of successive generations of ardent young men and women, his memory will withstand critical depreciation. His style has ease, suppleness, limpidity, felicity—every virtue save that of strength. If the art of it is not always completely concealed, it is very seldom irritatingly obtrusive; and one has to seek far to find so perfect a use of the English language to convey the simpler emotions and ideas of life.

BIBLIOGRAPHY

PROSE WORKS

1866 'The Pentland Rising.'
1878 'An Inland Voyage.'
1879 'Edinburgh: Picturesque Notes.'
1879 'Travels with a Donkey.'
1881 'Virginibus Puerisque.'
1882 'Familiar Studies of Men and Books.'
1882 'New Arabian Nights.'
1883 'The Silverado Squatters.'
1883 'Treasure Island.'
1885 'Prince Otto.'
1885 'The Dynamiter.'
1886 'Dr. Jekyll and Mr. Hyde.'
1886 'Kidnapped.'
1887 'Memories and Portraits.'
1888 'The Black Arrow.'
1889 'The Master of Ballantrae.'
1889 'The Wrong Box.'
1890 'Father Damien.'
1892 'Across the Plains.'
1892 'The Wrecker.'
1892 'A Footnote to History.'
1893 'Island Nights Entertainments.'
1893 'Catriona.'
1894 'The Ebb Tide.'
1895 'Vailima Letters.'
1896 'Weir of Hermiston.'
1896 'Lay Morals and Other Papers.'
1898 'St. Ives.'

POEMS

1885 'A Child's Garden of Verses.'
1887 'Underwoods.'
1890 'Ballads.'
1896 'Songs of Travel.'

PLAYS

1880   'Deacon Brodie.'
1884   'Beau Austin.'
       'Admiral Guinea.'
1885   'Macaire.'

COLLECTED   EDITIONS

The Edinburgh Edition, 27 vols., 1894–97.
The Pentland Edition, 20 vols., 1906–07.
The Swanston Edition, 26 vols., 1911–12.

BIOGRAPHY AND CRITICISM

Sidney Colvin, 'The Letters of Robert Louis Stevenson,' 1899.
Graham Balfour, 'The Life of Robert Louis Stevenson,' 1901.   Revised edition, 1915.
H. B. Baildon, 'Robert Louis Stevenson: A Life Study in Criticism,' 1901.
Lloyd Osbourne and Isobel Osbourne Strong, 'Memories of Vailima, 1903.
A. H. Japp, 'R. L. Stevenson: A Record, an Estimate and a Memorial,' 1905.
J. A. Hammerton, 'Stevensoniana,' 1910.
E. B. Simpson, 'Stevenson Originals,' 1912.
R. L. B. Stevenson, 'R. L. Stevenson,' 1913.
F. Swinnerton, 'R. L. Stevenson: A Critical Study,' 1914.
Mrs. R. L. Stevenson, 'The Cruise of the Janet Nichol among the South Sea Islands,' 1914.
Sir A. W. Pinero, 'Robert Louis Stevenson as a Dramatist,' 1914.
Sir Walter A. Raleigh, 'Stevenson,' 1915.
Clayton Hamilton, 'On the Trail of Stevenson,' 1915.
Nellie van de Grift Sanchez, 'The Life of Mrs. Robert Louis Stevenson,' 1920.
Charles John, Lord Guthrie, 'Robert Louis Stevenson. Some Personal Recollections,' 1920.

'A Bibliography of the Works of Robert Louis Stevenson' by Colonel W. F. Prideaux is very full and detailed up to the date of its publication (1903), and has been revised by Mrs. Luther S. Livingston (1917).

CHAPTER VI

GEORGE GISSING (1857–1903)

THE literary reputation of George Gissing, never very high during his lifetime, has been rather enhanced since his death. Most of his successful contemporaries have vanished into oblivion, but Gissing's personality, his methods, and his achievement continue to engage the serious attention of students of literature, though one judges from the infrequency of editions of Gissing that he has still few readers. His personality was indeed an elusive and puzzling one, and it is only in the light of revelations made since his death by his friends that we are able to arrive at a just estimate of his peculiar nature. The popular impression of him as a poverty-stricken writer of realistic and sympathetic studies of English working-class life is, of course, altogether astray. He regarded with loathing the working people with whom he was obliged to associate, and wished only "to wander endlessly amid the silence of the ancient world, to-day and all its sounds forgotten." His favourite subject of study and conversation was Greek metres, and he despised people who did not know "the difference between dochmiacs and antispasts."

His temper was that of the aristocratic scholar, and if he had taken the ways open to him to earn a modest living by means of his classical culture, he could have done so. This is made abundantly clear by the testimony of Frederic Harrison and H. G. Wells, who knew him and held him in high esteem, and above all by the curious book written by his fellow-student and life-long friend Morley Roberts, 'The Private Life of Henry Maitland.' This is not a good book; it is badly arranged and poorly written. The thin pretence of speaking of Gissing as "Maitland" and of his principal books under slightly changed titles; of Frederic Harrison as "Harold Edgewood," of John Morley as "John Harley," of H. G. Wells as "G. H. Rivers," of Edward Clodd as "Edmund Roden," and so on, is an irritating futility; but it does give us the biographical facts; and the facts are necessary to an understanding of Gissing's personality and his work.

The son of a Wakefield chemist, Gissing at fourteen won an entrance scholarship at the Owens College, Manchester (now one of the leading universities), and distinguished himself there as a student, carrying off many prizes. He had then and retained all his life the true mark of the scholar, a disinterested passion for learning, which is somewhat rare in Anglo-Saxon youth. He did himself no more than justice when he wrote in 'The Private Papers of Henry Ryecroft': "With leisure and tranquility of mind, I should have amassed learning. Within the walls of a college, I should have lived so happily, so harmlessly, my imagination ever busy with the old world."

How was it that Gissing, with these remarkable capacities and inclinations and his foot bravely set on the first rung of the ladder of learning, failed to realize an aim so ardently desired and apparently not so difficult of attainment? The answer is to be found in defects of character rare in combination with his scholarly

qualities. He had a strongly developed sexual nature
and strange weakness of judgment. He was a shy,
timid, sensitive, lonely boy, and before he was nineteen
or had taken his degree, he had formed a connection with
a woman of the town, which ruined his whole life.
With that strange mixture of idealism and sensuality
characteristic of him, he married her, and when he
found himself in financial straits owing to her demands
upon him, he was driven to stealing from his fellow-
students. Caught in the act by a detective who was set
to watch, he was imprisoned, and his academic career, of
course, came to an end.

It was the year of the Centennial Exhibition at Phil-
adelphia, and Gissing went to begin his fortunes again in
the New World. He sold short stories to the 'Chicago
Tribune' at a fair rate till he had written himself out, and
then he betook himself to Troy, N. Y., as some of his work
had been reprinted in a paper there. But the Troy editor saw no reason why he should buy what he could borrow from his contemporaries, and Gissing was driven to
earning money, first as assistant to a travelling photog-
rapher, then as a gas fitter. Intolerably homesick, he
made his way by Germany back to London and began to
write novels—not because he liked it, but because he
needed money, and for journalism, the only other way
open to him, he had little gift and no inclination. The
fault of his youth had left him with impaired health and
a wife who continued her career of vice and drunkenness
until it was brought to an end by her death. It is to
Gissing's credit that he contributed a small weekly sum—
between two and three dollars—to her support; but
small as it was, he found it a burden, and he had often

great difficulty in providing himself with the necessities
of life. Of these early struggles, from which he sought
temporary respite in the British Museum Reading Room,
he has given us a scrupulously accurate account in 'New
Grub Street':—

"No native impulse had directed him to novel-writing. His intellectual temper was that of the student, the scholar, but strongly
blended with a love of independence which had always made him
think with distaste of a teacher's life. The stories he wrote were
scraps of immature psychology—the last thing a magazine would
accept from an unknown man.

"His money dwindled, and there came a winter during which he
suffered much from cold and hunger. What a blessed refuge it was,
there under the great dome, when he must else have sat in his windy
garret with the mere pretence of a fire! The Reading-room was his
true home; its warmth enwrapped him kindly; the peculiar odour
of its atmosphere—at first a cause of headache—grew dear and delightful to him. But he could not sit here until his last penny
should be spent. Something practical must be done, and practical-
ity was not his strong point.

"Friends in London he had none; but for an occasional conversation with his landlady he would scarcely have spoken a dozen words
in a week. His disposition was the reverse of democratic, and he
could not make acquaintances below his own intellectual level.
Solitude fostered a sensitiveness which to begin with was extreme;
the lack of stated occupation encouraged his natural tendency to
dream and procrastinate and hope for the improbable. He was a
recluse in the midst of millions, and viewed with dread the necessity
of going forth to fight for daily food."

A legacy of five hundred dollars falling to him, he
spent the money in publishing his first novel, 'Workers in
the Dawn.' It was unsuccessful, but incidentally secured him an engagement as tutor to the two sons of
Frederic Harrison, to whom he had sent a presentation
copy. More tutorial work was offered to him, together

with the opportunity of contributing regularly to the
'Pall Mall Gazette,' then edited by John Morley. But
Gissing despised journalism, and begrudged the time
he had to spend on teaching. Though his real desire
was not to write, but to amass knowledge, he believed
himself capable of literary work of the first order. He
wrote to Mrs. Frederic Harrison in 1884:—

> "The conditions of my life are preposterous. There is only one
> consolation, that, if I live through it, I shall have materials for a
> darker and stronger work than any our time has seen. If I can hold
> out till I have written some three or four books, I shall at all events
> have the satisfaction of knowing that I have left something too
> individual in tone to be neglected."

His early novels brought him in about two hundred
and fifty dollars each, and when 'Demos' attained a
second edition owing to contemporary interest in working-class problems, Gissing spent the proceeds on a
long-desired trip to Italy. "There came into my hands
a sum of money (such a poor little sum) for a book I had
written. It was early autumn. I chanced to hear
some one speak of Naples—and only death would have
held me back." For 'The Nether World' (1890) he
received a thousand dollars, and for 'New Grub Street'
(1891) a little more; but in this year Gissing yielded to
another of those mad impulses which would ruin the
lives of the most gifted. His wife was dead and he
was unable to endure the loneliness in which he lived.
"I could stand it no longer," he said at the time to Morley Roberts, "so I rushed out and spoke to the very first
woman I came across." She happened to be a girl of no
education or natural attractiveness and a bitter scold—
H. G. Wells, who knew her, describes her as a "poor,

tormented, miserable, angry servant girl"—but in spite of all warnings Gissing married her. To the remonstrances of his friends, who urged that he was making "an unpardonable fool of himself in marrying so much beneath him; that he might well have waited until his income improved," he offered the same justification that he pleaded for one of his characters in 'New Grub Street':—

"This was all very well, but they might just as reasonably have bidden him reject plain food because a few years hence he would be able to purchase luxuries; he could not do without nourishment of some sort, and the time had come when he could not do without a wife. Many a man with brains but no money has been compelled to the same step. Educated girls have a pronounced distaste for London garrets; not one in fifty thousand would share poverty with the brightest genius ever born. Seeing that marriage is so often indispensable to that very success which would enable a man of parts to mate equally, there is nothing for it but to look below one's own level, and be grateful to the untaught woman who has pity on one's loneliness."

The result in Gissing's case was what might have been expected, and after two children had been born there came the inevitable separation.

A few years before his death Gissing formed a third tie with a French lady, a woman of education and refinement whose acquaintance he made through her offer to translate one of his novels. He went to live in the South of France, and here at last he found a short period of happiness. Relinquishing his realistic studies of the poor and his psychological analyses of struggling souls "well-educated, fairly bred, but without money," he wrote a volume of autobiographical essays 'The Private Papers of Henry Ryecroft,' and a romance of humble life

'Will Warburton'; he left unfinished at his death 'Veranilda,' a historical novel describing Roman society in the sixth century, a period in which he had long been interested and about which he had been planning a book for some twenty years.

It is clear that Gissing's temperament was as peculiar as the circumstances of his life, which were due indeed in large part to defects of character. He disliked teaching; he disliked writing, and if he had had the fortune he desired he would probably have lived and died an unproductive scholar. Only the direst necessity drove him to literary composition. What Gissing complained of was not lack of appreciation, but "the accursed struggle for money." "It amazes me," he wrote within five years of his death, "that a man secure from penury should lament the failure of his work to become popular." He did not write easily—"not a line that does not ask sweat of the brain"; and if, like Coleridge, he could have found a Gillman to lodge him and board him for nothing, he would never have touched a pen again. His one desire was to "pass my days in a garden, or by the fireside, merely reading. Now and then I have such a hunger for books that I loathe the work which forbids me to fall upon them." So he declared towards the end of his life, and at the beginning of his career he spent days at the British Museum, with a crust for breakfast and another crust for dinner, reading Ancient Philosophy, "Apuleius and Lucian, Petronius and the Greek Anthology, Diogenes Laertius and—heaven knows what!" At the age of twenty-four he jotted down a list of "things I hope to know, and to know well," including such "modest" items as "the history of the Christian Church up to the Reformation," "all Greek poetry," "the field of Mediæval Romance," "German literature from Lessing to Heine," and "Dante." From these congenial studies, out of which it was obviously impossible to make money by way of publication, Gissing turned to stories of working-class life—not that he really liked the people, or was interested in social questions. He says himself: "I am no friend of the people. . . . Every instinct of my being is anti-democratic." But he had to write, and what was he to write about? As he feared and distrusted Demos, he hated and feared Science as "the remorseless enemy of mankind." He wrote in passionate words to which later history has given the tone of prophecy:—

"I see it destroying all simplicity and gentleness of life, all the beauty of the world; I see it restoring barbarism under a mask of civilization; I see it darkening men's minds and hardening their hearts; I see it bringing a time of vast conflicts, which will pale into insignificance 'the thousand wars of old,' and, as likely as not, will whelm all the laborious advances of mankind in blood-drenched chaos."

While the scientific movement of his time moved him only to wrath, and he was far from accepting the mechanistic theory of the evolutionist, he had an equally violent antagonism to orthodox Christianity; the portraits of clergymen in his novels are invariably unsympathetic and sometimes prejudiced. He emerged from an extensive study of Greek and German philosophers without any philosophy of life beyond a vague agnosticism. He writes:—

"That there is some order, some purpose, seems a certainty; my mind, at all events, refuses to grasp an idea of a Universe which means nothing at all. But just as unable am I to accept any of the solutions ever proposed. Above all it is the existence of natural beauty which haunts my thought. I can, for a time, forget the world's horrors; I can never forget the flower by the wayside and the sun falling in the west. These things have a meaning—but I doubt, I doubt—whether the mind of man will ever be permitted to know it."

So far as he had a creed at all, it may be described as a mild pessimism. "Art, nowadays," he says in his second novel, 'The Unclassed,' "must be the mouthpiece of misery, for misery is the keynote of modern life." He was acquainted with the work of the French realists, Flaubert, Maupassant, and Zola, but he had neither the artistic detachment of the first two, nor the moral and social indignation of the third. He was quick to discern the difference between Zola's practice and his precepts. "Zola," he says, "writes deliberate tragedies; his vilest figures become heroic from the place they fill in a strongly imagined drama." Zola's theory of observation and experiment seems to have appealed to Gissing, for in his third novel, 'Isabel Clarendon,' he sets forth something very like it as his method:—

"He who is giving these chapters of her history may not pretend to do much more than exhibit facts and draw at times justifiable inference. He is not a creator of human beings, with eyes to behold the very heart of the machine he has himself pieced together; merely one who takes trouble to trace certain lines of human experience, and, working here on grounds of knowledge, there by aid of analogy, here again in the way of colder speculation, spins his tale with what skill he may till the threads are used up."

But there is a marked contrast in the confidence— one might say the wrongheaded confidence—with which Zola sets forth his theory, and the modesty—almost amounting to discouragement—with which Gissing

presents his view of his own work.   What he seems to have
had in mind when he began to write novels was the aim
he ascribes to Harold Biffen—"absolute realism in the
sphere of the ignobly decent."   Speaking of a love-scene
he had overheard in Regent's Park, Biffen says:—

"Now, such a love-scene as that has absolutely never been written
down; it was entirely decent, yet vulgar to the nth power.   Dickens
would have made it ludicrous—a gross injustice.   Other men who
deal with low-class life would perhaps have preferred idealising it—
an absurdity.   For my own part, I am going to reproduce it verbatim,
without one single impertinent suggestion of any point of view save
that of honest reporting.   The result will be something unutterably
tedious.   Precisely.   That is the stamp of the ignobly decent life.
If it were anything *but* tedious it would be untrue."

In his earlier novels he depicts the life of the poor
with scrupulous fidelity, finding his material in his enforced contact with them, and in visits, after the manner
Zola recommended and practised, to slums and police
courts.   It was conscientious work in the artistic sense,
but lacking in sympathy and power of imagination, and
there is in it neither faith nor hope.   Gissing "thought
nothing could be done" about the misery he represented,
and he "did not desire to do it."   It is no wonder that he
found no real satisfaction in it, and that his manner
changed to that of "a psychological realist in the sphere
of culture"—the manner of Reardon, who is the nearest
of the struggling authors in 'New Grub Street' to being
Gissing himself.   Biffen, who embodies Gissing's earlier
self, says to Reardon:—

"What are we—you and I?   We have no belief in immortality;
we are convinced that this life is all; we know that human happiness is the origin and end of all moral considerations.   What right
have we to make ourselves and others miserable for the sake of an

obstinate idealism? It is our duty to make the best of circumstances.
Why will you go cutting your loaf with a razor when you have a
serviceable bread-knife?"

But Gissing, like Reardon, while he was driven to write
for money, was always striving to satisfy his artistic
conscience. Like Reardon, as Morley Roberts tells us,
he would begin a novel over and over again, tearing up
the early chapters because he felt he could not go on—
"endless circling, perpetual beginning, followed by frustration."

Gissing's views of art were not always the same. It is
surprising to find him at the end of his life defining art
in 'The Private Papers of Henry Ryecroft' as "an expression, satisfying and abiding, of the zest of life."
His theory, as it is here presented, presents a curious contrast to his previous practice:—"The artist is moved and
inspired by supreme enjoyment of some aspect of the
world about him; an enjoyment in itself keener than that
experienced by another man, and intensified, prolonged,
by the power—which comes to him we know not how—of
recording in visible or audible form that emotion of rare
vitality." Gissing does convey, in his too rare passages
of description, his delight in natural beauty of scene, and
his growing love of trees, birds, and flowers; but the
"zest of life," in any broad sense, was a thing he never
knew. He realized, however, that "the artist ought to be
able to make material out of his own sufferings, even
while the suffering is still at its height." And out of his
own sufferings he did eventually make a great novel,
'New Grub Street' (1891). It is in the main the story
under a thin disguise of his own sufferings. Reardon,
the scholar, driven to write for money, Biffen, the con-

scientious realist, Alfred Yule, the unsuccessful author, burdened and irritated with an ignorant wife—they are all himself, regarded from different points of view, and in the case of Reardon the parallel is remarkably close. It is really his own cause he is pleading, and in one passage he pleads it almost directly:—

"The chances are that you have neither understanding nor sympathy for men such as Edwin Reardon and Harold Biffen. They merely provoke you. They seem to you inert, flabby, weakly envious, foolishly obstinate, impiously mutinous, and many other things. You are made angrily contemptuous by their failure to get on; why don't they bestir themselves, push and bustle, welcome kicks so long as halfpence follow, make place in the world's eye— in short, take a leaf from the book of Mr. Jasper Milvain?

"But try to imagine a personality wholly unfitted for the rough and tumble of the world's labour-market. From the familiar point of view these men were worthless; view them in possible relation to a humane order of society, and they are admirable citizens. Nothing is easier than to condemn a type of character which is unequal to the coarse demands of life as it suits the average man. These two were richly endowed with the kindly and the imaginative virtues; if fate threw them amid incongruous circumstances, is their endowment of less value? You scorn their passivity; but it was their nature and their merit to be passive. Gifted with independent means, each of them would have taken quite a different aspect in your eyes. The sum of their faults was their inability to earn money; but, indeed, that inability does not call for unmingled disdain."

The direct plea is perhaps unconvincing, but the book as a whole is, unlike Gissing's previous work, not so much described as felt. It is a painful and depressing picture of the life of the unsuccessful man of letters, but its power is unmistakable. The successful authors of 'New Grub Street' are more thinly realized, and so are the women, with the significant exception of the literary hack, Marian Yule, who in the familiar atmosphere of the

British Museum Reading Room, thinks the thoughts which must have occurred, in some hour of more than ordinary discouragement, to Gissing in his own person:—

"One day at the end of the month she sat with books open before her, but by no effort could fix her attention upon them. It was gloomy, and one could scarcely see to read; a taste of fog grew perceptible in the warm, headachy air. Such profound discouragement possessed her that she could not even maintain the pretence of study; heedless whether anyone observed her, she let her hands fall and her head droop. She kept asking herself what was the use and purpose of such a life as she was condemned to lead. When already there was more good literature in the world than any mortal could cope with in his lifetime, here was she exhausting herself in the manufacture of printed stuff which no one even pretended to be more than a commodity for the day's market. What unspeakable folly! To write—was not that the joy and the privilege of one who had an urgent message for the world? Her father, she knew well, had no such message; he had abandoned all thought of original production, and only wrote about writing. She herself would throw away her pen with joy but for the need of earning money. And all these people about her, what aim had they save to make new books out of those already existing, that yet newer books might in turn be made out of theirs? This huge library, growing into unwieldiness, threatening to become a trackless desert of print—how intolerably it weighed upon the spirit!

"Oh, to go forth and labour with one's hands, to do any poorest, commonest work of which the world had truly need! It was ignoble to sit here and support the paltry pretence of intellectual dignity. A few days ago her startled eye had caught an advertisement in the newspaper, headed 'Literary Machine'; had it then been invented at last, some automaton to supply the place of such poor creatures as herself, to turn out books and articles? Alas! the machine was only one for holding volumes conveniently, that the work of literary manufacture might be physically lightened. But surely before long some Edison would make the true automaton; the problem must be comparatively such a simple one. Only to throw in a given number of old books, and have them reduced, blended, modernised into a single one for to-day's consumption."

In general Gissing had a low estimate of women and no real acquaintance with them. What opportunity for real acquaintance did his narrow life afford? In his next book, 'Born in Exile,' another reminiscent study beginning with an elaborate account of prize day at the Owens College during the time Gissing was a student there, the hero (really again Gissing himself) is described as "one of those upon whose awaking instinct is forced a perception of the brain-defect so general in women when they are taught few of life's graces and none of its serious concerns,—their paltry prepossessions, their vulgar sequaciousness, their invincible ignorance, their absorption in a petty self." With much less grip upon the reader's attention than 'New Grub Street,' 'Born in Exile' is of considerable interest as a novel of self-revelation. Primarily, as the title indicates, it sets forth Gissing's resentment at the social disqualifications he suffered. His hero, Godwin Peak, like himself, leaves college without a degree, not, however, through any fault of his own, but through the indiscretion of a relative, who insists on opening a cheap restaurant opposite the college gates. Peak suffers, as Gissing suffered, among the London vulgar, whom he "abominates, root and branch," and holds "essentially the basest of English mortals." It is not of the vicious he speaks but of the "ignobly decent" lower classes:—

"The people who earn enough for their needs, and whose spiritual guide is the Sunday newspaper—I knew them, because for a long time I was obliged to lodge in their houses. Only a consuming fire could purify the places where they dwell. Don't misunderstand me; I am not charging them with what are commonly held vices and crimes, but with the consistent love of everything that is ignoble, with utter deadness to generous impulse, with the fatal habit of low mockery. And these are the people who really direct the democratic movement. They set the tone in politics; they are debasing art and literature; even the homes of wealthy people begin to show the effects of their influence. One hears men and women of gentle birth using phrases which originate with shopboys; one sees them reading print which is addressed to the coarsest million. They crowd to entertainments which are deliberately adapted to the lowest order of mind. When commercial interest is supreme, how can the tastes of the majority fail to lead and control?"

One would have to search far for a more uncompromising expression of the anti-democratic faith, and there is no doubt that it was held as fervently and vehemently by Gissing himself as he says it was by Peak. With the whole democratic movement he is entirely out of sympathy:— "A ludicrous pretence of education is banishing every form of native simplicity. In the large towns, the populace sink deeper and deeper into a vicious vulgarity, and every rural district is being affected by the spread of contagion. To flatter the proletariat is to fight against all the good that still characterises educated England— against reverence for the beautiful, against magnanimity, against enthusiasm of mind, heart, and soul." Peak "hates the very word majority; it is the few, the very few, that have always kept alive whatever of effectual good we see in the human race. There are individuals who outweigh, in every kind of value, generations of ordinary people." Such an individual he believes himself to be, and his grievance is not against the social system—he believes in it firmly—but merely against his own place in it. Again we have a reminiscence which is obviously Gissing's own experience:—

"He chanced once to be in Hyde Park, on the occasion of some public ceremony, and was brought to pause at the edge of a gaping

plebeian crowd, drawn up to witness the passing of aristocratic ve-
hicles. Close in front of him an open carriage came to a stop; in
it sat, or rather reclined, two ladies, old and young. Upon this
picture Godwin fixed his eyes with the intensity of fascination; his
memory never lost the impress of these ladies' faces. Nothing very
noteworthy about them; but to Godwin they conveyed a passionate
perception of all that is implied in social superiority. Here he stood,
one of the multitude, of the herd; shoulder to shoulder with boors
and pickpockets; and within reach of his hand reposed those two
ladies, in Olympian calm, seeming unaware even of the existence of
the throng. Now they exchanged a word; now they smiled to each
other. How delicate was the moving of their lips! How fine must
be their enunciation! On the box sat an old coachman and a young
footman; they too were splendidly impassive, scornful of the mul-
titudinous gaze.—The block was relieved, and on the carriage rolled.
    "They were his equals, those ladies; merely his equals. With
such as they he should by right of nature associate.
    "In his rebellion, he could not hate them. He hated the malo-
dorous rabble who stared insolently at them and who envied their
immeasurable remoteness. Of mere wealth he thought not; might
he only be recognized by the gentle of birth and breeding for what
he really was, and be rescued from the promiscuity of the vulgar!"

Peak avows that he respects hereditary social standing, independently of the individual's qualities. "Birth
in a sphere of refinement is desirable and respectable;
it saves one, absolutely, from many forms of coarseness.
The masses are not only fools, but very near the brutes.
Yes, they can send forth fine individuals-—but remain
base."

Feeling himself "an aristocrat of nature's own making—one of the few highly favoured beings who, in
despite of circumstance, are pinnacled above mankind,"
Peak as a boy visioned for himself a triumphant career,
with no lack of faith in his power to become an aristocrat
in the common sense, as he already felt himself "an

aristocrat *de jure.*" His independent temper and intellectual maturity save him from the temptations to which Gissing himself fell a victim and to which he makes one significant reference:—"A youth of less concentrated purpose, more at the mercy of casual allurement, would probably have gone to wreck amid trials so exceptional."

Gissing endows his hero with a colder nature, with more practical ability, and more constancy of purpose than he had himself; but Peak is none the less a victim of circumstance. He earns a decent living in the employment of a London chemical manufacturer, travels abroad, and determines to marry a woman of gentle birth and education. It is in this way that temptation comes to him, and he falls, committing an act, not of material, but of intellectual dishonesty by professing an intention to become a clergyman when he is really an agnostic. The falsity of his position is revealed, and though Sidwell Warricombe, the woman for whose sake he has lied, is willing to forgive him, her social position separates her from him, even when an unexpected legacy places Peak in a position to offer her a not unequal alliance. He dies as he has lived "in exile," conscious not so much that "dishonour still clings to him" for his past duplicity as that the disqualification of his origin is irremediable. On none of the counts suggested is the case Gissing presents convincing. A man of Peak's native ability and education, provided with a sufficient income, would have found the life he desired open to him in the England of the eighties, and it is inconceivable that a woman really in love would have rejected him for reasons so insufficient. But Gissing had no realization, as he had no experience, of the compelling emotion involving the whole nature, which overcomes easily such small obstacles as are here suggested. Godwin Peak analyses his own state of mind desperately and exhaustively before he arrives at the conclusion that he is really in love, and his letters to Sidwell convey no spark of real passion—they are excellently reasoned, but cold as ice. Lack of experience, lack of sympathy, prevented Gissing from writing a love-story, which 'Born in Exile,' in its main intention, purposed to be. Gissing only felt himself a free spirit when he was momentarily relieved "from the temptations and harassings of sexual emotion," and he adds, very significantly, "What we call love is mere turmoil." In a more reflective passage he echoes Flaubert's protest against romanticism:—

"If every novelist could be strangled and thrown into the sea we should have some chance of reforming women. The girl's nature was corrupted with sentimentality, like that of all but every woman who is intelligent enough to read what is called the best fiction, but not intelligent enough to understand its vice. Love—love—love; a sickening sameness of vulgarity. What is more vulgar than the ideal of novelists? They won't represent the actual world; it would be too dull for their readers. In real life, how many men and women fall in love? Not one in every ten thousand, I am convinced. Not one married pair in ten thousand have felt for each other as two or three couples do in every novel. There is the sexual instinct, of course, but that is quite a different thing; the novelist daren't talk about that. The paltry creatures daren't tell the one truth that would be profitable. The result is that women imagine themselves noble and glorious when they are most near the animals."

Granted that the *grande passion* is as rare as Gissing here makes out, it exists, and he nowhere succeeded in portraying it. He attempted it in a later novel, 'The Crown of Life,' but it is a failure. And Gissing is obviously wide of the mark when he suggests, as he does in the passage above quoted, that among ten thousand women who imagine themselves in love, all but the solitary exception are mere victims of sexual instinct. There is that element, of course, in all passion, but in the conclusion that it was the only element he was generalizing from his own exceptional nature. The result is that when he attempts to describe affectionate women, he either idealizes them, as in 'Thyrza,' 'A Life's Morning' and Jane Snowdon, the *belle fleur* who redeems the dunghill of 'The Nether World,' or brutalizes them, or leaves them mere lay figures, described from the outside without any touch of life.

Closely allied with the intense self-consciousness which is the source at once of Gissing's strength and weakness is his lack of humour. It is this which gives to all his pictures of lower class and middle class life the same impression of grayness. He depicts their squalour and their material straits, their sufferings and anxieties, never their innocent pleasures and merrymakings. In a holiday crowd at the Crystal Palace he sees only the desolation of ignorance and degradation. To Gissing it is all the more dreadful because they are unconscious of their own misery. He was in fact incapable of imagining happiness outside of his own ideal of material comfort and intellectual opportunity. The courage and cheerfulness of the poor, the humour with which they accept discomfort and their readiness to enjoy any alleviation of their toil lie beyond his ken.

This being so, it is surprising that his critical study of Dickens, who knew the poor as well as Gissing and represented them in an altogether different light, should have been full of sympathetic insight and understanding.

His book is not merely by far the best analysis of the genius of Dickens, but is one of the finest works of its kind in the English language. Gissing's appreciation of the work of other men was always generous, and he had a profound admiration for his great Victorian predecessors, except for George Eliot, whose moral and philosophical tone he disliked. He would have liked, he said, to write a similar book about Thackeray, and he remained a staunch Tennyson devotee when the worship of Tennyson had ceased to be fashionable. It is to be regretted that Gissing did not do more criticism, for the critical remarks interspersed in the novels are singularly acute and intelligent. His knowledge of the world of books—the only world he really knew—his vigorous mind, and his somewhat severe but careful and luminous style made him an admirable critic.

It is interesting to speculate on what Gissing would have accomplished in literature if he had had the easy circumstances he coveted. Perhaps nothing. His latest work, done in comparative comfort and freedom from anxiety, is somewhat lacking in intellectual vigour, possibly owing to his failing health. Though 'By the Ionian Sea,' 'The Private Papers of Henry Ryecroft,' 'Will Warburton,' and 'Veranilda' are all pleasantly written, they have not the grip and power of 'New Grub Street.' Perhaps the fact is that he succeeded not in spite of but because of his sufferings. His early ambition to write "something too individual in tone to be neglected" was not frustrated. He eventually triumphed over all obstacles, even those which he had himself created, he was never false to his own artistic standards, and his work, though likely never to win wide attention, will always be valued by those able to appreciate his intellectual honesty and vigour and his self-sacrificing devotion to scholarly and literary ideals.   It is the audience he would himself have desired, and the place allotted to him, above all but the very few great masters of his time, would not have disappointed his own mature judgment of his powers and achievement.

BIBLIOGRAPHY

1880   'Workers in the Dawn.'
1884   'The Unclassed.'
1886   'Isabel Clarendon.'
       'Demos.'
1887   'Thyrza.'
1888   'A Life's Morning.'
1889   'The Nether World.'
1890   'The Emancipated.'
1891   'New Grub Street.'
1892   'Born in Exile.'
       'Denzil Quarrier.'
1893   'The Odd Women.'
1894   'In the Year of Jubilee.'
1895   'Eve's Ransom.'
1897   'The Whirlpool.'
1898   'Charles Dickens: A Critical Study.'
1899   'The Crown of Life.'
1901   'By the Ionian Sea.   Notes of a Ramble in Southern Italy.'
       'Our Friend the Charlatan.'
1903   'The Private Papers of Henry Ryecroft.'
1904   'Veranilda.'
1905   'Will Warburton.'
1906   'The House of Cobwebs and other Stories.'

BIOGRAPHICAL AND CRITICAL

Frank Swinnerton, 'George Gissing, A Critical Study,' 1912.
Morley Roberts, 'The Private Life of Henry Maitland,' 1912.
Edward Clodd, 'Memories,' 1916.
Introductions by Frederic Harrison to 'Veranilda,' 1904, and by
      Thomas Seccombe to 'The House of Cobwebs,' 1906.
May Yates, 'George Gissing, An Appreciation,' (Publications of the
      University of Manchester, England), 1922.

   Articles by A. S. Wilkins in the 'Owens College Union Magazine,'
January, 1904; by H. G. Wells in the 'Monthly Review,' August,
1904; and by Austin Harrison in the 'Nineteenth Century,' September, 1906.

CHAPTER VII

GEORGE BERNARD SHAW (1856-)

BERNARD SHAW is regarded by many of his admirers as nothing if not original, and even the few who still decry him as a mere turner of paradoxes are at a loss to explain the literary genesis of his wit. He himself—no doubt, rightly—dismissed the "vague cacklings about Ibsen and Nietzsche," and acknowledged his indebtedness to Samuel Butler's "extraordinarily fresh, free, and future-piercing suggestions." In literature, no man is, to use Butler's phrase, "a born orphan," like Melchisedec, and Shaw's suggestion as to his literary parentage may be extended beyond the two points he specified—"the necessity and morality of a conscientious Laodiceanism in religion and of an earnest and constant sense of the importance of money." Shaw's attitude of antagonism not only to religious, but to scientific orthodoxy, his insistence on the factor of health as of primary importance in marriage, his scorn of parental authority were all anticipated by Butler, who has the same fondness for epigram and paradox, and is, like Shaw, the master of a brilliant style, especially in the exposition of an unpopular point of view. But while Butler was, like another famous forerunner, "the voice of one crying in the wilderness," Shaw quickly won public attention. It was not merely that a new generation had sprung up, eager for revolutionary doctrine; unlike Butler, Shaw was not at all averse to practising the noble art of self-advertisement; he had a keen interest in and soon acquired a competent knowledge of public affairs, which his great predecessor neither professed nor desired.

Shaw's literary beginnings were by no means propitious. He was born in Dublin of English Protestant middle-class stock. "I am a typical Irishman," he says; "my family come from Yorkshire. My father was an ineffective, unsuccessful man, in theory a vehement teetotaler, but in practice often a furtive drinker." His mother, much more gifted and independent-minded, left Dublin to establish herself as a successful teacher of singing in London—a fact of cardinal importance in Bernard Shaw's future career. The religious atmosphere of his childhood—though sometimes enlivened by a heretical uncle—was narrow and dreary, but at the age of ten he gave up going to church, and his first appearance in print was a letter to the newspapers protesting against the methods and doctrines of the popular religious revivalists, Moody and Sankey, who visited Dublin in 1875. His school days were, according to his own verdict "the most completely wasted and mischievous part of my life."

"I never learnt anything at School, a place where they put Cæsar and Horace into the hands of small boys, and expect the result to be an elegant taste of knowledge of the world. I took refuge in total idleness at school, and picked up at home, quite unconsciously, a knowledge of that extraordinary literature of modern music, from Bach to Wagner, which has saved me from being to the smallest disadvantage in competition with men who only know the grammar and mispronunciation of the Greek and Latin poets and philosophers. For the rest, my parents went their own way and let me go mine. Thus the habit of freedom, which most Englishmen and Englishwomen of my class never acquire and never let their children acquire, came to me naturally."

At fifteen he entered the office of a Dublin land-agent, and stayed there five years; he proved a competent clerk, in spite of his heretical opinions and his devotion to music and art, but it is not surprising that life at a Dublin desk was distasteful to him, and in 1876 he followed his mother to London. He worked for a while with the Edison Telephone Company, but subsisted mainly on his mother's bounty, his earnings during the first nine years by his pen amounting to only six pounds, of which five were paid for writing the advertisement of a patent medicine. These were the years of his novels, of which the first was, "with merciless fitness," entitled 'Immaturity.' The manuscript still remains, partially devoured by mice, "but even they have been unable to finish it." The other four found their way into print in obscure Socialist reviews, and have since been republished, both in England and America, but beyond showing a turn for heresy and paradox, they are of slight literary significance, and their author has always refused to take them seriously. He says:

"I recall these five remote products of my nonage as five heavy brown-paper parcels, which were always coming back to me from some publisher, and raising the very serious financial question of the sixpence to be paid to Messrs. Carter, Paterson & Company, the carriers, for passing them on to the next publisher."

Shaw was really engaged in acquiring the education for which he had found no opportunity in Dublin— haunting the National Gallery and the British Museum, hearing good music, joining revolutionary societies and meeting radical thinkers, reading Karl Marx and Henry George, speaking at street corners and in Hyde Park in support of Socialism, vegetarianism and teetotalism, and

so clarifying his opinions by learning how to express
them. He gave up novel-writing for reasons he must be
allowed to explain himself:—

"I had no taste for what is called 'popular art,' no respect for popular morality, no belief in popular religion, no admiration for popular
heroics. As an Irishman, I could pretend to patriotism neither for
the country I had abandoned nor the country that had ruined it.
As a humane person I detested violence and slaughter, whether in
war, sport, or the butcher's yard. I was a Socialist, detesting our
anarchical scramble for money, and believing in equality as the only
possible permanent basis of social organization, discipline, subordi-
nation, good manners, and selection of fit persons for high functions.
Fashionable life, open on indulgent terms to unencumbered 'brilliant'
persons, I could not endure."

Shaw's next venture was into journalism, for which he
was admirably qualified by talent and education and in
which he scored a brilliant success, first as reviewer for
the 'Pall Mall Gazette' and art critic for the London
'World' (1885), next as musical critic for the 'Star' (1888–
9), then in the same capacity for the 'World' (1890–94),
and finally as dramatic critic for the 'Saturday Review'
(1895–98). A selection of his dramatic notices, under
the title 'Dramatic Opinions and Essays' was published
in New York with an admirable preface by James Huneker, himself a very competent critic, and still enjoys
a wide circulation on both sides of the Atlantic. It would
be difficult to find in any language—and impossible in
English—a set of criticisms which contain so much of
permanent value. It was a time of crisis in the history
of the London stage, which was beginning to emerge from
the swaddling bands of sentimentalism and conventionality. A reviving breath came from the Continent in the
dramas of Ibsen, and Shaw did his utmost to open the

mind of the public to the new inspiration. Pinero and
Henry Arthur Jones were writing plays of compromise
which attempted to adapt new ideas to the popular
palate, and Shaw encouraged or chided them as he found
them true or false to the new ideals. The idolatry of
Shakespeare, inherited from the critics of the Romantic
movement, was an obstacle to progress, and Shaw did
his best to destroy it, though he acknowledges that
'Othello,' 'Lear,' and 'Macbeth' are masterpieces, and
that Shakespeare is "unsurpassed as poet, story-teller,
character draughtsman, humourist, and rhetorician."
Rightly considered, and due allowance being made for
Shaw's love for the position of devil's advocate, there is
little in his criticisms a modern Shakespeare scholar would
object to; but at the time they aroused attention by their
apparent extravagance—just what the author was aiming at—and ultimately they contributed powerfully to a
juster appreciation of Shakespeare's real genius. Nothing is gained by attributing, even to masterpieces, virtues
they do not really possess, and much of the Shakespeare
worship current at the time had no solid foundation.

Shaw was justly proud of his achievements as a journalist, "convinced that nothing that is not journalism
will live long as literature, or be of any use while it does
live," but he has nothing but contempt for the journalists
who profess that "it is their duty to 'reflect' what they
believe to be the ignorance and prejudice of their readers,
instead of leading and enlightening them to the best of
their ability." When Max Nordau gained a passing
popularity by a superficial essay on the degeneracy of
modern art, Shaw took a holy delight in reversing his
usual rôle and exposing the fallacies of Nordau's devil's

advocacy—an easy task for Shaw, with his more thorough acquaintance with modern music, art, and literature and his greater command of invective. This paper, originally published in 1896 as a contribution to an American review, was reprinted in 1908 with a preface and some revisions, and is one of Shaw's most characteristic productions. It is amusing to find him asserting the necessity and usefulness of conventions and warning the "emancipated" young enthusiast who flings duty and religion, convention and parental authority to the winds that she will find herself plunged into duties, responsibilities and sacrifices from which she may be glad to retreat "into the comparatively loose life of an ordinary respectable woman of fashion." We have characteristic outbreaks by the way on the one hand against "the popular conception of God as an omniscient, omnipotent, and frightfully jealous and vindictive old gentleman sitting on a throne above the clouds," and on the other against the "crop of cheap syllogisms excogitated by a handful of raw Rationalists in their sects of 'Freethinkers,' and 'Secularists' and 'Positivists' and 'Don't Knowists' (Agnostics)." An incidental defence of special pleading throws light on Shaw's habitual method—"the way to get at the merits of a case is not to listen to the fool who imagines himself impartial, but to get it argued with reckless bias for and against." This explains much that readers find disconcerting in Shaw as mere extravagance and perversity. But more significant still is a sober and yet eloquent passage in which he sets forth his ideas as to the aim of art:—

" The claim of art to our respect must stand or fall with the validity of its pretension to cultivate and refine our senses and faculties until seeing, hearing, feeling, smelling, and tasting become highly conscious and critical acts with us, protesting vehemently against ugliness, noise, discordant speech, frowzy clothing, and re-breathed air, and taking keen interest and pleasure in beauty, in music, and in nature, besides making us insist, as necessary for comfort and decency, on clean, wholesome, handsome fabrics to wear, and utensils of fine material and elegant workmanship to handle. Further, art should refine our sense of character and conduct, of justice and sympathy, greatly heightening our self-knowledge, self-control, precision of action, and considerateness, and making us intolerant of baseness, cruelty, injustice, and intellectual superficiality or vulgarity. The worthy artist or craftsman is he who serves the physical and moral senses by feeding them with pictures, musical compositions, pleasant houses and gardens, good clothes and fine implements, poems, fictions, essays, and dramas which call the heightened senses and ennobled faculties into pleasurable activity. The great artist is he who goes a step beyond the demand, and, by supplying works of a higher beauty and a higher interest than have yet been perceived, succeeds, after a brief struggle with its strangeness, in adding this fresh extension of sense to the heritage of the race."

Associated with Shaw's journalistic activity are two books, 'The Quintessence of Ibsen' (1891) and 'The Perfect Wagnerite' (1898). The first interprets Ibsen from the point of view of Shaw's anti-idealism, and contains many entertaining flashes of light on and about the struggle then proceeding to secure a foothold for the Ibsen plays on the English stage; but it is Shaw's philosophy rather than Ibsen's that is set forth, and the essay is far from being a sufficient or safe guide to the ideas and purposes of the Scandinavian poet. In the second volume the Nibelung cycle is interpreted from the point of view of Wagner's revolutionary opinions. But Shaw, in spite of his versatility and keen intelligence, is no more successful than a mere professor in applying an allegorical key to a work of art. At the time, however, the book no doubt contributed to a better understanding of Wagner's genius.

While Shaw was earning his livelihood as a journalist and doing good service by winning attention for work of real merit, as well as by exposing old shams and new bores,—a task for which he had prepared himself by years of study—his real intellectual interest lay in the social questions which later became the predominant factor in his work. It would be easy to convict him of inconsistency under this head by disregarding dates, but the better plan is to attempt to make clear the successive stages of opinion through which he passed. Of the earlier phases of his socialistic enthusiasm, which may be dated about the late seventies and earlier eighties, he gives us a striking picture in his address to the British Association at Bath (1888):—

"Numbers of young men, pupils of Mill, Spencer, Comte, and Darwin, roused by Mr. Henry George's 'Progress and Poverty,' left aside evolution and free thought; took to insurrectionary economics; studied Karl Marx; and were so convinced that Socialism had only to be put clearly before the working-classes to concentrate the power of their immense numbers in one irresistible organization, that the Revolution was fixed for 1889—the anniversary of the French Revolution—at latest. I remember being asked satirically and publicly at that time how long I thought it would take to get Socialism into working order if I had my way. I replied, with a spirited modesty, that a fortnight would be ample for the purpose. When I add that I was frequently complimented on being one of the more reasonable Socialists, you will be able to appreciate the fervour of our conviction, and the extravagant levity of our ideas."

When the Fabian Society was founded in 1884 with the motto: "For the right moment you must wait, as Fabius did most patiently when warring against Hannibal, though many censured his delays. But when the time comes you must strike hard, as Fabius did, or your waiting will be in vain, and pointless," Shaw joined the ranks of these middle class intellectuals, whom he natu rally found more congenial than the Social Democrats led by Hyndman. He at once took an active part in the Society's propaganda and contributed two of its first tracts, one of them a brief manifesto setting forth its principles, from which the following may be quoted as indicative of his position in 1884:

"That it is the duty of each member of the State to provide for his or her wants by his or her own Labour.

"That a life-interest in the Land and Capital of the nation is the birth-right of every individual born within its confines; and that access to this birth-right should not depend upon the will of any private person other than the person seeking it.

"That the State should compete with private individuals—especially with parents—in providing happy homes for children, so that every child may have a refuge from the tyranny or neglect of its natural custodians.

"That the State should secure a liberal education and an equal share in the National Industry to each of its units.

"That the established Government has no more right to call itself the State than the smoke of London has to call itself the weather.

"That we had rather face a Civil War than such another century of suffering as the present one has been."

The last two propositions reflect a phase of Anarchism out of which Shaw passed very speedily. A deeper study of economics led him to reject the Marxian theory of "surplus value," which had at first attracted him, and in 1887 he exposed its weaknesses in a series of papers in the 'National Reformer'; he had never been in favour of the "class war," another cardinal principle of Marxian Socialism, and he passed out definitely into the ranks of those who believed in the gradual municipalization of industry and the transference of rent and interest to the State, not in one lump sum, but by instalments.   This is the position taken by him in the British Association paper of 1888, published, together with another on the economic basis of Socialism, in the 'Fabian Essays' of 1889.   By this time he was ready to ridicule the revolutionary Socialist as "My friend Fitzthunder," and to speak of the extremists as "romantic amateurs who represent nobody but their silly selves."   A paper in 1896 on "The Illusions of Socialism" alienated and disconcerted many of his old comrades still further by its appalling frankness.   In a lighter effort, 'Socialism for Millionaires' (1896) he advises them to give the public "something they ought to want and don't"—and some American millionaires have followed his counsel.   The Fabian Society had become more moderate in its expectations and demands and among these moderates Shaw attached himself to the more conservative wing, assisting Sidney Webb to resist the unsuccessful campaign of H. G. Wells in favour of a more vigorous policy, including the endowment of motherhood.   Shaw had enlarged his acquaintance with practical problems of administration by six years' service on the St. Pancras Borough Council, the main literary outcome being one of his most solidly reasoned Socialistic pamphlets, 'The Common Sense of Municipal Trading' (1904).   About this time his interest in Socialism was waning under the competition of a new enthusiasm for eugenics, but this belongs to the later period of his success as a dramatist and will be most conveniently discussed in that connection.   In 1911 he declared himself still theoretically in favour of "a system of society where all the income of the country is to be divided up in exactly equal proportions," but as he was not very clear whether the share of every man, woman and child would be £500 a year or £50 a year, this avowal of a pious belief attracted little attention. The exposition of this view in a later address, 'The Case for Equality' (1914) was overshadowed by the outbreak of the Great War.

As early as 1885, the eminent dramatic critic and translator of Ibsen, William Archer, who secured for Shaw his first footing in journalism, had attempted to collaborate with him in a play. Its subject was to be the power of money in modern social and industrial organization—the theme of the 'Rheingold,' as afterwards developed by Shaw in 'The Perfect Wagnerite'—and its manner was to be that of the well-made play, a French comedy, '*La Ceinture Dorée*,' being actually chosen for a suggestion of the plot. Archer made the scenario, and Shaw wrote the dialogue for the first act. At this point the two collaborators found themselves hopelessly at variance, but Shaw insisted on finishing the second act and reading it to Archer, who promptly went to sleep. This silent criticism discouraged Shaw more than his collaborator's comments, and he put the manuscript aside. Then came, in the wake of the new theatre movement abroad and the controversy about the production of the Ibsen plays on the English stage, the foundation of the Independent Theatre in London by J. T. Grein. The theatre was there, but where were the new English plays? None were to be found, and Shaw bethought himself of his rejected manuscript. He added a third act, gave it the mock-scriptural title of 'Widowers' Houses,' and it was produced. "It made a sensation out of all proportion to

its merits and even its demerits; and I at once became
infamous as a dramatist." The Socialists applauded on
principle; the public hooted; the critics followed suit;
and the play was immediately withdrawn. Shaw himself accurately describes it as "a grotesquely realistic exposure of slum landlordism, municipal jobbery, and the
pecuniary and matrimonial ties between it and the pleasant people of 'independent' incomes who imagine that
such sordid matters do not touch their own lives." The
characters are grotesquely impossible, the plot is conventional romance reversed so as to show all manner of
ugliness, the dialogue is adorned with "silly pleasantries"
(the author's own phrase). Shaw admits that in these
"farcical trivialities" he had not taken the theatre seriously, and he determined to try again.

Ibsenism, now become a craze, was misunderstood both
by its reactionary opponents and its "emancipated"
devotees, and Shaw undertook in his next play to show
both sides their misconceptions. 'The Philanderer,' of
which the central scenes pass in a supposed Ibsen club in
London, exhibits in its characters various degrees of in-
fatuated hero-worship and blind condemnation, the
heroine, Grace Tranfield, representing the intelligent
appreciation of Ibsen's ideas as interpreted by Shaw himself. The play also serves to illustrate the fundamental
difference in method between Shaw and the great Scandinavian whom he has been accused of copying. Ibsen
is primarily the poet-dramatist, whose aim is "to depict
human beings, human emotions, and human destinies,
upon a groundwork of certain of the social conditions and
principles of the present day." Shaw is first of all a
propagandist, who uses the stage as a pulpit to set forth

his opinions. In 'The Philanderer,' in addition to the exposition of popular misconceptions about Ibsen, Shaw indulges his prejudices against vivisection and the medical profession. The dialogue shows a considerable advance on 'Widowers' Houses,' but the characters, though more subtly conceived, are still mechanical. Grein declined to produce it on the excuse that it was beyond the capacity of his company, and it remained unacted until its real significance was almost unintelligible to either a New York or a London audience, the Ibsen craze having passed.

Shaw had too much determination and intellectual vigour to be discouraged. He returned to his earlier model in 'Mrs. Warren's Profession,' which purports to deal with the question of prostitution, but really discusses much wider questions of social and commercial organization. Mrs. Warren, in her account of herself first as a poor working girl and then as a successful manager of a white slave syndicate, sets forth the apologue of modern industrialism, as Shaw viewed it. The other characters are much less powerfully realized, and the rifle episode introduces an unnecessary element of melodrama; the doubtful paternity of Mrs. Warren's daughter also introduces unnecessary elements of "unpleasantness," but as a piece of dramatic construction and character drawing the play is by far the best thing Shaw had yet done. The British censor, however, interfered and prohibited its performance, but of the prohibition and the newspaper controversy that resulted when the play was produced in New York Shaw did not fail to make literary capital.

Within a year Shaw returned to the attack on the stage,

and this time he succeeded. 'Arms and the Man' traves-
ties only conventional romanticism and militarism, and
as the scene was laid in Bulgaria, about which the British
public knew little and cared less, critics and audiences
alike were willing to be amused. It ran for three months
in London, and Richard Mansfield later made it popular in
the United States. It reverses the traditional theory of
playmaking, for the plot rises to its height in the first act
and wanders off into mere dialogue; but the dialogue is
easy and sparkling, and found ready acceptance as it
clashed with no cherished convictions and attacked no
revered institutions. The libretto of 'The Chocolate
Soldier' was borrowed from it and has helped to make
'Arms and the Man' one of Shaw's best known plays.

Christian Socialism was again in the air, and Shaw,
refusing to continue on the line of popular success, chose
this as the background for his next play, 'Candida.'
London managers praised its originality and verve, but
refused to produce it, and it waited nearly ten years before it was acted by Arnold Daly in New York and established Shaw's reputation as a popular dramatist.
New York women took their husbands to 'Candida' as to
a lecture on the secret of matrimonial felicity, and the
"shawl" speech—"put your trust in my love for you,
James, for if that went I should care very little for your
sermons"—became a commonplace of American conversation. Shaw was outraged at this popular appreciation, protested that that "minx" Candida had taken
in the New York public, and cast further obscurity on
the situation by a supplementary play, 'How He Lied to
Her Husband.' The main significance of 'Candida,'
apart from its popular interpretation, is not very clear,

but there are amusing and enlightening reflections on love, marriage, socialism, Christianity, and art, and the play has held the stage by the excellence of its character drawing—"minx" or heroine, Candida is admirably conceived—an emotional power in the main situation unusual in Shaw's plays, and the unfailing vivacity of its dialogue.

While it was still unproduced and unpublished, and Shaw was at work on 'The Man of Destiny,'—a conversation between Napoleon Bonaparte as Shaw conceived him and a lady in the likeness of Ellen Terry, which was acted a few years later and failed—he was approached by Cyril Maude, manager of the Haymarket Theatre, with an inquiry about this new play. Shaw answered that it would not suit the Haymarket—it was intended for Richard Mansfield, who did not like it—but that he would write one that would. Of the rehearsals Maude published in 'The Haymarket Theatre' the following account, since known to have been written by Shaw himself, and put into the mouth of Maude as a joke:—

"In the winter of 1897 this play, which was called 'You Never Can Tell,' came to hand. Some of our friends thought well of the author, and Harrison (who, as my readers have doubtless already gathered, is a perfect ignoramus in all matters connected with plays and acting) liked the play. In short, I allowed myself to be overpersuaded, and we actually put the play into rehearsal.

"From the first the author showed the perversity of his disposition and his utter want of practical knowledge of the stage. He proposed impossible casts. He forced us into incomprehensible agreements by torturing us with endless talk until we were ready to sign anything rather than argue for another hour. Had I been properly supported by my colleagues I should not have tolerated his proceedings for a moment. I do not wish to complain of anybody, but as a matter of fact I was not so supported. I expected nothing better from Harrison, because with all his excellent qualities he is too vain—I say it though he is my best friend—to be trusted in so delicate an under-taking as the management of a theatre. The truth is, Shaw flattered him, and thus detached him from me by playing on his one fatal weakness.

"The world knows, I think, that whatever my faults may be, I am an affectionate and devoted husband. But I have never pretended that my wife is perfect. No woman is, and but few men. Still, I do think she might have supported me better than she did through our greatest trial. This man from the first exercised a malign influence over her. With my full consent and approval she selected for her-self a certain part in his play. He had privately resolved—out of mere love of contradiction—that she should play another. When he read the play he contrived to balance the parts in such a way that my unfortunate and misguided wife actually there and then gave up her part and accepted the one he had determined to throw upon her. I then recognized for the first time that I had to deal with a veritable Svengali.

"Our mistake in admitting an author of this type to our theatre soon became apparent. At the reading, that excellent actor, Jack Barnes, whose very name calls up the idea of sound judgment, with-drew, overpowered by fatigue and disgust, at the end of the first act, and presently threw up the part with which we proposed to insult him—and I now publicly apologize to him for that outrage. Miss Coleman soon followed his example, with a very natural protest against a part in which, as she rightly said, there were 'no laughs and no exits.' Any author with the slightest decency of feeling would have withdrawn in the face of rebuffs so pointed as these. But Mr. Shaw—encouraged, I must say, by Harrison—persisted in what had now become an intolerable intrusion.

"I can hardly describe the rehearsals that followed. It may well be that my recollection of them is confused; for my nerves soon gave way; sleep became a stranger to me; and there were moments at which I was hardly in possession of my faculties. I had to stage-manage as well as act—to stage-manage with that demon sitting beside me casting an evil spell on all our efforts!

"On one occasion Mr. Shaw insulted the entire profession by want-ing a large table on the stage, on the ground that the company would fall over it unless they behaved as if they were coming into a real room instead of, as he coarsely observed, rushing to the float to pick up the band at the beginning of a comic song. This was a personal attack on me, as my vivacity of character and *diable au corps* make me specially impatient of obstacles.

"Mr. Shaw was one of those persons who use a certain superficial reasonableness and dexterity of manner to cover an invincible obstinacy in their own opinion. We had engaged for the leading part (I myself having accepted an insignificant part as a mere waiter) no less an artist than Mr. Allan Aynesworth, whose reputation and subsequent achievements make it unnecessary for me to justify our choice. Mr. Shaw had from the first contended that one of the scenes lay outside Mr. Aynesworth's peculiar province. There can be no doubt now that Mr. Shaw deliberately used his hypnotic power at rehearsal to compel Mr. Aynesworth to fulfil his prediction. In every other scene Mr. Aynesworth surpassed himself. In this he became conscious and confused; his high spirits were suddenly extinguished; even his good-humour left him. He was like a man under a spell—as no doubt he actually was—and his embarrassment communicated itself most painfully to my dear wife, who had to sit on the stage whilst Svengali deliberately tortured his victim.

"At the same time I must say that Mrs. Maude's conduct was not all I could have desired. I greatly dreaded an open rupture between her and the author; and the fiend somehow divined this, and used it as a means of annoying me. Sometimes, when he had cynically watched one of her scenes without any symptom of pleasure, I would venture to ask him his opinion of it. On such occasions he invariably rose with every appearance of angry disapproval, informed me that he would give his opinion to Miss Emery herself, and stalked up the stage to her in a threatening manner, leaving me in a state of apprehension that my overstrained nerves were ill able to bear. Not until afterwards did I learn that on these occasions he flattered my wife disgracefully, and actually made her a party to his systematic attempt to drive me out of my senses. I have never reproached her with it, and I never shall. I mention it here only because it is the truth; and truth has always been with me the first consideration.

"At last Aynesworth broke down under the torture. Mr. Shaw, with that perfidious air of making the best of everything which never deserted him, hypnotized him into complaining of the number of speeches he had to deliver, whereupon Mr. Shaw cut out no less than seventeen of them. This naturally disabled the artist totally. On the question of cutting, Mr. Shaw's attitude was nothing less than Satanic. When I suggested cutting he handed me the play, begged me to cut it freely, and then hypnotized me so that I could not collect my thoughts sufficiently to cut a single line. On the other hand, if I showed the least pleasure in a scene at rehearsal he at once cut it out on the ground that the play was too long. What I suffered from that man at that time will never be fully known. The heart alone knoweth its own bitterness.

"The end came suddenly and unexpectedly. We had made a special effort to fulfil our unfortunate contract, of which even Harrison was now beginning to have his doubts. We had brought back Miss Kate Bishop from Australia to replace Miss Coleman. Mr. Valentine had taken the part repudiated by Mr. Barnes. The scenery had been modelled, and a real dentist's chair obtained for the first act. Harrison, whose folly was responsible for the whole wretched business, came down to the rehearsal. We were honestly anxious to retrieve the situation by a great effort, and save our dear little theatre from the disgrace of a failure.

"Suddenly the author entered, in a new suit of clothes!!"

Maude's judgment in rejecting 'You Never Can Tell' was at fault, for it has since proved one of Shaw's most popular productions, both in England and America, combining a delightfully comic waiter and a grotesque barrister (his son), impossible twins and a dental chair as a novelty in stage device with a modicum of philosophy about the relations of parents and children. But as the frontal attack on the stage had apparently failed, Shaw tried the flank by publishing his one success and half dozen failures under the title of 'Plays Pleasant and Unpleasant,' with elaborate stage directions and still more elaborate prefaces, intended for the edification of readers and as "first aid to critics." The success of this venture established the modern practice of publishing plays and gave Shaw access to the English-reading public all over the world. He repeated the experiment, adding three prefaces this time, in 'Three Plays for Puritans' (1901)—'The Devil's Disciple,' 'Cæsar and Cleopatra,' and 'Captain Brassbound's Conversion,' the first and last mere burlesques—conventional melodrama with the spice of Shavian wit,—and the middle play written in emulation of Shakespeare, who had presented the Romans as contemporary Elizabethans. Shaw presents Cæsar as a modern statesman, Cleopatra as a naughty English school girl, and Britannus as a conventional Victorian. As acted later by Sir Johnston Forbes-Robertson's company, this travesty won much applause on both sides of the Atlantic, but all three plays, when originally produced in 1899 and 1902, had to be classed as failures. At the opening of this century, when Shaw was forty-five, he was still an unsuccessful dramatist so far as stage production was concerned.

The turn of the tide came in 1903–4 with the successful production of 'Candida,' 'The Man of Destiny,' and 'You Never Can Tell' in the New York season of Arnold Daly, and the revival of 'Arms and the Man' by Richard Mansfield. About the same time German translations of 'The Devil's Disciple,' 'The Man of Destiny' and 'Candida,' made by an Austrian playwright at the instance of William Archer, were successfully acted at Vienna, Frankfort, Dresden, and Berlin. There was a natural reaction in London, and Barker at the Court Theatre produced 'Candida,' 'The Man of Destiny,' 'You Never Can Tell,' and then the older plays (except the prohibited 'Mrs. Warren's Profession') with unvarying success. The plays were translated into Swedish, Danish, Magyar,

Polish, Russian, and Dutch, and Shaw's position as an international playwright became as incontestable as his supremacy on the English stage.

'Man and Superman' had been published in 1903 with 'Epistle dedicatory, the Revolutionist's Handbook, and Maxims for Revolutionists.' With the third act ('Don Juan in Hell') omitted, Forbes-Robertson made it the success of the season 1904–5, both in England and the United States. The telling situation of the first act, though against all theatrical tradition (in that the secret of Violet's marriage is held back from the audience) and contrary to popular morality, delighted the public, and the suggestion that woman is the pursuer rather than the pursued had enough truth in it to win favour. Shaw's more serious purpose was to set forth his new doctrine of the Life Force, which impels Ann to seek in John Tanner a father for the Superman. "For art's sake" alone, he tells us in the 'Epistle dedicatory' he "would not face the toil of writing a single sentence." By comparing the Epistle with 'The Revolutionist's Handbook' we learn that what Shaw wished to convey was that education, progress, democracy, socialism are all illusions, and that "the only fundamental and possible socialism is the socialization of the selective breeding of Man: in other terms, of human evolution." The "method" is apparently to be "a joint stock human stud farm" under a State Department of Evolution. It is safe to say that very few of the thousands who enjoyed the play in England and the United States saw anything of this in the submission of John Tanner and Ann Whitefield to "the Life Force" when they "renounce happiness, renounce freedom, renounce tranquillity, above all, renounce the romantic possibilities of an unknown future, for the cares of a household and a family." They say to Shaw, as Ann said to Tanner, "Go on talking," and the final stage direction, "universal laughter," includes the audience as well as the actors.

After a political dissertation on the Irish question, 'John Bull's Other Island,' much more favourably regarded in London than in Dublin, for which it was written,—Shaw returned to sociology in 'Major Barbara.' The introduction of the Salvation Army is merely incidental, and Shaw apparently chose the manufacture of munitions as Undershaft's business because it was the modern industry he disliked most; but behind Undershaft stands the Life Force, regarded no longer as an impulse to propagation but as the Will of God—"a will of which I am a part." The real burden of the play (and of the preface) is, however, the doctrine of the evil of poverty, taken over (with due acknowledgment) from Samuel Butler. In the preface we read:

"Now what does this Let Him Be Poor mean? It means let him be weak. Let him be ignorant. Let him become a nucleus of disease. Let him be a standing exhibition and example of ugliness and dirt. Let him have rickety children. Let him be cheap and let him drag his fellows down to his price by selling himself to do their work. Let his habitations turn our cities into poisonous congeries of slums. Let his daughters infect our young men with the diseases of the streets and his sons revenge him by turning the nation's manhood into scrofula, cowardice, cruelty, hypocrisy, political imbecility, and all the other fruits of oppression and malnutrition."

So in the play Undershaft enumerates the seven deadly sins as "food, clothing, firing, rent, taxes, respectability and children," and describes poverty as "the worst of crimes":

"All the other crimes are virtues beside it: all the other dishonours are chivalry itself by comparison. Poverty blights whole cities; spreads horrible pestilences; strikes dead the very souls of all who come within sight, sound or smell of it. What you call crime is nothing: a murder here and a theft there, a blow now and a curse then: what do they matter? they are only the accidents and illnesses of life: there are not fifty genuine professional criminals in London. But there are millions of poor people, abject people, dirty people, ill fed, ill clothed people. They poison us morally and physically: they kill the happiness of society: they force us to do away with our own liberties and to organize unnatural cruelties for fear they should rise against us and drag us down into their abyss. Only fools fear crime: we all fear poverty."

The public found Shaw's doctrines as expounded by Undershaft much less interesting than 'The Revolutionist's Handbook,' and the Salvation Army lass who was the granddaughter of an earl was no more convincing than the Greek professor who turned from beating the big drum to running a huge concern for the manufacture of munitions. There was a further falling-off in 'The Doctor's Dilemma,' which repeats on a large scale and in a preface of nearly a hundred pages the misrepresentation of the medical profession Shaw had already been guilty of in the earlier sketch of Dr. Paramore ('The Philanderer'). The professional dilemma is non-existent, there being no question as to the conduct of a doctor who kills a patient because he wants to marry the patient's wife; but the problem really posed is "how much selfishness we ought to stand from a gifted person for the sake of his gifts." In the preface to 'The Sanity of Art,' written about this time, Shaw says that he does not believe in allowing license to genius, but in the play the rascally artist makes out a very good case for himself, and dies in "indescribable peace" protesting his faith "in

Michael Angelo, Velasquez, and Rembrandt; in the might of design, the mystery of colour, the redemption of all things by Beauty everlasting, and the message of art that has made these hands blessed."

'The Doctor's Dilemma' was acted as soon as it was written, and so were the two plays that followed it. Shaw was in a position to say what he liked, for revolutionary opinion was growing, and many people who enjoyed his fun regarded his paradoxes merely as part of the performance. In 'Getting Married' he not only said what he liked, but said it how he liked. There is no plot—merely the setting of a continuous conversation on marriage, fortified by the customary preface, in which polygyny, polyandry, promiscuity, and every other sexual arrangement are discussed, and the following are offered as practical proposals:

"Make divorce as easy, as cheap, and as private as marriage.

"Grant divorce at the request of either party, whether the other consents or not; and admit no other ground than the request, which should be made without stating any reasons.

"Place the work of a wife and mother on the same footing as other work: that is, on the footing of labour worthy of its hire; and provide for unemployment in it exactly as for unemployment in shipbuilding or any other recognized bread-winning trade."

The play presents the inequalities and subterfuges of the existing marriage system in a sufficiently extravagant fashion, and is remarkable for a passage in which Mrs. George is inspired to picture the raptures of passion with an ardour Shaw succeeded in conveying only in this instance—and that in retrospect.

In 'The Shewing-up of Blanco Posnet' Shaw returned to melodrama, this time in a Wild Western setting, with the Life Force figuring under the name of God. This the

Censor objected to and prohibited the performance of the play; but as the Lord Chamberlain's writ did not run in Dublin, it passed successfully into the repertory of the Irish National Theatre, and was produced by the Irish Players on their American tour without a shadow of offence. Shaw took occasion to make hay of the British censorship, which was then being investigated by a parliamentary committee, in a characteristic preface.

The Censor also fell foul of Shaw's next play, 'Press Cuttings,' which ridiculed the suffragette agitation, then at its height, and represented Premier Balsquith as chaining himself to the scraper at General Mitchener's door. As the Censor had objected to the "sermon in crude Melodrama" because it discussed religion, a forbidden subject for the English theatre, he interposed in this instance another long-standing tradition which prohibited the introduction of contemporary personages on the stage. Shaw protested that he had no intention of caricaturing Mr. Asquith and Lord Kitchener and changed the names to Johnson and Bones; the play is an amusing skit on contemporary political difficulties, but has no philosophic or dramatic significance.

The same might be said of 'Misalliance,' except that it gave the opportunity for a preface on 'Parents and Children' (Samuel Butler again) of more than ordinary length, and of 'The Dark Lady of the Sonnets,' a Shakespearian extravaganza, both of which failed to please; but with 'Fanny's First Play' Shaw scored the most remarkable success of his career. It had a record run in London, and in the United States ran for an even longer period. Shaw availed himself of the Elizabethan device of "the play within the play" for a setting in which he made fun of the London critics, A. B. Walkley, Gilbert Cannan, and A. E. Vaughan; and the expedient of attributing the play proper to an aspiring amateur enabled him to combine the extravagant heresies he had already inflicted on the public with a conventional plot. The son of a respectable tradesman is sentenced to fourteen days' imprisonment with the option of a fine for assaulting the police, on the same day that the daughter of another respectable tradesman, to whom he is engaged, receives a similar penalty for the same offence, independently committed by her on her way home from a religious meeting. In the end the boy marries "Darling Dora," a "daughter of joy," and the girl a disguised footman who is the brother of a Duke. In the two-page preface, which was all he deemed the play worth, Shaw described it as a mere "pot-boiler," and so it was, in the sense that it contained no propaganda that Shaw had not made before; but the public liked the familiar heresies about family life all the better in a setting obviously absurd, and accepted them as a not unwelcome part of a capital evening's entertainment.

By this time Shaw had communicated to the public, indirectly and directly, all that he really had to say. He had realized the need for saying it entertainingly, and in some cases the sugar-coating of the pill had been so substantial as to overmaster completely the bitter instruction it was intended to convey, but this was remedied by the prefaces, if people could be induced to read them. There was no subject, however, on which his versatile intellect could not reflect gleams of wit and wisdom, and the temptation of the open stage, to be used as a pulpit to his heart's desire, was too great to be resisted. 'Over-

ruled,' which was first entitled 'Trespassers will be Prose-
cuted,' is a continuation of the interminable conversation
of 'Getting Married,' and 'Great Catherine' introduces a
Victorian Englishman to the Russian court of the eighteenth century, but both these are mere sketches. The
substantial additions to Shaw's dramatic achievement
up to the outbreak of the War are 'Pygmalion,' which
had its original production at Berlin in 1912, and 'Androcles and the Lion.' Both were put on the London and
New York stages in 1913, and met with general approval,
though they did not attain to the popular success of
'Fanny's First Play.'

'Androcles and the Lion' presents the Shavian view of
primitive Christianity, with some glances at religion in
general in the finely conceived character of Lavinia, but
its real attraction consists in the dramatization of the
nursery tale which 'Sandford and Merton' had made
familiar to Shaw's own generation. The Lion (really
the principal rôle) and Androcles, both admirably acted,
were irresistibly funny, and a comic Emperor with comic
subjects (including the Christian martyrs) contributed
to the enjoyment of those who did not mind the profana-
tion of subjects traditionally sacred.

'Pygmalion,' "a romance in five acts," presents the
conversion of a London flower girl into a possible duchess
by three months' training in phonetics. Her trial appearance in a London drawing room provides some excellent fooling, but the real delight of the play is the
character of her father, the dustman Doolittle, spokesman
of the undeserving poor until a legacy from a misguided
American philanthropist lands him in an unhappy respectability. The suggestion of the idle dustman may

have come from a recollection of Shaw's boyhood—a cynical tramp who was asked by Shaw's uncle why he did not work and "frankly replied that he was too lazy"; but the conception is worked out with inimitable humour. Oddly enough, this burlesque character is much more humanized than the boorish professor of phonetics, who is so indistinctly realized that Shaw had to add not merely a preface about him, but a supplementary note of sixteen pages to explain the outcome of the educational experiment which forms the centre of the play.

It would be idle to appraise Shaw's dramatic work by the standards accepted when he began to write for the stage, for his main purpose was precisely to remove those standards and his main service that he largely succeeded. The question whether his stage entertainments are "plays" belongs to a past age. He is certainly careless about plot construction, but as his aim was not to tell a story but to convey ideas, an analysis showing that some of his plays have no plot and some very bad plots, technically considered, would be beside the mark. He is not without gifts of characterization, but most of his characters are mere burlesques, with just enough life to embody or convey some thesis dear to the author. A number of critics and interpreters have analysed Shaw's philosophy and made it clear that he has a set of very definite ideas—that he is anti-moralist, anti-utilitarian, anti-Darwinist, anti-scientist, anti-sentimentalist, anti-hedonist, anti-militarist, anti-vivisectionist, and so on; on the positive side, he is a vitalist, a mystic, a socialist (as to commercial and industrial relations), an anarchist (as to personal relations), an individualist, a realist, an ascetic, a humanitarian, and a eugenist. The notion

that his criticism of society is merely negative is as untenable as the older view that he is a mere jester. But
his wit and humour, his intellectual keenness and brilliance of epigram will probably continue to be admired
when most of his doctrines have either been absorbed or
rejected by the common sense of mankind.

During the War Bernard Shaw's reputation was under a cloud. When the War broke out, he wrote a series
of articles which classed the British Imperialists with
the German Junkers, and scoffed at the idea that re-
garding treaties as "scraps of paper" was at all unusual.
He pictured the British Lion as only shamming sleep in
order to tempt Germany to provocative action, "and the
Lion, with a mighty roar, sprang at last, and in a flash
had his teeth and claws in the rival of England, and will
not now let her go for all the pacifists or Socialists in the
world until he is either killed or back on his Waterloo
pedestal again." Shaw took off his hat to the noble old
beast as he made his last charge, and applauded his
splendid past and valiant breed; but in future, he added,
"we must fight, not alone for England, but for the welfare of the world." To anyone versed in Shaw's hyper-
bolical manner and capable of penetrating to the real
meaning lying behind his exaggerations, there was little
in what he said to give offence,—but the British public
was in no mood to make allowances and distinctions.
Shaw's utterances were regarded as lending aid and comfort to the enemy—absurdly enough, for he was as far
removed as the poles from pro-Germanism—and his
license as a popular entertainer was tacitly withdrawn.
Many, even among his own followers, held him blame-
worthy in failing to respond to the national emotion and

assuming an unseasonable attitude of detachment. It
was a situation in which his keen intelligence did not make
up for his lack of emotional sympathy. It is the fault of
all his work—his characters talk about love, but they
never give the impression of being in love, and their anger
like their fear seems to be put on from the outside, often
with a heavy hand; they do not move from within. But
the particular revelation of the defect at a critical moment
in the nation's history hardly merited the bitter resentment it aroused, and calmer times brought back a juster
appreciation of the offender's real genius, with a general
return of his older successes to the stage.

'Playlets of the War' did not tend to conciliate public
opinion, or indeed add to the author's reputation, and
'Heartbreak House' was a puzzle to most readers on its
first publication. The preface, with its reference to
Chekof's 'The Cherry Orchard,' of which the play is an
English transcription, was enlightening. "The same nice
people, the same utter futility." When it was put on the
stage by the Theatre Guild in New York, the play was
surprisingly successful and had a good run, but it was less
warmly welcomed on its reproduction in London. Probably English audiences were better able to realize the
distance between Shaw's caricatures and the reality, and
were in too serious a mood to be diverted by the satire.
The American audiences took the play more objectively
and were amused by its quick movement and intellectual
extravagances, which they no doubt regarded as mere
absurdities, without any relation to any society they knew.
As a work of art it falls far short in delicacy and dramatic
skill of 'The Cherry Orchard' on which it was modelled.

'Back to Methuselah' is a return, on an unprecedented

scale for a drama, to Shaw's own manner. In a review of his dramatic activities in the preface he catalogues as subjects he has discussed in a series of comedies of manners in the classic fashion "slum landlordism, doctrinaire Free Love (pseudo-Ibsenism), prostitution, militarism, marriage, history, current politics, natural Christianity, national and individual character, paradoxes of conventional society, husband hunting, questions of conscience, professional delusions and impostures." 'Man and Superman' he had intended to make a dramatic parable of Creative Evolution, believing that this was the religion of which mankind stood in need; but "being then at the height of my invention and comedic talent, I decorated it too brilliantly and lavishly." Now, in his old age, he abandons the erotic associations of the Don Juan legend, and goes back to the legend of the Garden of Eden "without distractions and embellishments." The embellishments are not altogether lacking, fortunately for those who regard Shaw's decorations as more important than his Gospel. As presented by the Theatre Guild in New York in three instalments (and two of these lasted for nearly four hours), Shaw's version of the Garden of Eden legend proved quite entertaining, so long as it stayed in or near the Garden. When it wandered into the future— A. D. 2170, A. D. 3000, and A. D. 31,920—it was often tiresome; the central idea that man needs a longer life to enable him to solve the problems of existence was not sufficient to bear the strain put upon it, and the final solution in 'As Far as Thought can Reach' offered a view of human society which was singularly unattractive. As a critic of other people's 'isms, Shaw had shown extraordinary versatility and comic power; when he came to propound his own religion, his hand seemed to lose its cunning, and he was sometimes dull.

This does not, of course, disallow his claim that he found the English stage with "clandestine adultery" as its one serious subject, and opened the way for his contemporaries and successors to deal with the myriad issues of modern life. Many of these issues he himself presented with a daring and brilliance that have not been excelled. His intellectual acuteness and his dialectical skill enabled him to influence modern thought as profoundly as his talent for comedy enabled him to broaden and vitalise the modern drama. Incidentally he furnished, not merely for the English-speaking nations but for the whole civilised world, a succession of sparkling intellectual entertainments some of which are likely to hold the stage for many years to come.

BIBLIOGRAPHY

NOVELS

'The Irrational Knot.' Written 1880. Serial publication 1885-7. American and English edition 1905.

'Love among the Artists.' Written 1881. Serial publication 1887-8. American edition 1900. English edition 1914.

'Cashel Byron's Profession.' Written 1882. Serial publication 1885-6. English edition 1886.

'An Unsocial Socialist.' Written 1883. Serial publication 1884. English edition 1887.

SOCIALISM

1884   Fabian Tract No. 2, 'Manifesto.'

1885   Fabian Tract No. 3, 'Warning to provident Landlords and Capitalists.'

1887   Articles on Marxian Socialism in the 'National Reformer.'

1888   Address to the Economic Section of the British Association. Published as 'The Transition' with another chapter on the economic basis of Socialism in a volume of 'Fabian Essays' (1889) edited by Shaw.

1888   'My Friend Fitzthunder' in 'To-day.'

1891   'The Legal Eight Hours Question.' A public debate with J. W. Foote.

  'The Impossibilities of Anarchism.'

1892   'The Fabian Society; its Early History.'

1894   'Socialism and Superior Brains' (in 'Fortnightly Review' for April).

1896   'Socialism for Millionaires' (in 'Contemporary Review' for February.   Published as a Fabian Tract, 1901).

  'The Illusions of Socialism.'

1904   'Fabianism and the Fiscal Question.'

  'The Common Sense of Municipal Trading.'

1914   'The Case for Equality.' An Address to the Political and Economic Circle of the National Liberal Club.

CRITICISM

1891 'The Quintessence of Ibsenism.' New edition 'Now completed to the Death of Ibsen,' 1913.

1896 'A Degenerate's View of Nordau' in New York 'Liberty.' Published as 'The Sanity of Art: An Exposure of the current Nonsense about Artists being Degenerate,' revised, with new preface, 1908.

1898 'The Perfect Wagnerite.'

1906 'Dramatic Opinions and Essays,' selected from the 'Saturday Review' by James Huneker.

PLAYS

1893 'Widowers' Houses' (Independent Theatre Series of Plays, No. 2), written 1885–92, produced 1892, first of three 'Unpleasant Plays' (1898) including
'The Philanderer' (written 1893, produced 1907) and
'Mrs. Warren's Profession' (written 1894, produced 1902).

1898 'Arms and the Man' (written and produced 1894), published together with 'Candida' (written 1894-5, produced 1897),
'The Man of Destiny' (written 1895, produced 1897), and
'You Never Can Tell' (written 1896, produced 1900) as the second volume of 'Plays Pleasant and Unpleasant.'

1901 'Three Plays for Puritans':
'The Devil's Disciple,' written 1897, produced 1899.
'Cæsar and Cleopatra,' written 1898, produced 1899.
'Captain Brassbound's Conversion,' written 1899, produced 1902.

1903 'Man and Superman.'

1907 'John Bull's Other Island,' written and produced 1904.
'Major Barbara,' written and produced 1905.
'How he Lied to her Husband,' written 1904, produced 1905.

1909 'Press Cuttings.'

1911 'The Doctor's Dilemma,' written and produced 1906.
'Getting Married,' written and produced 1908.
'The Shewing-up of Blanco Posnet,' written and produced 1909.

1911 'Misalliance,' written and produced 1910.
'The Dark Lady of the Sonnets,' written and produced 1910.

'Fanny's First Play,' written and produced 1911.

'Androcles and the Lion,' written 1912; produced 1913.

'Over-ruled,' written 1912; produced 1913.

'Pygmalion,' written 1912; produced 1913.

'Great Catherine,' written 1912; produced 1913.

1919 'Heartbreak House, Great Catherine and Playlets of the War.' The last-mentioned included 'O'Flaherty V. C.,' 'The Inca of Perusalem' (produced 1917), 'Augustus does his Bit' (produced 1917), and 'Annajanska, the Bolshevik Empress' (produced 1918). 'Heartbreak House' was produced in New York in 1920.

1921 'Back to Methuselah'; produced, New York, 1922.

There are books about Shaw by Holbrook Jackson (1906), Renée M. Deacon (1910), G. K. Chesterton (1910), A. Henderson (1911), Joseph McCabe (1914), P. P. Howe (1915), John Palmer (1915), Richard E. Burton (1916), Herbert Skimpole (1918), H. C. Duffin (1920); in French, by Charles Cestre (1912), and Augustin Hamon (1913), the latter translated by Eden and Cedar Paul (1916).

CHAPTER VIII

J. M. BARRIE (1860-   )

BARRIE has had two careers—one as yet happily unfinished. At the beginning of this century his enthusiastic
admirer and expositor, J. A. Hammerton, in 'J. M. Barrie
and his Books,' could without compunction give all his
attention to the novels and express the opinion that
"Barrie is not, and is not likely to be, a serious factor in
the contemporary drama." This opinion, like so many
other literary prophecies, has now been completely reversed, and the inclination of present-day critics is to
regard Barrie primarily as a playwright; the novels have
fallen into the background.

But in addition to having a double career, Barrie enjoys
a double personality. His novel-writing period may be
divided conveniently enough from his play-writing period,
with only a little overlapping; the two personalities are
harder to distinguish; here he himself is our best helper.
In his admirable Rectorial Address at St. Andrews on
'Courage' in 1922, he explained that McConnachie "is the
name I give to the unruly half of myself—the writing
half. We are complement and supplement. I am the half
that is dour and practical and canny, he is the fanciful
half; my desire is to be the family solicitor, standing firm
on my hearthrug among the harsh realities of the office
furniture, while he prefers to fly around on one wing."

Born at Kirriemuir, a Scottish manufacturing town
he was afterwards to make famous under the name of

"Thrums," Barrie graduated at the University of Edinburgh in 1882, and after waiting some months found an opportunity as editorial writer on the 'Nottingham Journal' in 1883 at the modest salary of three guineas a week. From Nottingham he sent special articles to the London papers, and Frederic Greenwood, then editor of the 'St. James's Gazette,' published his first "Thrums" sketch, 'An Auld Licht Community,' in November, 1884. Greenwood did not encourage him to come to London on the strength of the early "Thrums" articles, but Barrie went, and in the St. Andrews address from which quotation has been made above he drew a lively picture of his first adventures on Fleet Street:—

"The greatest glory that has ever come to me was to be swallowed up in London, not knowing a soul, with no means of subsistence, and the fun of working till the stars went out. To have known anyone would have spoilt it. I didn't even quite know the language. I rang for my boots and they thought I said a glass of water, so I drank the water and worked on. There was no food in the cupboard, so I didn't need to waste time in eating. The pangs and agonies when no proof came. How courteously tolerant was I of the postman without a proof for us; how McConnachie on the other hand wanted to punch his head. The magic days when our article appeared in an evening paper. The promptitude with which I counted the lines to see how much we should get for it. Then McConnachie's superb air of dropping it into the gutter. Oh, to be a free lance of journalism again—that darling jade!"

Barrie insists that the "grisette" (as he calls journalism elsewhere) must be served faithfully for the time being, but he was not long in transferring his allegiance to "the other lady" whom he had worshipped from afar, for since his boyhood he had known that "literature was my game." His first book 'Better Dead' (1887) was a rather elaborate *jeu d'esprit* which passed almost unnoticed, but 'Auld Licht Idylls' (1888) speedily attracted public attention. The book was in the main re-cast from articles already published in the 'St. James's Gazette,' and but for the encouragement of the editor of that paper, Barrie says himself, "there is little doubt that they would never have appeared anywhere." This is important, not merely because these sketches gave the author his first hold on the public, but because their success affected the bent of his genius. "As unlooked for as a telegram," Barrie writes in 'Margaret Ogilvy,' "there came to me the thought that there was something quaint about my native place. A boy who found that a knife had been put into his pocket in the night could not have been more surprised." Dixon Scott seems to be right in the suggestion that the word "Idylls" was at first used ironically, and that what Barrie aimed at to begin with was sober, circumstantial realism. But it soon became evident that what the British public wanted was not Kirriemuir as Barrie really saw it, but the "Thrums" of his imaginative boyish recollections, created and revivified by his mother's talk. "I have seen many weary on-dings of snow," he writes, "but the one I seem to recollect best occurred nearly twenty years before I was born." When this was found to be a paying vein, Barrie appealed to his mother for more and more romantic recollections until her shrewd and honest Scottish soul almost revolted. "It's perfect blethers," she said in a moment of compunction, and she had always a sort of terror about each Auld Licht article that it would be the last. But Barrie had confidence in himself and the public, and as the public asked for romantic sentiment, he gave it to them with both hands. Possibly the public only drove Barrie to follow his own natural bent instead of the critical tendency of the time in the direction of realism. In any case the fanciful half-self, McConnachie, was encouraged in his inclination towards "playing hide-and-seek with angels," and 'A Window in Thrums' was outdone by 'The Little Minister,' in which a Scottish clergyman is irregularly married to a highborn lady who wanders about "Thrums" disguised as a gipsy. The public was delighted, and would no doubt have honoured further demands upon its credulity, but the dour, practical, canny Scot in Barrie apparently became weary of McConnachie's extravagances, and in 'Sentimental Tommy' and its sequel 'Tommy and Grizell' a vein of cynicism mingled with the sentimental romance; Barrie disappointed his old public without gaining a new one, and he turned his attention away from fiction to devote himself to drama, in which he had for some years been experimenting with varied success. Perhaps the most likely work of his first period to endure is the biographic sketch of his mother, 'Margaret Ogilvy.' Even in this, a scrupulous critic might discern an occasional inclination to extract exaggerated humour or pathos out of some familiar detail of domestic life, but in connection with the leading figure, who is realized with unfailing delicacy and charm, any tendency to sentimentality is held in check by the unmistakable sincerity of feeling which inspires the whole. Barrie owed a great debt to his mother, and the difficult task of expressing his consciousness of it is discharged with a tact, sensibility, and refinement which are beyond praise.

His first ventures upon the stage were not happy. In 1891 he produced a romantic drama of the eighteenth century 'Richard Savage' (in collaboration with H. B.

Marriot-Watson), an Ibsen burlesque, and a dramatised version of 'Vanity Fair'—all failures. He first made a hit in 1892 with a farce, 'Walker, London,' which sets forth the innocent amatory adventures of a London barber, alone on his honeymoon because there was not money enough for two, and entangled in the superior society of a houseboat on the Thames in the assumed character of an African explorer. It achieved with eminent success its purpose of providing a part in which a popular actor of that day (J. L. Toole) could display his powers.

After an intermediate failure with the libretto of a comic opera (in which he collaborated with Conan Doyle), Barrie scored great popular successes with 'The Professor's Love-Story' and his dramatisation of his own novel 'The Little Minister,' which were acclaimed on both sides of the Atlantic in spite of (and sometimes perhaps because of) their excessive sentiment and extravagant romance. In 'The Wedding Guest' (1900) Barrie tried, not altogether successfully, to deal with a serious problem seriously, and he returned to the farcical in 'Little Mary,' to the fanciful in 'Quality Street'—the latter a sympathetic reproduction of the sentimental atmosphere of the early nineteenth century; it was highly praised by the critics and stood the test of revival twenty years later. But it was not until 'The Admirable Crichton' was put on the stage later in the same year (1902) that Barrie succeeded in that blend of the ironic with the romantic which is peculiarly his own. The romance is chiefly in the setting; irony and satire run all through the treatment of the characters and the plot. The critics treated the play seriously—perhaps too seriously—and on its revival in 1918 there were loud outcries against Barrie's attempt to

take the edge off his own satire. A. B. Walkley's protest
in the 'Times' deserves quotation:—

"[Barrie] ought to have been too conscientious an artist to 'touch
up' his old work. He ought to have left the original ending alone,
not merely because it was the original—though that is reason good
enough—but because it was the right, congruous, appropriate ending. The wheel had come full circle. It was a case of 'As you were.'
The butler of the first act, after being a superman, had, in the fourth,
become the butler again, and nothing but the butler. He left you
with the announcement of his intention of settling down with Tweeny
in a little 'pub' in the Harrow Road. This struck the perfect note,
the final word of irony.

"You didn't need to be reminded of the superman. You could
do that for yourself. But now the author insists upon superfluously
reminding you. The Harrow Road 'pub' has been dropped out.
Crichton glares at his old island subjects, and they cower with
reminiscence. He glares at the formidable Lady Brocklehurst, and
she, even she, quails. Lady Mary reminds him of the past, and even
a *redintegratio amoris* is hinted at. In short, the author 'hedges'—
'hedges' against his own old irony, that perfect thing. This *is* a
butler, he seems to say, but remember, Oh, please remember, he
was a superman. As though we should forget it!

"And Crichton is even made to be wise after the event. He
foresees the late war, and predicts that if England should ever
hear the roll of the drums, then all the Bill Crichtons will get their
chance. With more about England, &c., Crichton, our imperturbable *homme fort*, turned mouthing, sentimental 'patriot'! Good
heavens!"

In the printed versions of the play (1915 and 1918)
there is no mention of "the 'pub' in the Harrow Road
and there is no patriotic outburst at the end. "Poor
Tweeny" in both versions is deprived (by a stage direction) of any expectation of joining Crichton in married
bliss as a London landlady, and Crichton's ultimate fate
is left in doubt. In the earlier printed version he is al-

lowed to snub Lady Mary just before the final curtain;
in the later one, he remains the imperturbable butler to
the end, and simply assures her that he has not lost his
courage. The patriotic prophecies of the 1918 revival
were doubtless a mistake, accounted for by war excitement, and the author has done well to omit them in the
permanent copy. As the text stands, it is still true that
"beneath the fun and friendliness of this delightful comedy
we get a glimpse of a very queer, very unhappy conception
of the world and of human nature."

The 'Times' review, from which the above sentence is
quoted, finds again in 'What Every Woman Knows' "a
clear cruelty, a strong hint of sneering." "We are shut
up in a cage of makeshift, of a clear-sighted, tolerant despair . . . We can find no faith—not even faith in womanhood, for all Maggie's ability—in 'What Every Woman
Knows.'" If this is true—and there may well be some
truth in it—it is curious that no hint of it reached the
thousands of people in England and America who enjoyed the humour and sentiment of this delightful comedy.
No doubt there is more under the surface than the ordinary
spectator sees or the ordinary reader discerns, but one
doubts whether it is so "bitter, cruel, despairing" as the
'Times' reviewer thinks. As in 'The Admirable Crichton,' the characters and situations are alike impossible,
and we get as far off the track by attempting to press their
significance to a logical issue as the ordinary theatre-goer
does by accepting them for the sake of the humour and
pathos and homely wisdom the words and acts convey.
The opening situation in 'What Every Woman Knows'—
the Scottish railway porter who commits burglary for the
acquisition of knowledge—is an admirable example of

Barrie's art; both on the stage and in the printed version— half dialogue, half narrative with the characteristic comments of the author—it is a delight, not because of its probability—no one would be bold enough to claim for it that virtue—but by reason of a whimsical relation to fact which is the peculiar charm of Barrie at his best.

When the relation to fact becomes too tenuous, as in 'The Legend of Leonora,' the common sense of the public revolts, though it has shown itself perfectly willing and able to follow Barrie's lead into flights of pure fancy such as 'Peter Pan' and 'A Kiss for Cinderella.' 'Dear Brutus' and 'Mary Rose' occupy again the more difficult intermediate ground between fact and fancy where Barrie's playful tenderness is cunningly combined with a view of life which is stern without being harsh.

One finds the same range and variety in the one act plays. 'The Will' and 'The Twelve Pound Look' carry satire almost to the point of cynicism; 'The Old Lady Shows her Medals' touches the deepest springs of human emotion with a hand unfailing in tact and delicacy.

Perhaps there is no author of our own time about whom it is harder to forecast the verdict of posterity. Contemporary differences of opinion about Barrie are a sufficient warning against dogmatism. There are still those who accuse him of a belated Victorian sentimentality; there are others who carry their worship to the other side of idolatry. Professor William Lyon Phelps, of Yale University, suggests that the most intelligent attitude to take towards his work is "unconditional surrender," and goes on to say:—

"J. M. Barrie is the foremost English-writing dramatist of our time, and his plays, taken together, make the most important con-

tributions to the English drama since Sheridan. He unites the chief
qualities of his contemporaries, and yet the last word to describe his
work would be the word eclectic. For he is the most original of them
all. He has the intellectual grasp of Galsworthy, the moral earnestness of Jones, the ironical mirth of Synge, the unearthly fantasy of
Dunsany, the consistent logic of Ervine, the wit of Shaw, the technical excellence of Pinero. In addition to these qualities, he has a
combination of charm and tenderness possessed by no other man."
('North American Review,' December, 1920.)

Such praise is at once too general and too extravagant
to be helpful; and it is not enough to refer doubters to
"the published plays" at large. It is likely that future
critics will make careful distinctions between Barrie at his
best and Barrie in his off moments. Considered as a
whole, his work is curiously uneven, and even in the plays
in which his whimsical genius carries us away, especially
during stage-presentation, the reader who has not adopted
the attitude of "unconditional surrender" will find weaknesses which may not be so readily pardoned by a generation less under the sway of Barrie's popular reputation and
personal charm. It hardly seems possible that the plays
will follow the novels into comparative neglect. The form
he has adopted for their publication—half drama, half
novel—is peculiarly suited to his genius, and will probably
secure their preservation, even if many of them fail to
hold the stage. Barrie's own generation certainly owes
him a great debt for numberless hours of unexpected delight. His magic touch has ennobled and endeared the
common things of life, and his fancifulness has rarely been
completely divorced from common sense. Recent critics
have gone too far in ascribing to his plays a cynical interpretation which is probably very far from his intention,
but they could not bear that so delicate and true an artist

should be classed among the sentimentalists. It is in the combination of tenderness and humour with keen satire that he has made a unique contribution to British drama.

BIBLIOGRAPHY

NOVELS AND SKETCHES

1887   'Better Dead.'
1888   'Auld Licht Idylls.'
1889   'A Window in Thrums.'
1891   'The Little Minister.'
1896   'Margaret Ogilvy.'
      'Sentimental Tommy.'
1900   'Tommy and Grizell.'

PLAYS (DATES OF PRODUCTION)

1891   'Ibsen's Ghost.'
1892   'Walker, London.'
1894   'The Professor's Love-Story.'
1897   'The Little Minister.'
1900   'The Wedding Guest.'
1902   'Quality Street.'
      'The Admirable Crichton.'
1903   'Little Mary.'
1904   'Peter Pan.'
1905   'Alice Sit-by-the-Fire.'
      'Pantaloon.'
1908   'What Every Woman Knows.'
1910   'The Twelve-Pound Look.'
1912   'Rosalind.'
1913   'The Will.'
      'Half an Hour.'
1914   'The Legend of Leonora.'
      'Der Tag.'
1915   'The New Word.'
1916   'A Kiss for Cinderella.'
      'A Slice of Life.'
1917   'The Old Lady Shows her Medals.'
      'Dear Brutus.'

1918 'A Well-remembered Voice.'
1920 'Mary Rose.'
1922 'Shall we Join the Ladies?'

BIOGRAPHICAL AND CRITICAL

J. A. Hammerton, 'J. M. Barrie and his Books,' 1900, 1902.
H. M. Walbrook, 'J. M. Barrie and the Theatre,' 1922.

CHAPTER IX

RUDYARD KIPLING (1865–   )

BRITISH Imperialism might be traced back to the Elizabethan Age or even earlier, but in the last quarter of the nineteenth century it awoke to a new consciousness. In politics this movement is associated with the names of Beaconsfield, Chamberlain and Cecil Rhodes; in the academic life of the time with that of Professor Seeley; but the man who gave the new imperialism its hold on the hearts of English-speaking people was Rudyard Kipling. He was born at Bombay in the Anglo-Indian community to which the imperial spirit is as natural as the air they breathe. His father was professor of architectural sculpture at the British school of art there and Bombay correspondent of the Allahabad 'Pioneer.' Kipling's mother and sister later published a joint volume of verses, and one can well believe the testimony that "the Kipling family were delightful people, all clever and artistic in their tastes, and the kindest and most gracious family I have ever known." Both Mr. and Mrs. Kipling were children of English Wesleyan ministers and to the religious atmosphere of his home Kipling owes the familiarity with the Bible which is one of his most effective literary resources. Another influence was that of the native nurse from whom he learnt Hindustani, and thus obtained a first hand knowledge of Indian life, to which his father, an enthusiastic student of Indian art and mythology, and later the author of 'Beast and Man in India,' no doubt contributed powerfully. Kipling says in the preface to 'Life's Handicap':

"These tales have been collected from all places, and all sorts of people, from priests in the Chubára, from Ala Yar the carver, Jiwun Singh the carpenter, nameless men on steamers and trains round the world, women spinning outside their cottages in the twilight, officers and gentlemen now dead and buried, and a few, but these are the very best, my father gave me."

Kipling's schooldays, of which he has given us a romantic account in 'Stalky & Co.,' were spent in England, but the same influences were at work, for the United Services College at Westward Ho, North Devon, to which he went, is a favourite resort for the children of Anglo-Indians. He won the prize for English Literature, edited the school magazine, and contributed to it imitations of Browning and Tennyson. A poem entitled 'Ave Imperatrix' written by him on the occasion of the last attempt on the life of Queen Victoria in 1882 shows at once his facility and the drift of his youthful thought:—

"Such greeting as should come from those
  Whose fathers faced the Sepoy hordes,
Or served you in the Russian snows,
  And, dying, left their sons their swords.

"And all are bred to do your will
  By land and sea—wherever flies
The flag, to fight and follow still
  And work your Empire's destinies."

When Kipling returned to India at the age of eighteen, his father was Principal of the school of art at Lahore, and there he began his professional career on the staff of the 'Civil and Military Gazette.' He was an untiring worker and found opportunity for varied experiences;

his reporting assignments brought him into contact with all classes of the native and Anglo-Indian population, and he had also abundant practice in journalistic writing of almost every kind, his daily duties including:

"To prepare for press all the telegrams of the day;
"To provide all the extracts and paragraphs;
"To make headed articles out of official reports, etc.;
"To write such editorial notes as he might have time for;
"To look generally after all sports, outstation, and local intelligence.
"To read all proofs except the editorial matter."

The Duke of Connaught, then military commander of the North Western district of India, became interested in Kipling during a visit to the home of his parents, and asked him if there was anything he could do for him. "I would like, sir, to live with the army for a time, and go to the frontier to write up Tommy Atkins." Permission was readily given, and Rudyard Kipling has been "writing up Tommy Atkins" ever since. Many of his early poems and stories were done as part of his journalistic task, and he had a share in two books published by members of the Kipling family in 1884 and 1885, but the real beginning of his literary career may be dated from the publication in 1886 of 'Departmental Ditties' as "a lean oblong docket, wire-stitched, to imitate a D. O. government envelope, printed on brown paper and secured with red tape." 'Plain Tales from the Hills' appeared in an equally modest fashion in 1888, and was followed in the same year by six other volumes of short stories of Anglo-Indian life. Both prose and verse met with a cordial reception in the Anglo-Indian community to which they specially appealed, and Sir William Hunter in 1888 warned the British public of "a new literary star of no mean magnitude rising in the East," but in England the warning passed unheeded. The seven little paper-bound volumes issued by Messrs. A. H. Wheeler & Co. of Allahabad in 'The Indian Railway Library' included "certain passages in the lives and adventures of Privates Terence Mulvaney, Stanley Ortheris, and John Learoyd" (among them 'The Taking of Lungtungpen'), such stories of horror as 'The Strange Ride of Morrowbie Jukes' and 'The Man Who Would be King,' and tales of child life such as 'The Story of Muhammed Din,' and 'The Drums of the Fore and Aft.'   It is a record not merely of promise, but of remarkable achievement, especially when it is remembered that Kipling wrote many of these stories while yet in his teens.   'The Phantom Rickshaw' was published in 'The Quartette' in 1885, when he was only twenty, and no less than twenty-eight out of the forty stories in 'Plain Tales from the Hills' appeared in the Lahore 'Civil and Military Gazette,' which he left in 1887 for the Allahabad 'Pioneer.'

It was with this substantial literary baggage that in 1889 Kipling set out for England by way of Japan and San Francisco.   He was still on the staff of the 'Pioneer' and the articles he sent back were afterwards published under the titles 'Letters of Marque' and 'From Sea to Sea.'   He did journalistic work in San Francisco and after his arrival in New York interviewed Mark Twain for the 'Herald'; but for his literary wares he found no market in either city; American publishers knew and cared as little about India as the American public.   In London he met with the same cold reception until a happy chance directed Edmund Yates of the 'World,' an

enterprising journalist always on the lookout for some
new thing, to seek the Anglo-Indian writer in his obscure
lodgings. The 'World' interview led to a notice of
Kipling's Indian booklets in the 'Times,' and 'Macmil-
lan's Magazine' published in one number in 1890 'The
Incarnation of Krishna Mulvaney' and 'A Ballad of
East and West.' It was at once recognized that a writer
had arisen in English literature of real genuis, remarkable
not merely for the fresh fields he opened up (Anglo-Indian
life had been treated in fiction before) but for a new spirit
and artistic faculties of no mean order.

The time was ripe for a reviving breath from a new
quarter. Romanticism had worn itself out, and the
cheerful meliorism of the early Victorian time was out of
fashion. Looking back, we see the beginnings of a new
era, but at the time the predominant cult was a self-
centred æstheticism. Walter Pater in the revised edition
of 'Studies of the Renaissance,' published in 1888, had set
forth the latest gospel:

"A counted number of pulses only is given to us of a variegated,
dramatic life. How may we see in them all that is to be seen in them
by the finest senses? How shall we pass most swiftly from point to
point, and be present always at the focus where the greatest number of vital forces unite in their purest energy? To burn always with
this hard, gem-like flame, to maintain this ecstasy, is success in life."

The French Decadents found English imitators, who
carried the search for mere sensations still further, and
æstheticism passed into sheer dandyism. The restless
curiosity of Aubrey Beardsley was as much a pose as the
self-conscious boredom of Oscar Wilde. "The first duty
of life is to be as artificial as possible; what the second
duty is no one has as yet discovered"—such flashy epi-

grams passed not merely as wit, but as wisdom. Wilde's tragic downfall was hardly needed to convince the public of the hollowness, as well as the unwholesomeness, of the movement, which never had any real hold except on a very small set, but the advent of a new writer who cared more about life than about art and who expressed himself, sometimes humorously, sometimes vigorously, but always in a way everyone could understand was hailed with enthusiasm by critics and populace. Kipling's immediate success was enormous, enough to turn the head of a young author less intent on getting out all he had in him.

Acknowledged forthwith as the greatest master of the short story in English, Kipling was challenged to attempt the more difficult art of the novelist. In response he wrote 'The Light that Failed,' with a happy ending for the supposed susceptibilities of the American public, and a more tragic one for the stronger nerves of the British. It was dramatized, and the stage version helped to spread Kipling's fame further, but while the public applauded, the critics ruled that he had not succeeded and must try again.

For the time being, Kipling had to be content with his acknowledged mastery of the short story, emphasized in 1891 by the publication of a new volume, 'Life's Handicap,' including 'The Courting of Dinah Shad,' 'On Greenhow Hill,' 'The Man Who Was,' 'At the End of the Passage,' 'The Mark of the Beast,' and 'Namgay Doola'—to mention only a few popular favourites. He asserted meanwhile his supremacy as a verse writer in the 'Barrack Room Ballads,' which at once caught the popular fancy, and were sung or recited all over the English-speaking world. About the same time he enlarged his knowledge of the Empire by a tour in South Africa, Australia and New Zealand, and married an American lady, building himself a house at Brattleboro, Vermont, which was his home for the next five years. With his wife's brother, Wolcott Balestier, he wrote a long story of adventure, 'The Naulahka,' which was judged much inferior to his unaided work. The next volume of short stories, 'Many Inventions,' revealed a new phase of his genius in his power to reveal the romantic side of our mechanical civilization, and then came in quick secession the two 'Jungle Books,' developed out of the suggestion of Mowgli, the boy brought up by the wolves, and in their own way the best romantic animal stories ever written.

All this was done before Kipling was thirty—an astounding achievement which should be borne in mind by those who lament the comparative barrenness of his later manhood. He was perhaps the most remarkable instance in English fiction of early maturity, for by this time his genius had taken its characteristic bent and his style was fully developed in all its sinewy strength and directness. The defects of his qualities were established and have remained unchanged—a love of striking, even brutal contrasts, the worship of mere force, a lack of sympathy for civilizations outside the English pale, and inability to render the finer sides of life within it. In spite of the apparent range and variety of his characters, the gentler and more intellectual men and women who represent the human race in its highest development are always inadequately realized, and often grotesquely caricatured. His psychology is never subtle, and he succeeds best with primitive peoples, children, and the coarser specimens of civilized humanity. Even with the military and official classes whom he knows best, altogether apart from the cheap cynicism which marred his earliest work, there is a hard and artificial smartness in their way of talking and a narrowness in their view of life which does them less than justice. His common soldiers have an exaggerated brutality which is unnecessary to set off their real qualities of hardihood and faithfulness. His colours are too glaring; his psychology is superficial; his characters do not develop. These are objections naturally evoked by his overwhelming popularity and they cannot be denied. But when all has been said, there remains his abounding vitality, his extraordinary power of invention, his skill in narration and description, and his genuine faith in the simple virtues which have made the English-speaking peoples the leaders of the modern world.

His later verse took on an added richness and depth of tone in 'The Seven Seas' and 'The Five Nations,' and 'The Recessional' reflected with sustained seriousness the sense of imperial responsibility and the love of justice and freedom—not the mere reliance on force which has sometimes seemed to be the centre of his thought. A closer acquaintance with the quieter scenery of Southern England and the gentler sides of English life—for the last twenty years he has lived at Rottingdean in Sussex—enlarged his horizon and tempered his original inclination to dwell on the coarser and more brutal sides of things. His sense of humour, always rich and strong, was developed and refined. The 'Just So Stories' breathed a new and more homely charm, which was continued, with some loss of freshness, in 'Puck of Pook's Hill' and 'Rewards and Fairies.'

The South African situation in 1897-8 took Kipling again across the sea, and the Boer War brought new material to his hand, which had by no means lost its cunning. On his return to England he published a new volume of short stories, 'The Day's Work,' but he had not relinquished the ambition of writing a good novel. 'Stalky & Co.' (1899) was a long story of school life, which won cordial appreciation from some of his old admirers, but was severely criticized by others as falling short not only in some matters of taste, but in its general conception. Undaunted, he returned to the field in which he had won his first success, and in 1901 published 'Kim,' a well-sustained novel touching upon the deeper as well as the more picturesque phases of Indian life, and universally acclaimed as his masterpiece in fiction.

It is too soon to pass any permanent judgment upon Kipling's genius, but it is safe to say that he will take an abiding place in literature as one of the most vigorous and original writers of his time. Though he was by no means the first to find romantic material in India and the Colonies, he made English-speaking people conscious of their imperial inheritance to a degree and to an extent unknown before. For good or ill he was a potent force in the development of the imperialistic spirit, with its high ambitions and heavy responsibilities. 'The Recessional' shows that he is not unaware of the graver side of the creed of power he has preached. Of the sincerity and forcefulness of his utterance there can be no question.

BIBLIOGRAPHY

1886 'Departmental Ditties' (Lahore). (London 1897.)
1888 'Plain Tales from the Hills' (Calcutta). (London 1890.)
       'Soldiers Three.' 'The Story of the Gadsbys.' 'In Black
       and White' (Calcutta). (Three volumes in one, London, 1895.)
          'Under the Deodars.' 'The Phantom Rickshaw.' 'Wee
       Willie Winkie' (Calcutta). (Three volumes in one, London,
       1895.)
1890 (U. S.) 'The Light That Failed' (London 1891).
1891 'The City of Dreadful Night.'
       'Life's Handicap.'
1891-2 'The Naulahka' (With Wolcott Balestier).
1892 'Barrack Room Ballads.'
1893 'Many Inventions.'
1894 'The Jungle Book.'
1895 'The Second Jungle Book.'
1896 'The Seven Seas.'
1897 'Captains Courageous.'
1898 'The Day's Work.'
       'A Fleet in Being.'
1899 'Stalky & Co.'
1901 'Kim.'
1902 'Just So Stories.'
1903 'The Five Nations.'
1904 'Traffics and Discoveries.'
1906 'Puck of Pook's Hill.'
1909 'Actions and Reactions.'
1910 'Rewards and Fairies.'
1911 'A School History of England' (With C. R. L. Fletcher).
1916 'Sea Warfare.'
1917 'A Diversity of Creatures.'
1919 'The Years Between.' 'Verse 1885-1918.'

There are many books about Kipling,—a 'Primer,' a 'Guide Book,'
and a 'Dictionary'; critical and biographical studies by G. F. Monk-
house (1899), Will M. Clemens (1899), Richard Le Gallienne (1900),
Cecil Charles (1911), Cyril Falls (1915), John Palmer (1915), and
Thurston Hopkins (1914, 1916, and 1921); Bibliography by E. W.
Martindell (1922).

CHAPTER X

JOSEPH CONRAD (1856–)

BY LELAND HALL

AMONG the English novelists of the present day Joseph Conrad is outstanding by reason of his extraordinary breadth of vision, intellectual power, and artistic sincerity. It would be perhaps more cynical than true to say that these qualities have stood in the way of his general popularity; but the fact remains that he is not a popular writer in the sense that Kipling, Wells, and Bennett are popular. A comparison between his work and theirs can hardly suggest itself, except in the momentary consideration that he, like Kipling, has written of life in the far East. As a creative artist he belongs in the company of Meredith, Hardy and Henry James; but here, too, his conception of his function as a novelist, as well as what may be called the outlandish character of much of his material, makes a comparison unlikely. Finally, although he writes in English, and although he is a loyal British subject, he is by birth and character a Pole; and his novels are unique because they are unmistakably cosmopolitan.

His life has been extraordinarily varied. He was born in the Ukraine on December 6th, 1856, and he grew up in Poland and Russia amid the changes and uncertainties which it has been the unhappy fate of Poland to undergo. After the death of his parents, for which the sufferings of

179

disappointment and exile were largely responsible, he was affectionately cared for by an uncle, his mother's brother. He was put in charge of an excellent tutor to be prepared for the University of Cracow; but he had been obsessed from childhood by an unaccountable desire to go to sea,— a desire which neither the incredulous amazement of his relatives, nor the reasoning of his tutor served to abate. Eventually, at the age of seventeen, just as he was ready to matriculate, he left Poland, having won his uncle's consent to do so, and shipped on a sailing vessel out of Marseilles,—an incorrigible Don Quixote.   From then on for more than twenty years he led the life of a deep-water sailor.   In 1884 he became a naturalized British subject, and in the same year was admitted to the rank of Master Mariner in the British Merchant Marine.   Some ten years later the effects of a tropical fever compelled him to give up his seafaring; and at this crucial time in his life, almost by chance, he submitted to a publisher the manuscript of a novel, 'Almayer's Folly,' which he had written at odd moments during several years, for no reason he can think of.   To his surprise it was accepted and published in 1895.   Since then he has led in England the quiet life of a writer, a life of which nothing in his experience up to the time he adopted it had given the slightest prediction. Two things Conrad himself finds inexplicable: that there should have stirred in the breast of Teodor Jozef Konrad Korzeniowksi, a Polish youth remote from any suggestion of the sea, the irresistible desire to be a sailor; and that Joseph Conrad, Master Mariner, should have turned writer of prose tales and romances.

The success of Conrad's first novel, written under such extraordinary conditions, was in itself sufficiently remarkable; but even more astonishing was his almost immediate mastery of the principles and methods of the art he came to practise late in life and in a language not his own. The preface he wrote for 'The Nigger of the Narcissus,' may be classed with de Maupassant's preface to 'Pierre et Jean' among the permanent contributions to literary theory, especially as it affects the art of modern fiction, and nothing else throws so much light on Conrad's own work—the aims he has in view and the means by which he strives to accomplish them.

He begins with a very clear definition of art, contrasting it with philosophy, which deals with ideas, and science, which deals with facts and theories, and leads up to the conclusion that

"the artist appeals to that part of our being which is not dependent on wisdom; to that in us which is a gift and not an acquisition—and, therefore, more permanently enduring. He speaks to our capacity for delight and wonder, to the sense of mystery surrounding our lives: to our sense of pity, and beauty, and pain: to the latent feeling of fellowship with all creation; and to the subtle but invincible conviction of solidarity that knits together the loneliness of innumerable hearts: to that solidarity in dreams, in joy, in sorrow, in aspirations, in illusions, in hope, in fear, which binds men to each other, which binds together all humanity—the dead to the living, and the living to the unborn."

He then goes on to justify fiction as an art:

"Fiction—if it at all aspires to be art—appeals to temperament. And in truth it must be, like painting, like music, like all art, the appeal of one temperament to all the other innumerable temperaments whose subtle and resistless power endows passing events with their true meaning, and creates the moral, the emotional atmosphere of the place and time. Such an appeal, to be effective, must be an impression conveyed through the senses; and, in fact, it cannot be made in any other way, because temperament, whether individual or collective, is not amenable to persuasion. All art, therefore, appeals primarily to the senses, and the artistic aim when expressing itself in written words must also make its appeal through the senses, if its high desire is to reach the secret spring of responsive emotions. It must strenuously aspire to the plasticity of sculpture, to the colour of painting, and to the magic suggestiveness of music—which is the art of arts. And it is only through complete unswerving devotion to the perfect blending of form and substance; it is only through an unremitting, never-discouraged care for the shape and ring of sentences that an approach can be made to plasticity, to colour; and the light of magic suggestiveness may be brought to play for an evanescent instant over the commonplace surface of words: of the old, old words, worn thin, defaced by ages of careless usage.

"The sincere endeavour to accomplish that creative task, to go as far on that road as his strength will carry him, to go undeterred by faltering, weariness, or reproach, is the only valid justification for the worker in prose. And if his conscience is clear, his answer to those who, in the fulness of a wisdom that looks for immediate profit, demand specifically to be edified, consoled, amused; who demand to be promptly improved or encouraged, or frightened, or shocked, or charmed, must run thus:—My task which I am trying to achieve is, by the power of the written word, to make you hear, to make you feel—it is, before all, to make you *see*. That—and no more, and it is everything. If I succeed, you shall find there according to your deserts: encouragement, consolation, fear, charm—all you demand and, perhaps, also that glimpse of truth for which you have forgotten to ask."

Every one of Conrad's novels and stories shows a fidelity to the ideal thus eloquently set forth. Books so conceived and executed do not fail to have definite and rather unusual characteristics, some of which are at first reading disconcerting. In the earlier works his style, for instance, is too consciously sonorous. It must be said, however, that this is due not so much to an excess of "care for the shape and ring of sentences" as to the fact that he has yet to realize that English prose has not the crystal resonance of French. Obviously this early style is founded on French models. The later works do not contain such conscious profusion of rhythm and regular cadence, though even in 'Victory' there is often a suspicion of timbre that is not English.

His desire to give to fiction as an art something of the plasticity of sculpture may account in a general way for another, and to some a more disconcerting characteristic, which becomes more and more prominent in the novels and stories after 'Lord Jim.' It is an extremely complicated method of telling a story by means of several observers and narrators. From one point of view this is Conrad's compromise with the convention of the novelist's omniscience; for compromise it is, though in 'Chance' he has achieved such results with it as to raise very pressingly the question whether or not he has broken quite away from tradition and created a new art of the novel. So far as story-telling is concerned, the simple assumption by a novelist of a complete knowledge of characters, motives, causes, and effects makes easy going for both the writer and the reader, and is indeed desirable for the sake of smoothness in narration. Conrad himself has assumed such knowledge in his first three novels, in 'The Secret Agent,' and in many of his short stories. But for the presentation of 'Lord Jim' he seems to have felt the need of a method that would give more relief, that would make his characters stand out from their background, and would endow them with a movement more varied than that of a marionette pulled in a straight groove across the stage. With this aim in view he created Captain Marlow. Marlow is a man past middle age, whose wide experience of life, similar to Conrad's own, has left him with a detached but thoroughly kind interest in human beings. He pieces the story of Jim out of what he has actually seen of him, what he has heard, and what he has thought. His tale is, of course, often straight narration, but the novel of 'Lord Jim' is the story of Marlow telling the story of Jim; and it is the creation of Jim out, as it were, of Marlow, and at the same time the creation of Marlow wholly apart from Jim, that give Jim all but the breath of life. Unfortunately the novel (which still retains its undeserved fame of being Conrad's masterpiece) suffers rather seriously from Marlow's interminable psychological speculations. Conrad has given him much too free a rein; and all such narrators are of the kind that given an inch will take an ell.

But his handling of Marlow and the like has since become prodigiously skilful. In 'Chance' he has employed at least four narrators: Marlow, Captain Powell, and Mr. and Mrs. Fyne, and there are others besides. Three of these characters play a part in the novel quite distinct from their parts as narrators; yet Conrad has handled all the complications which such a method must occasion so smoothly that the reader hardly realizes the difficulties that the author has surmounted. They are difficulties with which most authors would not choose to burden themselves. Indeed, Henry James wrote that 'Chance' had proved Conrad the votary of the "way to do a thing that shall undergo most doing." But Conrad's success is beyond question, and the vindication of the method may be found in the intricate and perfect counterfeit of reality which 'Chance' presents. It is a method which has given to the novel not a little of the plasticity of sculpture. 'Chance' as a whole is a perfectly rounded work of art, art in the abstract sense of form and structure. Moreover, the two central figures, Flora de Barral and Captain Anthony, are moulded, as it were, by the subtle touches of many pairs of hands, the source of whose single inspiration—Conrad's high creative force—is all but concealed by the method. Of course, these characters are more than statues; they have been endowed with faculties of movement and sensation. And the greatest triumph of the method is that they move, not against a background, but in the midst of a circumfluent reality.

It was perhaps as much the desire to present his characters so surrounded as the high artistic aim to give to his novels the plasticity of sculpture that impelled Conrad to devise and perfect the method of presentation of which 'Chance' is so splendid a result. Speaking of Marlow, who relates 'Heart of Darkness,' he has said:

"To him the meaning of an episode was not inside like a kernel, but outside, enveloping the tale, which brought it out only as a glow brings out a haze, in the likeness of one of these misty halos that are made sometimes visible by the spectral illumination of moonshine."

Such an envelopment of the chief episodes is one of the most striking characteristics of nearly all Conrad's novels and stories.

Less rich in suggestion to fellow-craftsmen than this perfected method, but not less important in the general effect of Conrad's work, is his incessant appeal to the senses, or rather to the sense imagination, of his readers. He has set before himself the task of making his readers feel, hear, and above all see. Therefore he is as scrupulously precise in naming a colour, in tracing a line, and in describing a sound, a taste, or a smell, as Meredith in polishing an aphorism, or Henry James in analyzing a manner; and he demands of the reader as concentrated an effort to imagine as Meredith or James to comprehend. For one who has made this effort his novels are uniquely vivid. The memories retained of them are as of things actually seen and heard, and in some places even experienced. His work necessarily abounds in passages of description, and a study of his development in the mastery of this special art of writing would be interesting. The descriptions in the early works often suffer from the consciousness of style. 'Youth,' for example, one of the most poetic of his stories, is marred by monotonousness of rhythm and cadence. One suspects deliberateness in the heaping on of colour. As his style grows more flexible, his descriptions become less sensuous but more vivid, less massive but more finely brilliant. Yet it must be added that he has never written finer description than in 'The Nigger of the Narcissus,' or anything more vivid than the account of the passage of the 'Patna' ('Lord Jim'), or than that of Jim himself before the court of inquiry. He handles colour as a painter; and adds to this such a suggestion of sound and smell as to convey to his readers in many passages the sensation of life itself.

This emphasis on the sensible attributes of all he wishes to write about is a marked positive result of his conception of the function of the novelist striving for artistic expression. A negative result, not less marked, is the absence from his books of much of what most novelists have deemed suitable matter for novels. Of criticism, of doctrine, and of general philosophy his novels contain little or nothing. He suggests no reform; he champions no ideal. For the most part he withholds both commendation and blame from his characters. Indeed it would be hard to find traces of even a personal sympathy with more than two or three of the many men and women he has created. As an artist he makes no compromise with life. To this extent he is a realist; and if he were nothing more, an estimate of his work might end here with admiration for its vividness and power. But he is more.

The realist deals with local actualities. The reality he portrays is circumscribed. He may achieve perfect verisimilitude, but he reveals no more than a fragment of the truth. In Conrad's work there is no hint of such circumscription. His life upon the sea and his varied experience in many lands and among many kinds of people have given him an extraordinary breadth of vision. The fragments of truth he has chosen here and there to reveal are arranged in perspective and in relation to all life. Consequently there are in his work qualities of general understanding and of general revelation which, though not uncommon in our best poetry, produce upon the ordinary reader of modern fiction an effect of strangeness.

Yet Conrad is not a visionary. He presents life as it is. His characters have nothing of the heroic, and they are extraordinarily real. Few are wholly despicable; none is idealized. It can be said of none that here is a standard-bearer for the race. They show no literary earmarks. He has drawn them without prejudice for race, colour, and social caste; and they are so distinct from each other that it is impossible to generalize about them, except to say that all, being in the midst of life, are compelled to struggle against a force that is not benevolent. It is the revelation of such a force, not visionary but real, influencing the lives of men in all circumstances and in all parts of the world, that Conrad's novels and stories have accomplished. The revelation is distinct and articulate. Conrad has not shown man miserable in conflict with the impersonal forces of nature. On the contrary, as a sailor he has seen how men in ships unite against the wind and sea when they are hostile, and become strong and noble in their union. That force which brings grief and misery upon the race rises out of man himself, out of man's greed, which turns him against his own kind and renders him distrustful, envious, and cruel. Here is the tragedy, harshly evident to the eyes of the sailor visiting the habitations of man after months on the sea.

Conrad's first four novels deal almost exclusively with life in the eastern archipelagoes, to which the search for profit and gold has brought the white man. The subtle disguises of western civilization have been left far behind. 'Almayer's Folly' tells of the slow moral degradation of a man who quite openly sold himself, who married a savage Malay girl for the sake of the money her protector, the powerful Captain Lingard, had promised should go with her. 'The Outcast of the Islands' is the story of a man who resorted to treachery to get hold of a treasure he believed hidden in the interior of Borneo, and who suffered a terrible vengeance in consequence. 'The Nigger of the Narcissus' stands by itself as a story dealing wholly with life on the sea; but even here, the miserable Donkin, who stirred up discontent and mutiny upon the ship, Conrad has only finally branded as utterly despicable in an act of thieving from a man dying alone and helpless. 'Lord Jim' is the story of a man whom one act of cowardice drove farther and farther from civilization; yet that act was due to the rottenness of a steamer which but for the hidden greed of men had never sailed the seas with its crowded mass of pilgrims.

The next novel, 'Nostromo,' is in some ways the most remarkable of Conrad's achievements. It has the qualities of an epic. It seems the complete expression of modern life, of life actuated by the far-reaching and powerful spirit of commercial enterprise. There are a dozen stories in it; there are a dozen sets of characters, astonishingly alive; there are success and failure, love and hate, true patriotism and selfish scheming, aspiration, defiance, tenderness, and cruelty. There is hardly a human passion but plays its part in the intricate tangle of the action; but through it all runs the dominating influence of the great San Tomé silver mine, the symbol of law and order, the cause of revolutions, the source of tragedy. Conrad has created a South American republic and has peopled it with men and women. There are the native inhabitants to whom the land belongs, of partly Spanish and partly Indian origin; there are men and women of various European nationalities who have drifted there, and there are men who have come there on purpose to develop the material possibilities of the land. The vast drama of their lives, enacting itself for the most part between the mine, back in the mountains, and the town of Sulaco on the shores of the Placid Gulf, Conrad has cast in the form of a novel for which, in the completeness of its revelation of modern life, it would be perhaps impossible to find a parallel.

In three of the four novels following 'Nostromo'— 'The Secret Agent,' 'Under Western Eyes,' and 'Chance,' —Conrad has turned his attention to life in Europe; and in 'Victory,' the chief characters have preserved their western subtleties. 'The Secret Agent' and 'Under Western Eyes' fill the space between 'Nostromo' on the one hand and 'Chance' on the other. Having in 'Nostromo' revealed once and for all, and on a scale that is truly colossal, the motive power of the spirit of avarice in human affairs, Conrad falls back for his next two novels upon the concentrated study of two brief episodes of special interest: an explosion in Greenwich, for which he imagines the anarchists in London are indirectly responsible; and a political assassination in Russia, with its effect upon a man who is essentially order-loving. The characters are, like all his characters, astonishingly definite and alive, but they are relatively few in number. The range of interest, too, is restricted, so that in spite of the brilliance of technique and the vitality of both novels, 'The Secret Agent' and 'Under Western Eyes' may be taken as the product of a period of replenishment, that is, of spiritual replenishment, since there is no sign in either of flagging energy or mental fatigue.

Having passed through this period, Conrad approaches his next novels with a changed, matured, and ever deepening interest in the mystery of human destiny. He is still the realist in method, representing life as it is. His drawing and modelling are still clear and firm; his colours still brilliant. But over both 'Chance' and 'Victory' there play shadows like those that fall upon the land from great clouds moving across the sky. Out of man's greed has risen a cloud of Fate, as the smoke rose from the genii's lamp. In both novels the instance of greed from which evil has grown may be found. That which first embittered Flora de Barral, and which proved to be the origin of most of the misery which she was forced to undergo, was the imprisonment of her father for dishonesty in pursuit of his financial ambitions. In 'Victory' that which brought evil and death to Samburan, a lonely island whither Axel Heyst had taken the girl Lena to save her from the vile persecutions of the hotel keeper, Schomberg, was a shameless lust for booty. But Conrad's interest is here not in the corroding influence of greed upon those who have given way to it, but in the struggle of unselfish men and women against the general power of evil which love of gain has turned loose upon the world. That power has been personified. Old de Barral, coming crazed from prison and full of murderous intent, and the utterly cold-blooded and malevolent Jones are more than standard villains in melodrama. They are symbols of all the evil in the world. Those who read 'Chance' and 'Victory' must look below the surface for their full meaning.

For Conrad, evil is that power which turns man against his kind, tearing that bond of fellowship, of solidarity as he has called it, in which is man's source of comfort and strength. The tragedy of human life he finds in its loneliness, in that particular loneliness of man living in the midst of his fellows. The tragedy of Almayer's life is not that it is passed in a remote quarter of the globe, far from men and women of his own class and race, but that he has lost the power to feel confidence, that he regards his fellow beings with suspicion and distrust. So it is in both 'Chance' and 'Victory.' Flora de Barral dares trust nobody. Hence the terrible loneliness of her life, which all but warps her soul. Lena, that pathetic figure of 'Victory' about whom alone of all his characters Conrad has allowed a radiance to shine, has from babyhood found no honest friend. In neither of these wan and helpless girls is there evil. They suffer under a malignant fate.

If evil is that force which turns man against his kind, then the force to oppose it must be one that unites the members of the race. Conrad has found many types of such a force: fidelity, the sense of obligation, common need in the face of common danger, and it is almost needless to add, love. These last two novels are the story of a victory of love over fate.

In neither 'Chance' nor 'Victory' does love achieve the radiant triumph of romance. The victory is not in that opposition has been wholly overcome, but in that two human beings have become united in spite of fate. Does that union, short-lived, but complete, symbolize the solidarity of the race, of which Conrad has written so eloquently in the preface to 'The Nigger of the Narcissus'? He has promised that if he succeeds in his self-appointed task as an artist, and there seems to be no reasonable doubt that he has succeeded, we shall find in the result of his work what we look for in art: something of encouragement and hope, among other things. On first thought there seems to be nothing for comfort in the gloomy novel of 'Chance'; and 'Victory' is indeed a tragedy, a match for 'Hamlet' in general mortality. Yet there is a hint in the title of the latter which points to a deep meaning not only in that novel but in all that Conrad has written. It is a meaning felt but not easily perceived, for it envelopes all life and is more vague and more vast than the act of all living. Conrad, sailor, novelist, realist, fatalist, mystic, or poet, call him what you will, stands revealed by his work as a prophet of one great truth: the solidarity of the human race, masked by social

distinctions, forgotten in national prejudice, terribly rent
by selfishness and greed, but eternally indestructible.

'The Rescue' stands apart in the list of Conrad's works,
not merely by the fact that twenty years elapsed between
its beginning and its completion. First published in 1920,
it was far advanced in 1898, when the author laid it aside
to begin and complete without a pause 'The Nigger of
the Narcissus.' The contents and the close of the story
he had clearly in mind at the earlier date; what he had
lost for the moment was "the sense of the proper formula
of expression, of the only formula that would suit"; in reality, he says, it was "the doubt of my prose, the doubt of its
adequacy." There can be no doubt of the adequacy of the
style of the finished work; it is Conrad at his highest perfection. What gives the novel its supreme value is, however, a certain brooding quality which Professor H. S.
Canby has singled out as that which distinguishes Conrad
from all other writers in English—a characteristic of the
Slav mind. In no other novel has the author displayed
greater skill as a psychologist. The problem he had set
before himself was a most difficult one—the impact of a
highly-sophisticated woman's soul upon that of a simple,
passionate, great-hearted adventurer—our old friend Captain Lingard, in the prime of his youth, still full of eager
ambitions, dreams, and plans. These high schemes of his
are troubled and brought to naught by his passion, which
confuses his mind, weakens his will, and saps his native
energy at the crucial moment so that he seems, even to
himself, to have broken his pledged word and betrayed his
friends. This inner conflict is analysed by Conrad with
mature power, while the subordinate interests of an exciting plot retain the verve and brilliance of an earlier

period. The Malay characters are vividly imagined, and
if the sophisticated Europeans are less completely realised,
they are still living enough to be convincing and to carry
on the story. The central figure is, of course, the youthful
Lingard; in the grip of an overwhelming enthralment, he
struggles manfully against the Fates, and retains the
fascinated and sympathetic interest of the reader until,
in the very last words of the novel, he gives the command,
"Steer north," which separates him for ever from the
woman, still the object of his devout adoration, who has
all but wrecked his life.

Notwithstanding the objective artistry of Conrad's
work, every page he has written is infused with a vivid
personality. The minute care in choice of words and
the prolonged yet intense pursuit of sensible revelation,
abstract craftsmanship in themselves, are brilliant tokens
of the craftsman. Rigorous fidelity to an artistic ideal
gives to his tales and romances an unmistakable personal
warmth. Upon the urging of friends, he once applied
this fidelity to the task of revealing himself, and the
result—'Some Reminiscences,' published in the United
States under the title, 'A Personal Record'—is one of the
most brilliant pieces of autobiography in English. Many
a self-constituted judge has kicked against the pricks of
its seemingly wanton disorder. The pages have been, to
use the author's own words, "charged with discursiveness,
with disregard of chronological order (which is in itself
a crime), with unconventionality of form (which is an
impropriety). I was told severely that the public would
view with displeasure the informal character of my recollections. 'Alas,' I protested, mildly. 'Could I begin
with the sacramental words, "I was born on such a date

in such a place"? The remoteness of the locality would have robbed the statement of all interest. I haven't lived through wonderful adventures to be related *seriatim.*'"

As it is with the episodes and characters in his stories, so it is with this disclosure of himself. The reader has not been given the inner secret nakedly. Conrad shines through his circumstances, giving them the shape and colour which they have for us and by which the character of the man within them is suggested. There are not lacking passages of keenly direct personal expression, but on the whole the most significant expression is indirect, a diffusion of spirit through transparencies of time and place. Circumstance after circumstance, episode after episode grow luminous before the reader. One moment it is a dingy London boarding house, the next it is a drive across the snowbound plains of Poland, the old family coachman on the box and the jingle of sleighbells in the cold air. Then it is far up a fever-haunted tropical river, or before an examining officer of the British shipping board; and at the last, for a profoundly moving, enchanted spell, it is a boy of seventeen in a boat full of Provençal pilots in *le vieux port,* Marseilles, the ancient houses, the quays, the waters of the harbour, the breakwater, the château d'If, the islets, all drenched in moonlight.

"Yet, these memories, put down without any regard for established conventions, have not been thrown off without system and purpose. They have their hope and their aim. The hope that from the reading of these pages there may emerge at last the vision of a personality: the man behind the books so fundamentally dissimilar as, for instance, 'Almayer's Folly' and 'The Secret Agent,' and yet a coherent, justifiable personality both in its origin and in its action. This is the hope. The immediate aim, closely associated with the hope, is to give the record of personal memories by presenting faithfully the feelings and sensations connected with the writing of my first book and with my first contact with the sea. In the purposely mingled resonance of this double strain a friend here and there will perhaps detect a subtle accord."

The accord is unmistakable. There is no dissonance between the unpremeditated rapture of the first contact with the sea and the prolonged, groping, mental effort to tell the story of Almayer. Neither is there between plastic youth and man whom life has roughly fixed; but the note to which they are attuned has a low ring, though sweet.

This note must have sounded often in Conrad's ear. 'Youth' makes it poignant, giving it the romantic sadness of disillusionment. A later book, 'The Shadow Line,' takes its key therefrom; but here there is no regret for illusions. Neither is there any metaphysical implication of the fading of a glory into the common light of day.

In most lives the essential quality of youth passes slowly; in others there comes an hour that takes it suddenly away, and life changes sharply. Youth crosses the Shadow Line. The pleasant gift of life becomes for an instant a crushing burden, soon lightened, perhaps, but the remembered weight of which accompanies man throughout the rest of his days more intimately than his shadow.

One ventures to say that 'The Shadow Line' is the record of an actual personal experience. It is called a confession, and it is written in a familiar, colloquial style. In the absence of conscious shape and ring of sentences, one finds a material corollary to the differences in mood and conclusion which distinguished it from 'Youth.'

The earlier work is fervid, sensuously poetic, and vibrant with regret; 'The Shadow Line' is calm and, though touched with sadness, full of that sort of hope which is courage.

There is something special in the ring of it. In view of the fact that it was published during the Great War, and in view of the dedication—to his son, at that time serving in the British army, and to all young men who must now cross the Shadow Line—one cannot escape the feeling that Conrad published it, if he did not actually write it, with the trust that it was timely. At any rate, the deepest and best of him are in it; and through the simple yet mysterious narrative there shines the solace of a strong spirit, the unshakable conviction that though in passing through the worst of life man may lose for ever much that was even dearer than he knew, his strength will become more augustly beautiful as he takes upon himself the responsibility of faith in the solidarity and in the common destiny of his fellow beings.

BIBLIOGRAPHY

NOVELS

1895   'Almayer's Folly.'
1896   'An Outcast of the Islands.'
1898   'The Nigger of the Narcissus.'
1900   'Lord Jim.'
1903   'Nostromo.'
1907   'The Secret Agent.'
1911   'Under Western Eyes.'
1914   'Chance.'
1915   'Victory.'
1917   'The Shadow Line: A Confession.'
1919   'The Arrow of Gold.'
1920   'The Rescue.'

IN COLLABORATION WITH FORD MADOX HUEFFER

1901   'The Inheritors: An Extravagant Story.'
1903   'Romance: A Novel.'

TALES AND SHORT STORIES

1898   'Tales of Unrest.'
1902   'Youth: A Narrative; and two other Stories.'
1903   'Typhoon: and other Stories.'
1908   'A Set of Six.'
1912   ''Twixt Land and Sea.'
1916   'Within the Tides.'

ESSAYS AND AUTOBIOGRAPHY

1906   'The Mirror of the Sea: Memories and Impressions.'
1912   'A Personal Record' (Published in England as 'Some Reminiscenses').
1921   'Notes on Life and Letters.'

DRAMA

Several of Conrad's novels have been dramatised by other hands. One, 'The Secret Agent,' he has himself made into a drama under the same title. It was acted at the Ambassadors Theatre, London, on November 2, 1922.

BIOGRAPHICAL AND CRITICAL

Richard Curle, 'Joseph Conrad: A Study,' 1914.
Hugh Walpole, 'Joseph Conrad,' 1916.

The limited edition of Conrad's works (1921) includes a preface by the author to each volume.

Bibliography by Thomas J. Wise (London, 1920) and in Ruth M. Stauffer 'Joseph Conrad and his Romantic Realism' (Boston, 1922).

CHAPTER XI

HERBERT GEORGE WELLS (1868-   )

If, as many think, sociological fiction is the character-istic literary product of the time, H. G. Wells has a fair claim to be considered its most representative writer, on account not merely of the extent and variety of his contacts with current thought, but of the power with which he has brought vague popular discontents to clear and artistic expression. He sprang from the lowest scale of the middle-class—barely divided in his birth and upbringing from the working class which dur-ing his youth and early manhood came into educational opportunity and political power. One of his grand-fathers was head gardener at Penshurst, the other an innkeeper at Midhurst, his father a professional crick-eter and small shopkeeper at Bromley, Kent. His earliest recollections are thus recorded in 'First and Last Things':—

"I recall an underground kitchen with a drawered table, a window looking up at a grating, a back yard in which, growing out by a dustbin, was a grape-vine; a red-papered room with a bookcase, over my father's shop, the dusty aisles and fixtures, the regiments of wine-glasses and tumblers, the rows of hanging mugs and jugs, the towering edifices of jam-pots, the tea and dinner and toilet sets in that emporium, its brighter side of cricket goods, of pads and balls and stumps. Out of the window one peeped at the more ex-terior world, the High Street in front, the tailor's garden, the butcher's yard, the churchyard and Bromley church tower behind; and one was taken upon expeditions to fields and open places. This limited world was peopled with certain familiar presences, mother and father, two brothers, the evasive but interesting cat, and by intermittent people of a livelier and more transient interest, customers and callers."

Upper-class life he saw (from the point of view of the servants' hall) when on his father's death in 1878 his mother became housekeeper in the family in which she had formerly been lady's maid at Up Park near Peters-field, the "Bladesover" of 'Tono-Bungay,' which also enshrines some early experiences in the chemist's shop (drug-store) at Midhurst.   He had a bitter struggle, both for livelihood and for education, beginning work as a draper's assistant (dry goods clerk) at the age of 15 and experiencing in his own person some of the humiliations he has described in 'Kipps.'   Striving to educate him-self, he took a humble post as assistant-master in an obscure school, and from this in turn he escaped with the aid of a Government Scholarship to the Royal College of Science, South Kensington.   It was his good fortune to come under Huxley, the leading exponent of the new science of biology and one of the most stirring spirits in the intellectual unrest of the time.   Economically and socially the immediate gain for Wells was the London B.Sc. degree with first class honours in zoölogy; upon his mental development, the effects were far-reaching.   It is really of himself under the name of Oswald that Wells speaks in 'Joan and Peter':

"Those were the great days when Huxley lectured on zoölogy at South Kensington, and to him Oswald went.   Oswald did indeed find science consoling and inspiring.   Scientific studies were at once rarer and more touched by enthusiasm a quarter of a century ago than they are now, and he was soon a passionate naturalist, consumed by the insatiable craving to know how.   That little, long upper laboratory in the Normal School of Science, as the place was then called, with the preparations and diagrams along one side, the sinks and windows along the other, the row of small tables down the windows, and the ever-present vague mixed smell of methylated spirit, Canada balsam, and a sweetish decay, opened vast new horizons to him. To the world of the eighteen-eighties the story of life, of the origin and branching out of species, of the making of continents, was still the most inspiring of new romances. Comparative anatomy in particular was then a great and philosophical 'new learning,' a mighty training of the mind; the drift of biological teaching towards specialization was still to come."

For the time being, however, Wells had to work hard for a living as a university coach—so hard that after three years his health broke down. He had already published a text-book on biology and had written for the 'University Correspondent,' the 'Educational Review' and the 'Fortnightly.' He now abandoned teaching and adventured boldly on journalism in the 'Pall Mall Gazette,' 'Saturday Review' and 'Nature.' By 1895 he had published his first romance and his first volumes of essays and of short stories, and was fairly launched on a literary career.

His early stories were a curious amalgam of scientific knowledge and riotous romance which he has himself compared to the "monstrous experimental imaginings" of children. The verve and technical skill with which they were written won for them a wide popularity, but it was inevitable that Wells should soon be discontented with the themes he was treating and the public to which he was appealing. Between 'The Time Machine' (1895) and 'When the Sleeper Wakes' (1899) he had reduced the scope of his imaginative flight from 30 million years to a mere matter of a century ahead, and as early as 1896 he had begun to turn his glance from the far future to the present. 'The Wheels of Chance' (1896), recounting the adventures, amorous and other, of a draper's assistant on a holiday, is slight, but it is a well-told story of contemporary life. 'Love and Mr. Lewisham' (1900) marks a distinct advance in the same direction, and after the interposition of two romances 'The First Men in the Moon' and 'The Food of the Gods' (the character of which is sufficiently indicated by their titles) Wells definitely committed himself to the sociological novel of contemporary life in 'Kipps' (1905). The misadventures and successes of the suddenly-enriched draper's apprentice are told with a humorous kindliness which is in itself a delight, but the novelist never loses sight of the social significance of his hero's vain endeavours to accommodate himself to the conventional requirements of a society to which he comes too late. It is a mere chance that he comes to it at all; but if by another chance he had come to it earlier he would have found his way perfectly smooth.

'In the Days of the Comet' (1906) is a partial return to Wells's older manner, but even in it the main interest is sociological, and the romantic science is merely an ill-fitting patch upon the presentation of the serious questions which were then occupying the writer's mind. The resulting combination is unsuccessful alike as a romance and as a novel.

In 'Tono-Bungay' (1909) the scientific element is less prominent and much less fantastic; if the flight of the hero in an aëroplane across the Channel was at the time of composition not very probable, it was only a step or two in advance of actuality. The career of the patent medicine promoter, in spite of some grotesque elements, was characteristic of the time (being, indeed, founded on the exploits of some recent commercial adventurers) and it gave Wells the opportunity to reveal both the powers and limitations of his genius as a novelist. The story is told with sustained sweep and vitality; the three main characters are originally conceived and finely drawn. The minor characters are less successful, especially Beatrice, who never has the touch of life, least of all in the love scenes. This appears to be due, not so much to lack of social experience on the part of the novelist, as to temperamental defect. The little stenographer with whom the hero comes so quickly to an understanding is real enough, but this affair can hardly be called romantic. It is when Wells tries to convey passion purified by its own fire that he fails most dismally. The lower forms of sex attraction he represents faithfully and sympathetically; for the portrayal of real passion in its higher, intenser moods he has no gift.

This is often exemplified in the novels, in none more clearly than in 'Ann Veronica,' which is a study of sex and of the efforts of an intelligent girl to free herself from the trammels of conventional surroundings. The novelist's picture of Ann's struggles to gain economic independence is not any more encouraging than Brieux's treatment of a somewhat similiar situation in 'La Femme Seule.' In both, man is represented as a predatory animal controlling economic opportunity and exercising that control to satisfy his sensual desires. The War has changed the economic situation for the better in both England and France, and it may be doubted whether at any time in the United States a

capable woman eager to earn her own living would have
found the path of virtue so difficult as Ann did. The
solution in her particular case, under an appearance of
unconventionality, is thoroughly in accord with conventional opinion. Only the existence of a discarded wife
prevents Capes from marrying Ann in the first instance,
and as soon as he is free, he does marry her. They settle
down to the conventional felicity of the hearth and the
cradle, and Ann's conventional relatives recognize that
her rebellion is condoned by her ultimate submission.
There is no sympathy wasted by the author on the more
extreme emancipators of her sex with whom Ann comes in
contact during her struggle for freedom; they are frankly
ridiculed. Take for instance this scrap of Miss Minifer's
conversation:—

"'We do not want the men, we do not want them, with their
sneers and loud laughter. Empty, silly coarse brutes. Brutes!
They are the brute still with us! Science some day may teach us a
way to do without them. It is only the women matter. It is not
every sort of creature needs—these males. Some have no males.'

"'There's green-fly' admitted Ann Veronica. 'And even then—'

"The conversation hung for a thoughtful moment. Ann Veronica
readjusted her chin on her hand. 'I wonder which of us is right?'
she said. 'I haven't a scrap—of this sort of aversion.'"

'The History of Mr. Polly' recounts with humour and
sympathy the misadventures of a small tradesman,
cursed with indigestion, an unsuccessful business, and a
shrewish wife, but blessed with a mild romantic imagina-
tiveness which lends his character a certain charm.
A much more ambitious effort from the sociological point
of view is 'The New Machiavelli,' which opens with a
searching analysis of social conditions in the later Victorian period, and proceeds to present, not without per-

sonal feeling, the clash between public ambition and irregular passion. There are amusing, if somewhat malicious, portraits of contemporary personalities, and some acute reflections on contemporary political tendencies, but the development of the novel, as not infrequently happens with Wells, fails to bear out the promise of its beginning, partly because of the author's inability, already noted, to convey adequately the overmastering passion which is the centre of the story.

'Marriage' deals again with a particular phase of the sex-question—the conflict between sexual attraction and devotion to science. The young scientist and his somewhat conventional bride are amusingly and not unsympathetically drawn in their earlier difficulties of courtship and housekeeping, but when they get out into the wilds of Labrador to discuss sex relations in the abstract, they cease to be either natural or entertaining, and their disquisitions on matrimony cannot be said to add anything new to a subject already well-worn.

'The Passionate Friends' is still another treatment of the same theme; in this case, romance is kept alive by enforced separation, but the resulting love-letters have neither the accent of passion nor the stimulus of intellectual inspiration. The didactic element is again overemphasized in 'The World Set Free,' 'The Wife of Sir Isaac Harman,' and 'The Research Magnificent,' and in none of these did the theme sufficiently stir the author's imagination to enable him to write more than a readable story, with occasional lapses into philosophical dullness.

'Bealby' is a mere extravaganza, and 'Mr. Boon,' (at first only half acknowledged), is simply a fling at some contemporaries Wells disliked but apparently did not care to attack openly. The Great War, however, really fired the novelist's imagination, and 'Mr. Britling Sees it Through' is by far the best of contemporary accounts of the social and intellectual conditions of the English middle-class immediately before and immediately after the opening of the new epoch. Britling, apart from being endowed with unnecessarily numerous amours before the story opens, is treated with that humorous sympathy which is one of the author's best gifts, and his searchings of heart are vitalized by the sudden change affecting his life, as it did millions of others at the same time. The widespread popularity of the story was not undeserved, for its sincerity of utterance gave it a universal appeal, and it will remain an invaluable and moving record of a mind sensitive to spiritual change in a great crisis of the world's history.

It was a pity that Wells did not leave this incursion into the spiritual field to stand by itself. 'The Soul of a Bishop,' with its superfluous potion, was as unhappy a venture into the domain of religion as 'God the Invisible King,' published about the same time, which had not even the novelist's narrative power to relieve its ineffectiveness. All that Wells did as a theologian was to present ancient heresies with the surprised air of a modern conjurer.

Wells has made large claims for the modern novel and he has done his best to occupy the wide territory he sketched out as its proper field. He writes:—

"It is to be the social mediator, the vehicle of understanding, the instrument of self-examination, the parade of morals and the exchange of manners, the factory of customs, the criticism of laws and institutions and of social dogmas and ideas. It is to be the home confessional, the initiator of knowledge, the seed of fruitful self-questioning. Let me be very clear here, I do not mean for a moment that the novelist is going to set up as a teacher, as a sort of priest with a pen, who will make men and women believe and do this and that. The novel is not a new sort of pulpit; humanity is passing out of the phase when men sit under preachers and dogmatize influences. But the novelist is going to be the most potent of artists, because he is going to present conduct, devise beautiful conduct, discuss conduct, analyse conduct, suggest conduct, illuminate it through and through. He will not teach, but discuss, point out, plead and display. And this being my view, you will be prepared for the demand I am now about to make for an absolutely free hand for the novelist in his choice of topic and incident and in his method of treatment; or rather, if I may presume to speak for other novelists, I would say it is not so much a demand we make as an intention we proclaim. We are going to write, subject only to our own limitations, about the whole of human life. We are going to deal with political questions and religious questions and social questions. We cannot present people unless we have this free hand, this unrestricted field. What is the good of telling stories about people's lives if one may not deal freely with the religious beliefs and organizations that have controlled or failed to control them? What is the good of pretending to write about love and the loyalties and treacheries and quarrels of men and women, if one must not glance at those varieties of physical temperament and organic quality, those deeply passionate needs and distresses from which half the storms of human life are brewed? We mean to deal with all these things, and it will need very much more than influential people in London, the scurrility of the 'Spectator,' and the deep and obstinate silences of the 'Westminster Gazette,' to stop the incoming tide of aggressive novel-writing. We are going to write about it all. We are going to write about business and finance and politics and precedence and pretentiousness and decorum and indecorum, until a thousand pretences and ten thousand impostures shrivel in the cold, clear air of our elucidations. We are going to write of wasted opportunities and latent beauties until a thousand new ways of living open to men and women. We are going to appeal to the young and the hopeful and the curious, against the established, the dignified, and defensive. Before we have done, we will have all life within the scope of the novel."

It is not surprising that his essays have been overshadowed by his novels, where his gift for vivid narrative and his imaginative sympathy found freer play, but these more direct and unadorned expressions of his political and social views are by no means to be neglected, and have rather gained in richness and power as the years passed while his novels have lost by being overburdened by unassimilated reasoning. In the earlier essays, too, there is still a considerable element of romantic prophecy which ministers rather to amusement than to serious thought; but the most recent series 'First and Last Things' and 'Social Forces in England and America' grapple with some of the most urgent problems of the day. He has an equal dislike for the planless individualism (as he sees it) of the United States, and for the "bureaucratic servile state" towards which, before the War, both Great Britain and Germany seemed to him to be tending. His ideal lies somewhere between these two —perhaps nearer the latter than the former—in what he describes as "the Great State":—

"A glance at the countryside conjures up a picture of extensive tracts being cultivated on a wholesale scale, of skilled men directing great ploughing, sowing and reaping plants, steering cattle and sheep about carefully designed enclosures, constructing channels and guiding sewage towards its proper destination on the fields, and then of added crowds of genial people coming out to spray trees and plants, pick and sort and pack fruits.

"The amount of regular labour, skilled and unskilled, required to produce everything necessary for everyone living in its highly elaborate civilization may, under modern conditions, with the help of scientific economy and power-producing machinery, be reduced to so small a number of working hours per head in proportion to the average life of the citizen, as to be met as regards the greater moiety of it by the payment of wages over and above the gratuitous share of each individual in the general output; and as regards the residue, a residue of rough, disagreeable and monotonous operations, by some form of conscription, which will demand a year or so, let us say, of each person's life, for the public service.   If we reflect that, in the contemporary state, there is already food, shelter and clothing of a sort for everyone, in spite of the fact that enormous numbers of people do no productive work at all because they are too well off, that great numbers are out of work, great numbers by bad nutrition and training incapable of work, and that an enormous amount of the work actually done is the overlapping production of competitive trade and work upon such politically necessary but socially useless things as Dreadnaughts, it becomes clear that the absolutely unavoidable labour in a modern community and its ratio to the available vitality must be of very small account indeed.

"It is possible to have this Great State, essentially socialistic, owning and running the land and all the great public services, sustaining everybody in absolute freedom at a certain minimum of comfort and well-being, and still leaving most of the interests, amusements and adornments of the individual life, and all sorts of collective concerns, social and political discussion, religious worship, philosophy, and the like to the free personal initiatives of entirely unofficial people."

On the subject of marriage, which he has discussed so often in his novels, he is as firmly opposed to the doctrinaire radicalism of Shaw as he is to the romantic idealism of the rigid and eternal bond:—

"In that world of Mr. Shaw's dreams, in which everybody is to have an equal income and nobody is to have children, in that culminating conversazione of humanity, his marriage law will, no doubt work with the most admirable results.   But if we make a step towards reality and consider a world in which incomes are unequal, and economic difficulties abound—for the present we will ignore the complication of offspring—we at once find it necessary to modify the first fine simplicity of divorce at either partner's request.   Marriage is almost always a serious economic disturbance for both man and woman; work has to be given up and rearranged, resources have to be pooled; only in the rarest cases does it escape becoming an indefinite business partnership.

"Marriage to me is no mystical and eternal union, but a practical affair, to be judged as all practical things are judged—by its returns in happiness and human welfare. And directly we pass from the mists and glamours of amorous passion to the warm realities of the nursery, we pass into a new system of considerations altogether. We are no longer considering A. in relation to Mrs. A., but A. and Mrs. A. in relation to an indefinite number of little A.'s, who are the very life of the State in which they live. Into the Case of Mr. A. and Mrs. A. come Master A. and Miss A. intervening. They have the strongest claim against both their parents for love, shelter and upbringing, and the legislator and statesman, concerned as he is chiefly with the future of the community, has the strongest reasons for seeing that they get these things, even at the price of considerable vexation, boredom or indignity to Mr. and Mrs. A. And here it is that there arises the rational case against free and frequent divorce and the general unsettlement and fluctuation of homes that would ensue.

"Divorce as it exists at present is not a readjustment but a revenge. It is the nasty exposure of a private wrong. In England, a husband may divorce his wife for a single act of infidelity, and there can be little doubt that we are on the eve of an equalization of the law in this respect. I will confess I consider this an extreme concession to the passion of jealousy, and one likely to tear off the roof from many a family of innocent children. . . . Of course, if our divorce law exists mainly for the gratification of the fiercer sexual resentments, well and good, but if that is so, let us abandon our pretence that marriage is an institution for the establishment and protection of homes. And while on the one hand existing divorce laws appear to be obsessed by sexual offences, other things of far more evil effect upon the home go without a remedy. There are, for example, desertion, domestic neglect, cruelty to the children, drunkenness or harmful drug-taking, indecency of living and uncontrollable extravagance."

'Joan and Peter, The Story of an Education' (1918) belongs in this section of Wells's works rather than among his novels, for it has barely enough thread of story to hold it together and the characterization is slight. Joan and Peter are any two young people growing up to womanhood and manhood, and Oswald is any guardian (as it might be Wells himself) with an inquiring mind and a sense of responsibility for the future of the Empire and of the world. The dons and schoolmasters Oswald interviews are types in the sense that they have no individuality—one hopes that they are not typical—and they say the kind of thing Wells wants them to say to bring out the points of his argument, not the kind of thing human beings would say—for schoolmasters are still human—if confronted by such a persistent questioner of all established principles as Wells is and Oswald is set out to be. A paper by Wells in the 'Fortnightly Review' of the previous year (April, 1917), 'The Case against the Classical Languages,' gives his view more clearly and concisely without the impression that he is setting up men of straw for the pleasure of bowling them over. He says:—

"I want . . . to see my country and my English-speaking race thinking more massively than it does at present, thinking more strongly and clearly. I want to see the hundred and fifty millions of English-speakers as one great unifying mind finding itself in expression. I do not want to see what should be the best thing in our university life, the philosophical teaching in the universities, the teaching that attracts the best intelligences of the country, perpetually cut off from the market-place because it is reading Greek, thinking partly in Greek and partly in English, with a partition between, and writing its thoughts sloppily and confusedly in an Anglo-Greek jargon. . . . These Greek monopolists have to get their trade and their prejudices and privileges out of the way of our sons and our people and our public services. It is their share in the sacrifices of these creative days."

In the United States the Greek monopolists have got out of the way—or rather they have been pushed into a corner—and still the educational problem is not solved.

For the rest, besides English and philosophy, Wells wants to have biology, physiology, hygiene, sociology, and history taught—all of which has been done already in many American schools. The advanced educationalist in the United States of to-day would find Wells's educational programme quite conservative. In one point, however, he is radical enough; he wants a new race of teachers. Those encountered by Joan and Peter "seemed to be for the most part little-spirited, gossiping men. They had also an effect of being underpaid; they had been caught early by the machinery of prize and scholarship, bred, as they say at the Zoölogical Gardens, 'in the menagerie'; they were men who knew nothing of the world outside, nothing of effort and adventure, nothing of sin and repentance." One wonders how the teachers Wells has in mind would find time to acquire knowledge, seeing that personal experience of "those graver and larger sins that really distress and mar mankind" makes heavy demands on health and energy. Hardly in this way could the problem be solved of "making the teacher of youth an inspiring figure," and under the present system it has not been found so insoluble as Wells seems to think.

Wells is too much of an artist not to relieve his dissertation by many lively and amusing passages of description and narration, and when in the course of some 500 pages he has got his young people educated—as well as he could, though not at all to his own satisfaction— just in time for the outbreak of the War, he turns to an account of the state of English society in 1914 almost as good as the sketch of later Victorian England at the beginning of 'The New Machiavelli'—not quite so good, for the author's personal feeling comes more into play and distorts the picture. But the restless excitement of the years before the War is vividly portrayed in its various manifestations; feminism, trades unionism, socialism, the Irish question are presented concretely, and there follows a graphic review of the various phases of public feeling and opinion as the great struggle proceeds. Intermixed with this there is inevitable philosophizing, and some theology—more modest in tone than Wells's first incursion into this field. Peter arrives at "a new conception, the conception of Man taking hold of the world, unassisted by God but with the acquiescence of God, and in fulfilment of some remote, incomprehensible planning on the part of God." At this point, however, Wells adds the saving clause:—"Probably Peter in thinking this was following one of the most ancient and well-beaten of speculative paths, but it seemed to him that it was a new way of thinking." The book ends with Oswald's 'Valediction,' a discourse on things in general with education as its kernel, given to us in two versions, first as Oswald devised it in bed, and then as he actually delivered it with the interruptions of Peter, which are so considerable that it takes an entirely different shape—the mind of Wells in its last phase, Oswald's midnight reverie representing the one before the last. Friendship with America, the League of Nations, yes, but for what? Not merely for peace, not for democracy, but for progress, "for the adventure of mankind." And this brings us back to education—"the State explaining itself to and incorporating the will of the individual" so as to fulfil the will of God.

In 1922 Wells announced to the students of Glasgow

University that he was "seriously thinking" of writing no
more novels. A captious critic might retort that he had
written none for some years, for 'The Undying Fire' and
'The Secret Places of the Heart' are really treatises with
an all too thin envelope of fiction. Admirers of Wells's
extraordinary verve and skill in imaginative narration
cannot but regret the diversion of his genius to current
issues of fact and opinion. His visits to Russia and to
Washington during the Conference produced excellent
journalism, but the interest in such work is necessarily
evanescent. 'The Salvaging of Civilisation,' embodying
the content of lectures Wells was prevented by illness
from delivering in the United States, is of more permanent
value, especially the first part, with its vivid and fresh
presentation of world problems and its ardent expression
of the author's desire for a world order of peace and
progress. He makes a suggestive contrast between the
United States, an essentially modern nation extending its
boundaries by the steamboat and the railway, and the
older countries of the European Continent, whose limits
were set by the horse and the high road. The size of the
latter has made them impossible of defence against modern
explosives and hampered them by restrictions of commerce and communication in time of peace. The British
Empire might be described as not a railway but a steam-
ship nation, but its communications and food supplies
are subject to attack by sea and air. The United States,
on the other hand, in addition to its enormous natural
resources, has the advantage of being practically safe from
external aggression.

The 'Outline of History,' undertaken at the suggestion
of a gathering of English and American writers and pro-

fessors in London at the end of the War, presents not merely the author's view of human evolution, but his main interest in a world order towards which the Babylonian, Persian, Greek, and Roman Empires, Christianity, Mohammedanism, the ambitions of Napoleon and the German Emperor, the British Empire and the United States are mere ineffectual beginnings. The book has been violently criticized by some professional historians for alleged errors in detail, but when all allowance is made for these and for some personal bias, it remains a most remarkable achievement in virtue of the skill shown in the arrangement and presentation of an unwieldy mass of material and the narrative power which carries the reader from century to century and gives him a clear and consistent view of human development and achievement.

In 1922 Wells was further diverted from his natural bent towards imaginative fiction by his candidacy for the Rectorship of Glasgow University, in the course of which he made the announcement mentioned above, and by standing as Labour candidate for the University of London at the parliamentary election. On both occasions he was unsuccessful, and to many of the admirers of his work his failure was not altogether a disappointment. He is not a good speaker, and one cannot believe that he would submit patiently to the tedium of debate and committee work in the House of Commons, to say nothing of the other labours incidental to any real achievement in constructive legislation. One rejoices therefore to hear of his return to fiction, even though it is to the scientific romance of his beginnings rather than to the social novels of his middle and best period.

Careful consideration of Wells's work as a whole justifies the central position in current literature ascribed to him at the beginning of this chapter. He widened the scope of the novel, and reflected powerfully many characteristic tendencies of the thought of his time. His direct contributions to that thought are stimulating and suggestive. He is something more than a good story-teller; and when the historian in a future age wishes to discover what were the material and spiritual discontents, the misgivings and aspirations of the more restless thinkers in England during the years immediately before and after the War, he will find them more adequately and vividly expressed in the works of Wells than in those of any other writer.

BIBLIOGRAPHY

ROMANCES

1895 'The Time Machine.'
1896 'The Island of Dr. Moreau.'
1897 'The Invisible Man.'
1898 'The War of the Worlds.'
1899 'When the Sleeper Wakes.'
1901 'The First Men in the Moon.'
1904 'The Food of the Gods.'
1906 'In the Days of the Comet.'
1908 'The War in the Air.'

SOCIOLOGICAL ESSAYS

1901 'Anticipations of the Reaction of Mechanical and Scientific Progress upon Human Life and Thought.'
1903 'Mankind in the Making.'
1905 'A Modern Utopia.'
1906 'The Future in America.'
1907 'This Misery of Boots.'
1908 'New Worlds for Old.' '
       'First and Last Things.'   (Revised and enlarged in 1917.)
1914 'Social Forces in England and America.'   (Published in England as 'An Englishman looks at the World.')
1916 'What is Coming?'
1917 'God the Invisible King.'
1921 'The Salvaging of Civilisation.'
       'Outline of History.'
1922 'A Short History of the World.'

NOVELS

1896 'The Wheels of Chance.'
1900 'Love and Mr. Lewisham.'
1905 'Kipps.'

1909 'Tono-Bungay.'
      'Ann Veronica.'
1910 'The History of Mr. Polly.'
1911 'The New Machiavelli.'
1912 'Marriage.'
1913 'The Passionate Friends.'
1914 'The World Set Free.'
      'The Wife of Sir Isaac Harman.'
1915 'Bealby.'
      'The Research Magnificent.'
1916 'Mr. Britling Sees it Through.'
1917 'The Soul of a Bishop.'
1918 'Joan and Peter.'
1919 'The Undying Fire.'
1922 'The Secret Places of the Heart.'
1923 'Men like Gods and Air like Wine.'

BIOGRAPHICAL AND CRITICAL

Alexander H. Crawfurd, 'The Religion of H. G. Wells,' 1909.

J. D. Beresford, 'H. G. Wells, A Biography and a Critical Estimate of his Work,' 1915.

Van Wyck Brooks, 'The World of H. G. Wells,' 1915.

Edwin E. Slosson, 'Six Major Prophets,' 1917.

(Shaw is the first author discussed, Wells the second. There are good bibliographies.)

Edouard Guyot, 'H. G. Wells,' Paris, 1920.

Sidney Dark, 'An Outline of Wells,' 1922.

R. Thurston Hopkins, 'H. G. Wells: Personality—Character—Topography,' 1922.

There is an interesting sketch of Wells's early career by Thomas Seccombe in the London 'Bookman,' vol. 46, pp. 13–24 (April, 1914).

CHAPTER XII

JOHN GALSWORTHY (1867–   )

Galsworthy has not Wells's narrative power or infectious enthusiasm for ideas or first-hand knowledge of the lowest middle class. The qualities which give him a permanent place in the literature of the period are a very real sympathy for the lowest working class—the oppressed and outcast—and skill in analysis of character and emotion, especially of amorous passion in people of intelligence and refinement.

The son of a leading London lawyer, born in Surrey and educated at Harrow and Oxford, a briefless barrister who completed his education by extensive travel, Galsworthy at early manhood had acquired an intimate knowledge of the habits and prejudices of the English upper middle class and a superficial acquaintance with various foreign types met in the course of his globe-trotting. It was unfortunately with the latter that he chose to deal in his first published work, which shows a curious immaturity and uncertainty. 'From the Four Winds,' printed when he was thirty, is a collection of sensational foreign adventures which give no promise of the power of analysis and criticism he developed later. 'Jocelyn' and 'Villa Rubein,' which followed, conduct love-stories of no special interest to happy endings; in each case the attempt is made to depict and analyse overmastering passion, but without success, for the characters have little grip on reality. The foreign

settings and the foreign English used in the dialogue—
the Americans talk a selection of slang apparently culled
from every State in the Union—add to the impression of
artificiality. In 'The Island Pharisees' the women are
still shadowy, but the two men—the hero Shelton and
the French vagabond, Louis Ferrand—are firmly drawn.
It is a pardonable impertinence to identify Shelton—
well-born, educated at Eton and Oxford, travelled and
detached from the cultivated society to which he belongs—with the author, whose point of view he obviously
presents. He and Ferrand—both greatly enriched and
developed—were later taken over into 'The Pigeon'—
Shelton as Wellwyn and Ferrand under his own name.
In the novel they produce a continuous stream of social
criticism—almost the only part of the book of any real
value—but it lacks the balance, subtlety and sympathy
of Galsworthy's later work.

It was in 'The Man of Property,' published when
Galsworthy was nearly forty, that the novelist first showed
complete mastery of his material and of his art. Soames
Forsyte, though he is not an agreeable character, is
represented not as a criminal (as are some of his typical
predecessors), but as a victim of his own nature, his
education and his environment. He is the embodiment
of middle class prejudices, limitations and virtues; he
regards everything—including his wife—from the point
of view of possession; he has no sense of beauty, no real
affection. With individual differences which are very
subtly indicated, the whole Forsyte family has the same
point of view. The women, though still not very profoundly realized, are more lifelike than the passionate
heroines Galsworthy had hitherto attempted; and the

men are admirably differentiated from each other; old Jolyon Forsyte, whose business capacity does not prevent him from remaining thoroughly human—he uses his money to indulge the domestic affections by which he really lives—is a masterpiece. The young architect who stands for love and beauty but has no financial sense, is beaten by the power of money as the woman he loves is undone by the lack of it, and the novel ends with "the man of property" in absolute control of the situation. The spirit of the story is one of bitter irony, and young Jolyon, who has rebelled against his class but is still part of it, sets forth openly and directly on behalf of the author the view which the whole story is intended to illustrate:—

"The Forsytes are the middle-men, the commercials, the pillars of society, the cornerstones of convention, everything that is admirable!! The great majority of architects, painters, or writers have no principles, like any other Forsytes. Art, literature, religion, survive by virtue of the few cranks who already believe in such things, and the many Forsytes who make a commercial use of them. . . . They are magnificently represented in religion; in the House of Commons perhaps more numerous than anywhere; the aristocracy speaks for itself. . . . My people are not very extreme, and they have their own private peculiarities, like every other family, but they possess in a remarkable degree those two qualities which are the real tests of a Forsyte—the power of never being able to give yourself up to anything soul and body, and the 'sense of property.'"

Galsworthy was well advised in continuing 'The Man of Property' more than ten years later in a charming sketch of the old age of Jolyon Forsyte entitled 'Indian Summer of a Forsyte.' Two novels, 'In Chancery' and 'To Let,' recount the further adventures and misfortunes of Soames

Forsyte, with an intervening sketch, 'Awakening,' devoted
to the childhood of a Forsyte of the next generation. The
three novels with the two interludes make up 'The Forsyte
Saga,' published in 1922 with a special preface and an
elaborate family tree of the Forsytes, extending from 1741
to the present day. The whole constitutes Galsworthy's
most substantial claim for endurance as a writer of fiction,
and is an important contribution to the social history of
the English upper middle class during the period which
ended with the War.

In 'The Country House,' which followed 'The Man of
Property' in order of composition and publication, the
author's satire is directed against the characteristic limitations of country house life. "They're crass," says
Mr. Paramor, who defines 'Pendycitis' as young Jolyon
in the previous novel made "the diagnosis of a Forsyte":
"they do things but they do them the wrong way! They
muddle through with the greatest possible amount of
unnecessary labour and suffering. It's part of the hereditary principle." This "crassness," the author says in
another passage, "common to all men in this strange
world, and in the Squire intensified, was rather a process
than a quality—obedience to an instinctive dread of what
was foreign to himself, an instinctive fear of seeing another's point of view, an instinctive belief in precedent."
This crass unintelligent traditionalism, adhered to with
invincible obstinacy, embroils old Pendyce—a much less
sympathetic figure than his parallel, old Jolyon Forsyte—
with his tenants, his wife, his son. When the son breaks
the tradition by falling in love with a married woman and
meets obstinacy with obstinacy, stupidity with stupidity,
all that his father can think of is that he wishes he had

sent George to Harrow instead of Eton! This, the author comments, was his simple creed:—

"I believe in my father, and his father, and his father's father, the makers and keepers of my estate; and I believe in myself, and my son, and my son's son. And I believe that we have made the country, and shall keep the country what it is. And I believe in the Public Schools and especially the Public School that I was at. And I believe in my social equals and the country house, and in things as they are, for ever and ever. Amen."

His son, equally unintelligent and unattractive, ruins himself for a worthless woman, and his single redeeming virtue, that of constancy, becomes a blind, unreasoning jealousy. Seldom has Galsworthy drawn father and son so wholly self-centred and disagreeable. With Mrs. Pendyce, who is not a Pendyce at all, but a Totteridge— not a provincial but a true aristocrat—a gentle soul, the author deals gently, almost lovingly—most lovingly of all with Mr. Pendyce's other devotee, the spaniel John. All these are strongly conceived and firmly drawn. The appendages of the country house and the outsiders— Gregory Vigil with his quixotic romance and his absurd philanthropic organization—have hardly—except perhaps the Rector—the breath of life.

From the "crassness" of country house life, Galsworthy turned the arrows of his satire on the artificiality of London artistic and philanthropic circles in 'Fraternity.' The title is of course ironical, the novelist's view being that no fellow-feeling is possible among classes so profoundly separated by education, habit, and convention. The note of division is struck in the account of 'Bianca's Day' with which the story opens, and the climax is reached when Hilary Dallison, estranged from his wife and attracted by the "little model," finds he has not the courage to run away with her. To begin with, her nails were not clean, and when she kissed him "the touch of her lips was moist and hot. The scent of stale violet powder came from her warmed by her humanity. It penetrated to Hilary's heart. He started back in sheer physical revolt."

'The Patrician' offers us the most winning family group Galsworthy has yet drawn, from the fascinating little Ann to her no less charming great-grandmother. Lord Miltoun is hardly the characteristic English aristocrat, and his father, who comes much nearer the modern type, plays a secondary rôle. The story suffers from a shift of central interest from Lord Miltoun in the first half to Lady Barbara in the second, and there is no real suspense in either case, as it is obvious from the beginning that both will remain true to the traditions of their class; but both characters are subtly analysed and powerfully as well as skilfully portrayed. The complete passivity of Mrs. Noel leaves her too much in the background to be distinctly realized, and Courtier never becomes altogether lifelike. In spite of much excellent craftsmanship, the novel won only a *succès d'estime*.

In 'The Dark Flower' Galsworthy concentrated on his strongest gift—the analysis of romantic passion. Besides the hero's affection for the gentle Sylvia whom he marries and to whom he constantly returns, he suffers the bitter experiences of disillusion with an older woman in his youth, of blighting tragedy in middle life, and of difficult renunciation in the years when his senses make their last effort to overcome his brain, his conscience and his will. Throughout he retains our sympathy and respect because of his essential humanity and refinement. The book suffers somewhat both from its division into three parts, each with its own heroine, and from dwelling continuously on the same note of passion, but it is originally conceived and powerfully as well as delicately executed.

'The Freelands' brings us back to the discussion of one of the most important social questions of the day—the question of the land and of the social tyranny exercised by landowners. The Freeland brothers are somewhat artificially set off against each other—Felix stands for intellectualism against officialism and industrialism, John for officialism against industrialism and intellectualism, Stanley for industrialism against officialism and intellectualism. But this is merely the setting for the conflict waged by the young rebels, Derek and Sheila Freelands, against the tyranny of Sir Gerald and Lady Malloring, the model landlords. The rebellion is, of course, a failure, and the arch rebel, Derek, gives up the unequal contest, but the story offers Galsworthy the opportunity of saying with feeling and emphasis much that he had in his heart. The contrast that he draws between the life of the landlord and that of the ordinary farm labourer will serve as an example:—

"Your Malloring is called with a cup of tea, at, say, seven o'clock, out of a nice, clean, warm bed; he gets into a bath that has been got ready for him; into clothes and boots that have been brushed for him; and goes down to a room where there's a fire burning already if it's a cold day, writes a few letters, perhaps, before eating a breakfast of exactly what he likes, nicely prepared for him, and reading the newspaper that best comforts his soul; when he has eaten and read, he lights his cigar or his pipe and attends to his digestion in the most sanitary and comfortable fashion; then in his study he sits down to steady direction of other people, either by interview or by writing letters, or what not. In this way, between directing people and eating what he likes, he passes the whole day except that for two or three hours, sometimes indeed seven or eight hours, he attends to his physique by riding, motoring, playing a game or indulging in a sport that he has chosen for himself. And, at the end of all that, he probably has another bath that has been made ready for him, goes down to a good dinner that has been cooked for him, smokes, reads, learns and inwardly digests, or else plays cards, billiards and acts host till he is sleepy, and so to bed in a clean, warm bed, in a clean fresh room.

"Now, to take the life of a Gaunt. He gets up summer and winter much earlier out of a bed that he cannot afford time and money to keep too clean or warm, in a small room that probably has not a large enough window; into clothes stiff with work and boots stiff with clay; makes something hot for himself, very likely brings some of it to his wife and children; goes out, attending to his digestion crudely and without comfort; works with his hands and feet from half-past six or seven in the morning till past five at night, except that twice he stops for an hour or so and eats simple things that he would not altogether have chosen to eat if he could have had his will. He goes home to a tea that has been got ready for him, and has a clean-up without assistance, smokes a pipe of shag, reads a newspaper perhaps two days old, and goes out again to work for his own good, in his vegetable patch, or to sit on a wooden bench in an atmosphere of beer and 'baccy.' And so, dead tired, but not from directing other people, he drowses himself to early lying again in his doubtful bed.

"Candidly, which of those two lives demands more of the virtues on which human life is founded—courage and patience, hardihood and self-sacrifice? And which of two men who have lived those two lives well has most right to the word 'superior'?"

'Beyond'—still the analysis of passionate love, this time from the woman's side—was coldly received by a public intent on more important matters. By this time, too (1917) the public and the critics had made up their minds that Galsworthy was better as a playwright than as a novelist. There is no doubt that the more concentrated and more plastic medium gives scope for his powers of character analysis and dialogue and supplements his besetting weakness—a certain flatness in the minor personages, who were rounded out by the skill of the actors he had the good fortune to secure for the interpretation of his dramatic successes alike in Manchester, London and New York.

His first play, 'The Silver Box,' was produced in the same year that his best novel 'The Man of Property' was published (1906). The play deliberately attempts a formal symmetry which is one of Galsworthy's favourite dramatic devices. Jones, an "out-of-work," has stolen in a drunken fit of resentment from Jack Borthwick, the idle son of a wealthy Liberal M. P., a purse of crimson silk which Jack in a drunken fit of resentment has stolen from "an unknown lady, from beyond." Jones has taken also the silver cigarette box, and adds to the complications of his own case by assaulting the police. Jack gets a scolding from an indulgent father; Jones gets a month's hard labour. Jones is removed from the dock shouting:—"Call this justice? What about 'im? 'E got drunk! 'E took the purse— 'e took the purse, but it's *'is money* got *'im* off—*Justice!*"

There are additional (and perhaps unnecessary) touches of pathos in the crying of Jones's child outside the Borthwick's house and the disposal of two forsaken little girls by the police magistrate before Jones's case comes on; but the real effect of the play consists in the contrast between the Borthwick household, purseproud and pampered, and the Jones family, driven to desperation by poverty. Mrs. Jones, who furnishes the connection be-

tween the two by acting as charwoman in the Borthwick
house, is an admirable character study, very effective
on the stage.

Passing by 'Joy,' which is merely a dramatization of
the psychological gulf which stretches between two generations, "a play on the letter 'I'," we have a similar
contrast in 'Strife'; the issue is a strike at the Trenartha
Tin-Plate works, whose chairman, John Anthony, is
balanced against the workmen's leader, David Roberts,
the Directors against the Workmen's Committee, the
Manager against the Trades Union Official. Anthony
and Roberts are both fighting to win, regardless of consequences, and both men are broken by the determination
of their supporters to end the struggle by compromise—
on the very terms that were suggested when the strike
began. So far Galsworthy holds the balance even between Capital and Labour, but it is obvious that his
sympathies are on the side of Labour, though he makes
the capitalist's son and daughter full of kindly eagerness
to do what they can for the workpeople. The real interest of the play lies in the conflict between the two
masterful characters, Anthony and Roberts, who are
both splendidly realised, the former with very few words,
the latter with burning eloquence about the wrongs of
his class.

'Justice' is a protest against the denial of the privilege
of divorce to the poor and against the severity of English
prison administration, which, indeed, it did something to
ameliorate. It was preceded in order of composition—
though not of production—by 'The Eldest Son' (written
1909, produced 1912), which transfers to the stage the
atmosphere and principal characters of 'The Country

House,' though the illicit tie formed by the son is not now with a married woman of his own class, but with his mother's maid. On the stage, father and son take on more humanity—they are more living people and less types than in the novel, and the father's determination is stiffened by previous severity to a keeper on his own estate who has been guilty of a similar offence; but the point insisted on is the same—the "crassness" of country house life, its immovable adherence to caste and tradition.

One other play of Galsworthy's belonging to the prewar group seems to call for comment on account of its social significance, 'The Pigeon.' Wellwyn is our old friend Shelton of 'The Island Pharisees,' richly humanised and provided with a sensible daughter. The Frenchman Ferrand is taken over under the same name without change, and is the spokesman of the outcasts for whom the drama makes an impassioned plea. By the side of these three,—the vagabond Frenchman, the broken-down cabman, and the loose-living flower-girl—the Professor, the Magistrate and the Clergyman are mere mechanical figures stuck into the play to prove the foolishness of the attempt "to make wild birds tame":—

"*Ferrand.* They do a good work while they attend with their theories to the sick, and the tame old, and the good unfortunate deserving. Above all to the little children. But, Monsieur, when all is done there are always us hopeless ones. What can they do with me, Monsieur, with that girl, or with that old man? Ah! Monsieur, we, too, 'ave our qualities, we others—it wants you courage to undertake a career like mine, or a life like that young girl's. We wild ones— we know a thousand times more of life than ever will those sirs. They waste their time trying to make rooks white. Be kind to us if you will, or let us alone like Mees Ann, but do not try to change our skins. Leave us to live, or leave us to die when we like in the free air. If you do not wish of us, you have but to shut your pockets and your doors—we shall die the faster.

Wellwyn (with agitation). But that, you know—we can't do—now can we?

Ferrand. If you cannot, how is it our fault? The harm we do to others—is it so much? If I am criminal, dangerous—shut me up! I would not pity myself, nevare. But we in whom something moves—like that flame, Monsieur, that *cannot* keep still—we others —we are not many—that must have motion in our lives, do not let them make us prisoners with their theories because we are not like them—it is life itself they would enclose."

During and after the War Galsworthy produced and published a number of plays, some of which did not meet with the approval either of the critics or of the public. Of these it is enough to say, in the words of St. John Ervine, that they belong to "the class of work done by a distinguished man on a wet day when he is rather tired." The list of comparative failures was, however, broken by two remarkable successes—'The Skin Game' and 'Loyalties.' The former sets forth the havoc wrought by the incursion of a pushing northern manufacturer into a county society, which succeeds in driving him out, but only at the sacrifice of every delicacy of feeling which makes an aristocracy worth its salt. The "Hillcrests" and the "Hornblowers" are admirably characterized and contrasted (perhaps with a little extra sympathy for the aristocratic side), and Galsworthy shows unusually clever stagecraft in the management of material which at times demanded very delicate treatment.

'Loyalties' is an even better play, with an exciting plot, which would have turned to melodrama but for the deftness of the handling. It revolves round the theft in a country house of £1000 from the bedroom of a young Jewish guest who makes himself sufficiently disagreeable to alienate the sympathies of his fellow-guests—and of the audience. He suspects a wild young officer who occupies the next room, and as, in spite of the social pressure brought to bear upon him, he does not keep his suspicions to himself, the matter becomes one for the club of which both are members and is ultimately the subject of an action for slander. In the middle of the action the young D. S. O.'s solicitor and counsel receive privately convincing proof of his guilt, and withdraw from the case. The young officer finds the only solution in suicide. The theme of the play is indicated by its title, but is not unduly stressed in the action, which brings out, subtly and naturally, the clashing loyalties of the various characters— loyalty to one's race, to one's caste, to one's friends, to one's profession, to one's regiment, to one's club, and so on.

Both these plays illustrate the theory of the drama which Galsworthy sets forth in one of his best essays. He says, "A drama must be shaped so as to have a spire of meaning. Every grouping of life and character has its inherent moral; and the business of the dramatist is so to pose the group as to bring that moral poignantly to the light of day." In this matter of the moral, there are three courses open to the serious dramatist: (1) He may set forth popular and accepted views; (2) He may set forth his own views, "the more effectively if they are the opposite of what the public wishes to have placed before it, presenting them so that the audience may swallow them like powder in a spoonful of jam." (3) He may set before the public "no cut-and-dried codes, but the phenomena of life and character, selected and combined, but not distorted by the dramatist's outlook, set down without fear, favour or prejudice, leaving the public to draw such poor moral as nature may afford." Obviously this third method is the one Galsworthy himself prefers—it requires detachment, sympathy, the far view, and it depends mainly on the interpretation of character.

"The dramatist's licence, in fact, ends with his design. In conception alone he is free. He may take what character or group of characters he chooses, see them with what eyes, knit them with what idea, within the limits of his temperament; but once taken, seen, and knitted, he is bound to treat them like a gentleman, with the tenderest consideration of their mainsprings. Take care of character; action and dialogue will take care of themselves."

It is not surprising to find that Galsworthy despises plot construction; but his frequent neglect of this element of drama has two resulting weaknesses. In the first place, his characters often fail to develop within the action of the play; the vast majority are the same at the end as they were at the beginning, the impression conveyed is that of a dramatic situation, not of the ever-moving current of life. In the second place, Galsworthy is inclined, for lack of a well-constructed plot, to build up his characters symmetrically, one balanced against the other, as in 'Strife,' 'The Pigeon,' and 'The Skin Game'—and this adds to one's sense of artificiality. He is not a born storyteller or dramatist, and though he always writes well— his style is a never-failing pleasure—one has often a consciousness of thinness in his imaginative work. The beauty of his prose and his artistic sincerity may save much of his work from oblivion when that of more successful competitors is forgotten, but it seems likely to be treasured by the few who can appreciate delicacy and subtlety and do not ask either for the excitement of a stirring action or for the intellectual stimulus of brilliant paradox. He has no 'ism to offer as a cure for all human ills. He sees men bound by class limitations—the poor by actual want, the rich by ignorance and prejudice—and he has found no remedy except understanding and sympathy. No critic has ever revealed the shortcomings of his own class with greater fearlessness; no social observer has set forth the wrongs and sufferings of the down-trodden with deeper sympathy. So long as the English social system produces such inequality, ignorance and suffering, English readers will not be lacking for an English critic who has had the courage and skill to turn on them a mind of singularly delicate and penetrating power. Some of these inequalities have been softened or diminished by the stress of the Great War; others are perhaps deeply founded in human nature and will never entirely disappear. But it will be long years before a generation will arise which has no need of the message of consideration and human kindness which Galsworthy has conveyed with so much subtlety and artistic charm.

BIBLIOGRAPHY

NOVELS

1898 'Jocelyn.'
1900 'Villa Rubein.'
1904 'The Island Pharisees.'
1906 'The Man of Property.'
1907 'The Country House.'
1909 'Fraternity.'
1911 'The Patrician.'
1913 'The Dark Flower.'
1915 'The Freelands.'
1917 'Beyond.'
1919 'Saint's Progress.'
1920 'In Chancery.'
1921 'To Let.'

ESSAYS AND STORIES

1897 'From the Four Winds.'
1901 'A Man of Devon.'
1908 'A Commentary.'
1910 'A Motley.'
1912 'The Inn of Tranquillity.'
1915 'The Little Man and other Satires.'
1916 'A Sheaf.'
1917 'Indian Summer of a Forsyte.'
1918 'Five Tales.'
1919 'Another Sheaf.'
1920 'Tatterdemalion.'
      'Awakening.'

PLAYS

1906 'The Silver Box.'
1907 'Joy.'
1909 'Strife.'
1910 'Justice.'
1911 'The Little Dream.'

235

1912 'The Pigeon.'
     'The Eldest Son.'
1914 'The Fugitive.'
     'The Mob.'
1915 'A Bit o' Love.'
1917 'The Foundations.'
1920 'The Skin Game.'
1921 'Six Short Plays.'
1922 'Loyalties.'
     'Windows.'

POEMS

1912 'Moods, Songs and Doggerels.'

BIOGRAPHICAL AND CRITICAL

Sheila Kaye-Smith, 'John Galsworthy,' 1916.

CHAPTER XIII

ARNOLD BENNETT (1867-   )

The greatest obstacle to the permanence of Arnold
Bennett's literary reputation is the mass of commonplace
production which threatens to distract attention from his
few masterpieces. One may pass an idle hour pleasantly
enough with what Bennett calls 'fantasies,' 'frolics,'
'melodramas,' 'idyllic diversions' (and some of the
books he calls novels really belong to the same class),
but what has the student of literature to do with such
pretentious pot-boilers (Bennett applies the word indis-
criminately to his own work and George Meredith's
novels) as 'How to Live on Twenty-four Hours a Day,'
'The Reasonable Life,' 'Friendship and Happiness,'
'The Married Life,' etc., which the author classes under
'Belles-Lettres,' and which his publishers (not, one
hopes, himself) heralded as containing "big, strong,
vital, thinking"? The danger is that this over-adver-
tised deadweight of platitudes will overwhelm Bennett's
reputation as a conscientious artist and hinder appreciation of his really significant work. To those who are
acquainted with both it must be an astonishment that
the author of these cheap popular essays should also be
the novelist of 'The Old Wives' Tale' and the 'Clayhanger' trilogy.

The key to the enigma is supplied by Arnold Bennett
himself. In 'The Truth about an Author,' originally
published anonymously in the columns of the 'Academy,'

237

and reprinted years afterwards under the author's name, Bennett gives an unblushingly veracious account of his early struggles and successes. He was born near Hanley, the 'Hanbridge' of the Five Towns which his novels were to launch into literary fame, and received a somewhat limited education at the neighbouring 'Middle School' of Newcastle, his highest scholastic achievement being the passing of the London University Matriculation Examination. Some youthful adventures in journalism were perhaps significant of latent power and literary inclination, but a small provincial newspaper offers no great encouragement to youthful ambition, and Enoch Arnold Bennett (as he was then called) made his way at 21 as a solicitor's clerk to London, where he was soon earning a modest livelihood by "a natural gift for the preparation of bills of costs for taxation." He had never "wanted to write" (except for money) and had read almost nothing of Scott, Jane Austen, Dickens, Thackeray, the Brontës, and George Eliot, though he had devoured Ouida, boys' books and serials. His first real interest in a book was "not as an instrument for obtaining information or emotion, but as a *book*, printed at such a place in such a year by so-and-so, bound by so-and-so, and carrying colophons, registers, water-marks, and *fautes d'impression*." It was when he showed a rare copy of 'Manon Lescaut' to an artist and the latter remarked that it was one of the ugliest books he had ever seen, that Bennett, now in his early twenties, first became aware of the appreciation of beauty. He won twenty guineas in a competition, conducted by a popular weekly, for a humorous condensation of a sensational serial, being assured that this was "art," and the same paper paid

him a few shillings for a short article on 'How a bill of
costs is drawn up.' Meanwhile he was "gorging" on
English and French literature, his chief idols being the
brothers de Goncourt, de Maupassant, and Turgenev,
and he got a story into the 'Yellow Book.' He saw that
he could write, and he determined to adopt the vocation
of letters. After a humiliating period of free lancing
in Fleet Street, he became assistant editor and later
editor of 'Woman.' When he was 31, his first novel, 'A
Man from the North,' was published, both in England
and America, and with the excess of the profits over the
cost of typewriting he bought a new hat. At the end of
the following year he wrote in his diary:—

"This year I have written 335,340 words, grand total; 224 articles
and stories and four instalments of a serial called 'The Gates of
Wrath' have actually been published, also my book of plays, 'Polite
Farces.' My work included six or eight short stories not yet published, also the greater part of a 55,000 word serial 'Love and Life'
for Tillotsons, and the whole draft, 80,000 words, of my Stafford-
shire novel 'Anna Tellwright.'"

This last was not published in book form till 1902
under the title of 'Anna of the Five Towns'; but in the
ten years that had elapsed since he came to London, Bennett had risen from a clerk at six dollars a week to be a
successful "editor, novelist, dramatist, critic, connois-
seur of all arts" with a comfortable suburban residence.
Still he was not satisfied; he was weary of journalism
and the tyranny of his Board of Directors. He threw up
his editorial post, with its certain income, and retired
first to the country and then to a cottage at Fontainebleau to devote himself to literature.

In the autumn of 1903, when Bennett used to dine

frequently in a Paris restaurant, it happened that a fat old woman came in who aroused almost universal merriment by her eccentric behaviour. The novelist reflected: "This woman was once young, slim, perhaps beautiful; certainly free from these ridiculous mannerisms. Very probably she is unconscious of her singularities. Her case is a tragedy. One ought to be able to make a heart-rending novel out of a woman such as she." The idea then occurred to him of writing the book which afterwards became 'The Old Wives' Tale,' and in order to go one better than Guy de Maupassant's 'Une Vie' he determined to make it the life-history of two women instead of one. Constance, the more ordinary sister, was the original heroine; Sophia, the more independent and attractive one, was created "out of bravado." The project occupied Bennett's mind for some years, during which he produced five or six novels of smaller scope, but in the autumn of 1907 he began to write 'The Old Wives' Tale' and finished it in July, 1908. It was published the same autumn, and though its immediate reception was not encouraging, before the winter was over it was recognized both in England and America as a work of genius. The novelist's reputation was upheld, if not increased, by the publication of 'Clayhanger' in 1910, and in June, 1911, the most conservative of American critical authorities, the 'New York Post' could pronounce judgment in these terms:—

"Mr. Bennett's Bursley is not merely one single stupid English provincial town. His Baineses and Clayhangers are not simply average middle class provincials foredoomed to humdrum and the drab shadows of experience. His Bursley is every provincial town, his Baineses are all townspeople whatsoever under the sun. He professes nothing of the kind; but with quiet smiling patience, with a multitude of impalpable touches, clothes his scene and its humble figures in an atmosphere of pity and understanding. These little people, he seems to say, are as important to themselves as you are to yourself, or as I am to myself. Their strength and weakness are ours; their lives, like ours, are rounded with a sleep. And because they stand in their fashion for all human character and experience, there is even a sort of beauty in them if you will but look for it."

The appreciation is a just one, and suggests the further elucidation of a side of Bennett's art which is often misunderstood. He is often regarded as the unsparing critic of provincialism; he is really its apostle. It is not because he dislikes and despises the life of the Five Towns that he describes it with such minute care, it is because he loves it. This is in accord with a well-established principle which Bennett has himself very clearly set forth:—

"The sense of beauty [is] indispensable to the creative artist. Every creative artist has it, in his degree. He is an artist because he has it. An artist works under the stress of instinct. No man's instinct can draw him towards material which repels him—the fact is obvious. Obviously, whatever kind of life the novelist writes about, he has been charmed and seduced by it, he is under its spell—that is, he has seen beauty in it. He could have no other reason for writing about it. He may see a strange sort of beauty; he may—indeed he does—see a sort of beauty that nobody has quite seen before; he may see a sort of beauty that none save a few odd spirits ever will or can be made to see. But he does see beauty." ('The Author's Craft.')

To suppose that the novelist, who was born and spent his youth in the Five Towns and made his own literary reputation at the same time as he made theirs, regards them with the superficial condescension of the ordinary London journalist is a complete misapprehension. Bennett says so himself in so many words. "It seems to me," he wrote in 1907, "the most English piece of England that I ever came across. With extraordinary clearness I see it as absurdly, ridiculously, splendidly English! All the English characteristics are, quite remarkably, exaggerated in the Potteries." To anyone who knows English provincial life, this is an obvious truth, and the fact that Bennett makes kindly fun of the oddities and limitations of his provincial characters says nothing to the contrary. Constance and Sophia are provincial heroines—but they are heroines. Unintelligent, self-centred, eccentric, if you like, but full of honesty and courage, of practical ability and sincere affection. Take, for instance, the first "Good Night" of the two sisters after their long years of separation:—

"They looked at each other again, with timid affectionateness. They did not kiss. The thought in both their minds was:—'We couldn't keep on kissing every day.' But there was a vast amount of quiet, restrained affection, of mutual confidence and respect, even of tenderness in their tones."

Above all, they have common sense, the knowledge how to live. When Madame Foucault makes her confession, Sophia thinks "What a fool you have been!" not, "What a sinner!" "If I couldn't have made a better courtesan than this pitiable woman I would have drowned myself." It is character that saves Sophia from the treachery of Gerald Scales and that makes her repulse Chirac. "The instinct which repulsed him was not within her control. Just as a shy man will obstinately refuse an invitation which is he hungering to accept, so, though not from shyness, she was compelled to repulse Chirac." It is an inherited and traditional instinct for decency and order. It is the same instinct that makes Sophia shrink from the dust in the corners of Madame Foucault's room, and the showiness of the furniture. "Nothing in it, she found, was 'good.' And in St. Luke's Square 'goodness' meant honest workmanship, permanence, the absence of pretence."

It is the same fundamental solidity of character which saves Hilda Lessways from the consequences of her own waywardness and enables her to make a success of life with Edwin Clayhanger in the old-fashioned provincial way of material advancement and family affection. The Orgreaves in the same series of novels are a model— almost an ideal—family, for they have, in addition to the everyday virtues, a keener sense of beauty than Bennett claims for the ordinary Five Towns families. He says in 'The Truth about an Author,' speaking of his own youth:—

"I had lived in a world where beauty was not mentioned, seldom thought of. I believe I had scarcely heard the adjective 'beautiful' applied to anything whatever, save confections like Gounod's 'There is a green hill far away.' Modern oak sideboards were called handsome, and Christmas cards were called pretty, and that was about all."

So, among the provincial characters of 'What the Public Wants,' only John Worgan is described as "highly educated," "with very artistic tastes," but we are told that "all these people are fundamentally 'decent˙ and sagacious," and it is their point of view that is upheld, despite their queer clothes, food and manners.

Substantially their point of view is Arnold Bennett's own point of view, and it is no wonder that his treatment of them is sympathetic, for he has remained a thorough provincial at heart. He admires their qualities of faithfulness and endurance, and is never tired of insisting on the essential wholesomeness and rightness of English provincial life, though he is not blind to its æsthetic shortcomings. Of its shortcomings on another side—its narrowness of vision and lack of spirituality—he is only half conscious. Religion plays a curiously small part in any of his books, and the great political and social questions of the period he describes find only a faint echo now and then, almost always on their mechanical or material side. We learn in 'The Old Wives' Tale' about such changes as the introduction of public baths, free libraries, municipal parks, telephones, and electric tramcars and automobiles, and in 'Clayhanger,' we have references to parliamentary elections, strikes, and religious revivals, but the reader would hardly gather that in the period covered by these two novels the intellectual, social and political life of England had undergone revolution.

There is the same defect in Bennett's novel dealing with the earlier years of the War, 'The Pretty Lady.' It is noteworthy that he chooses to see the great struggle through the eyes of a Parisian courtesan, flung upon Leicester Square by the tide of the Belgian invasion, and of a London man about town, sobered to serious work as a member of a war committee and carrying into his amours the systematic punctuality of business. G. J. Hoape may have acquired some London polish, but he was surely born in one of the Five Towns. The solid painting of this character contrasts with the sketchiness of the portraits of the neurotic London ladies who seek in war charities a new form of excitement. The 'pretty lady' herself is somewhat dimly realized; perhaps she

would be more convincing if she were allowed to talk
French, for the literal translation of her terms of en-
dearment fails as a literary device to give any touch of
actuality; but in any case it would be hard to away with
her mysticism, which is twice associated with purely
accidental coincidence. That she should obey the un-
uttered summons of a lover who happens, all unknown
to her, to be in the next street might be tolerated, but
that she should again hear his voice when he is not there
and thus by an evil chance wrongly convince her regular
protector, who happens to be looking out of his club
window at the time, of her faithlessness, is too much.
The external features of London in 1916–17 are vividly
presented—the dark streets and the Zeppelin raids,
committee meetings and war charities feverishly alter-
nating with revues and night clubs—but apart from these
incidental interests the story is unsatisfactory either as a
rendering of the English mind at a period of crisis or as
a study of particular persons under the strain of deep
emotion.

'The Roll Call' is a combination, not altogether successful, of the war interest with the fortunes of a minor
character in the Clayhanger series, George Cannon, now a
young architect in London, his mother (more familiar to
us as Hilda Lessways) and her husband, Edwin Clayhanger, being introduced only incidentally towards the
end of the book. It is almost the end, too, before Bennett
catches up with the subject of the novel as indicated by the
title, for George Cannon has only just got into the Army
and is still in England when the story comes to an abrupt
close.

Instead of continuing the adventures of George Cannon,

public and publishers being alike weary of war novels, Bennett, with his usual flair for a subject of current interest, took up in 'Mr. Prohack' the contrast between the "new rich" and the "new poor" after the War. If the hero had made a fortune by profiteering, the reader's sympathies would have been alienated, and Bennett would have been embarrassed, for he has never lost the "Five Towns" admiration for worldly success. So he ascribes Mr. Prohack's sudden accession to wealth to a windfall in the shape of a totally unexpected legacy. The social adventures of the hero, his wife, his son and his daughter are recounted with a good deal of verve and kindly humour, and we get a glimpse of the mad rush for pleasure and excitement that took place in certain circles in London after the War. As social documents, this novel and the two preceding it may have some value; as works of art, they are not worthy to rank with the studies of provincial life before the War on which the permanent fame of the author seems likely to rest.

BIBLIOGRAPHY

NOVELS

1898 'A Man from the North.'
1902 'Anna of the Five Towns.'
1903 'Leonora.'
1904 'A Great Man.'
1905 'Sacred and Profane Love.'   (Revised edition, U. S. 1911:
          'The Book of Carlotta.')
1906 'Whom God hath Joined.'
1908 'Buried Alive.'
      'The Old Wives' Tale.'
1910 'Clayhanger.'
1911 'The Card.'   (U. S.: 'Denry the Audacious.')
      'Hilda Lessways.'
1913 'The Regent.'
1914 'The Price of Love.'
1916 'These Twain.'
1918 'The Pretty Lady.'
1919 'The Roll-Call.'
1922 'Mr. Prohack.'
      'Lilian.'

SHORT STORIES

1905 'Tales of the Five Towns.'
1907 'The Grim Smile of the Five Towns.'
1912 'The Matador of the Five Towns.'

PLAYS

1908 'Cupid and Commonsense.'
1909 'What the Public Wants.'
1912 'Milestones.'   (With Edward Knoblauch.)
      'The Honeymoon.'
1913 'The Great Adventure.'
1918 'The Title.'
1919 'Judith.'
      'Sacred and Profane Love.'
1922 'The Love Match.'
      'Body and Soul.'

BELLES LETTRES

1903   'The Truth about an Author.'
1912   'Those United States.'   (U. S.: 'Your United States.')
1914   'The Author's Craft.'

There is a little book about Arnold Bennett by F. J. Harvey Darton, in the 'Writers of the Day' series.

CHAPTER XIV

THE IRISH MOVEMENT

From whatever point of view it may be studied, the Irish Renaissance is one of the most interesting literary movements of the time. It seems idle to discuss whether it really belongs to English or to Irish literature (the distinction between English and American literature being already recognized), and almost as idle to ask whether the poets produced the Movement or the Movement produced the poets. Yeats and Synge would have been men of letters without the Irish Revival, but without it they would not have been the same men of letters. Possibly they contributed more to the Movement than they gained from it, but that they were greatly influenced by it cannot be doubted.

The Movement is perhaps rather overweighted with literary history, but it is worth while to put on record its humble beginnings and the important steps in its development. Its first historian was W. P. Ryan, whose little book was published in 1894, when the Movement was hardly more than under way, as is indicated by his title: —'The Irish Literary Revival, its History, Pioneers and Possibilities.' According to Mr. Ryan, the Movement began in the early eighties, with the Southwark Irish Literary Club, which in 1890 moved to the neighbouring district of Clapham, and in 1891 changed its name to the Irish Literary Society, London. W. B. Yeats, who had been an active worker in the London Society, helped in

1892 in the foundation of the Irish National Literary Society at Dublin. Two addresses delivered by Sir Charles Gavan Duffy, as President, to the London Society in 1892–3, one by Dr. Sigerson, and one by Dr. Douglas Hyde to the Dublin Society in 1892 were published together in 1894 under the title 'The Revival of Irish Literature' and set forth, still somewhat vaguely, the aims of the founders. Sir Charles Gavan Duffy's principal theme was the 'New Irish Library,' of which a dozen volumes were published under his editorship by 1897; Dr. Sigerson dealt with the glorious past of Irish literature, but had no very definite plans for the future; Dr. Douglas Hyde's paper on 'The Necessity for De-Anglicizing Ireland' blew a trumpet blast, not merely reproaching the Irish people for their neglect of Irish tradition, language and literature for the past century, but urging every Irishman "to set his face against this constant running to England for our books, literature, music, games, fashions, and ideas" and "to do his best to help the Irish race to develop in future upon Irish lines." Meanwhile, at the inaugural lecture of the London Society in 1893, the Rev. Stopford Brooke had drawn up a definite programme. Taking it for granted that the work already done to preserve and edit old Irish Mss. would be continued, he urged:—(1) that the pieces of the finest quality should be accurately translated "with as much of a poetic movement as is compatible with fine prose, and done by men who have the love of noble form and the power of shaping it"; (2) that Irishmen of formative genius should take, one by one, the various cycles of Irish tales, and grouping each of them round one central figure, supply to each a dominant human interest to

which every event in the whole should converge, after
the manner of Malory's 'Morte d'Arthur'; (3) that suitable episodes in these imaginative tales should be treated
in verse, retaining the colour and spirit of the original;
(4) that the folk-stories of Ireland should be collected.
Douglas Hyde's 'Beside the Fire,' which had appeared
in 1890, was mentioned as exactly the thing that ought
to be done for the folk-tales of all Ireland, and it is possible that Stopford Brooke realized what Dr. Hyde had
already accomplished or was on the way to accomplish
—the discovery of a new literary idiom, Hibernian
English or Anglo-Irish. It is not the literal translation
of Gaelic, but the adoption of Irish idioms, "of the kind
used all over Ireland, the kind the people themselves
use," which rest ultimately, no doubt, upon translation
from that Irish which was the language of the speaker's
father, grandfather, or great-grandfather, and have per-
petuated themselves, "even in districts where you will
scarce find a trace of an Irish word." Hyde continued
and successfully developed the experiment in 'Love
Songs of Connacht' (1893) and the Movement found
itself endowed with the priceless boon of a medium of
expression which had the charm of literary freshness and
the ease and naturalness of a spoken tongue.

WILLIAM BUTLER YEATS (1865–   )

Of the third kind of work to be done on the Irish
cycles—the rendering of selected episodes in modern
verse—Stopford Brooke gave as one of the two best
examples he had seen 'The Wanderings of Oisin' by
William Butler Yeats, a young and then little known
poet who had been actively connected with both the

London and the Dublin Societies. Born in Dublin of a
Sligo Protestant family in 1865, Yeats had spent his
childhood and the most impressionable years of his youth
in Ireland, with the exception of some five years in England at school. He had written poetry when he was 16
and began to publish before he was 20 in Irish magazines
and newspapers. He was an ardent patriot, read old
Irish literature "in bad translations" (there were at
that time very few good ones), and gathered folk lore
from the lips of the Connaught peasantry by their turf
fires. He had edited 'Poems and Ballads of Young Ireland' and 'Fairy and Folk Tales of the Irish Peasantry'
in 1888, 'Stories from Carleton' in 1889, and two volumes
of 'Representative Irish Tales' in 1890. The early poems
included in 'The Wanderings of Oisin' volume (1889)
bear marks of the influence of Spenser and Shelley, Morris
and Rossetti; several of them were suppressed, and
others severely revised by their author, who had already
discovered his individual bent and very soon perfected
his style. He had dabbled in theosophy with a wander-
ing Brahmin who came to Dublin, and in 1893 completed
a three-volume edition of Blake. He read all this mystical lore into the peasant tales he gathered, being "at no
pains to separate my own beliefs from those of the peasantry." ('The Celtic Twilight,' 1893.) Similarly in
his poetry, Yeats found the way to express his mysticism
by means of the mythology which old Irish literature had
in common with the traditional superstitions of the Irish
peasant. Contact with a mass of material so long unused
for literary purposes that it had been almost forgotten
gave his work freshness of appeal, his devotion not merely
to Ireland as a nation, but to the Irish spirit as he inter-

preted it gave him sincerity and authority of utterance, and his philosophy, though it was one of escape from life rather than a resolute attempt to face its problems and agitations, was not unwelcome to a generation world-weary and somewhat oppressed with a sense of its own meaningless materialism. Yeats had a genuine lyrical gift and his inspiration was supplemented by conscientious and skilful craftsmanship. The volume of 'Poems' he published in 1895 established not merely his own reputation, but the position of the literary movement of which he now became the protagonist, and won a hearing for his friend and fellow mystic "A. E." (George William Russell), whose 'Homeward Songs by the Way' (1894-5) and 'The Earth Breath' (1897) gained wide acceptance. Probably few of the English readers of either poet paid much attention to the mystical doctrine involved in the new mythology, and the critic's task was left to an Irish transcendentalist "John Eglinton" (W. K. Magee), who in the columns of the Dublin 'Daily Express' raised a doubt whether "a determined pre-occupation" with the ancient legends of Ireland was likely to produce "anything but belles lettres as distinguished from a national literature." There followed a lively and instructive controversy, which was collected under the title 'Literary Ideals in Ireland' (1899) and is one of the most important documents of the Movement. "John Eglinton" distinguished between two conceptions of the poet, the first "as a seer and a spiritual force," the second, "as an aristocratic craftsman."

"The first looks to man himself as the source of inspiration; the second to tradition, to the forms and images in which old conceptions have been embodied—old faiths, myths, dreams. The weakness of the first is an inclination to indifference toward the form and comeliness of art, as in Whitman; while the second, if it hold aloof from the first, cuts itself asunder from the source of all regeneration in art. The bias of the first is toward naked statement, hard fact, dogmatism; the bias of the second toward theory, diffuseness, insincerity. The latter appears to me to be the bias of belles lettres at present. The poet looks too much away from himself and from his age, does not feel the facts of life enough, but seeks in art an escape from them. Consequently, the art he achieves cannot be the expression of the age and of himself—cannot be representative or national."

The attack was direct and was driven home. Yeats met it with an answer no less outspoken: —

"I believe that the renewal of belief, which is the great movement of our time, will more and more liberate the arts from 'their age' and from life, and leave them more and more free to lose themselves in beauty, and to busy themselves, like all the great poetry of the past and like religions of all times, with 'old faiths, myths, dreams,' the accumulated beauty of the age. I believe that all men will more and more reject the opinion that poetry is 'a criticism of life,' and be more and more convinced that it is a revelation of a hidden life."

After this, the issue seemed likely to be lost in the sound and fury of battle, but "A. E." intervened to recall both combatants to a recollection of the subject and to offer a reconciling view. The Old Irish legends, he urged, have gained rather than lost by the lapse of time.

"They have crept through veil after veil of the manifold nature of man, and now each dream, heroism, or beauty has laid itself nigh the divine power it represents, the suggestion of which made it first beloved; and they are ready for the use of the spirit, a speech of which every word has a significance beyond itself, and Deidre is like Helen, a symbol of eternal beauty, and Cuculain represents as much as Prometheus the heroic spirit, the redeemer in man."

Yeats, in an essay on 'The Literary Movement in Ireland' written about the same time, although not published till 1901 (in a volume edited by Lady Gregory, entitled 'Ideals in Ireland') took much the same line of defence:—

"Irish literature may prolong its first inspiratior without renouncing the complexity of ideas and emotions which is the inheritance of cultivated men, for it will have learned from the discoveries of modern learning that the common people, wherever civilization has not driven its plough too deep, keep a watch over the roots of all religion and all romance. Their poetry trembles upon the verge of incoherence with a passion all but unknown among modern poets, and their sense of beauty exhausts itself in countless legends and in metaphors that seem to mirror the energies of nature. . . .

"It may be that poetry is the utterance of desires that we can only satisfy in dreams, and that if all our dreams were satisfied there would be no more poetry. Dreams pass from us in childhood, because we are so often told they can never come true, and because we are taught with so much labour to admire the paler beauty of the world. The children of the poor and simple learn from their unbroken religious faith, and from their traditional beliefs, that this world is nothing, and that a spiritual world, where all dreams come true, is everything; and therefore the poor and simple are that imperfection whose perfection is genius."

"A. E." later defended himself and Yeats against these and other attacks, in a spirited poem 'On behalf of some Irishmen not followers of tradition.' It is not the historic Ireland that claims the allegiance of the new school, but "the Ireland in the heart," the ideal of the far past and of the future; their fealty is "to unseen kings or unimaginable light." So in a prose passage no less eloquent he says:—

"During all these centuries the Celt has kept in his heart some affinity with the mighty beings ruling in the unseen, once so evident to the heroic races who preceded him. His legends and fairy tales have connected his soul with the inner lives of air and water and earth, and they in turn have kept his heart sweet with hidden influence. . . . So this Isle, once called the Sacred Isle and also the Isle of Destiny, may find a destiny worthy of fulfilment; not to be a petty peasant republic, nor a miniature duplicate in life and aims of great material empires, but that its children out of their faith, which has never failed, may realize this immemorial truth of man's inmost divinity, and in expressing it may ray their light over every land."

It was perhaps unfortunate for Yeats's lyric fame that in 'The Wind among the Reeds' (1899) he passed under the influence of the French Symbolist School, and came to use the heroes of Irish mythology "more as principles of the mind than as actual personages." Thus Hanrahan is "fire blown by the wind," and Aedh "fire burning by itself."

"To put it in a different way, Hanrahan is the simplicity of an imagination too changeable to gather permanent possessions, or the adoration of the shepherds; and Michael Robartes is the pride of the imagination brooding upon the greatness of its possessions, or the adoration of the Magi; while Aedh is the myrrh and frankincense that the imagination offers continually before all that it loves."

Later he adopted a mode of thought and a style, which, if not simpler, were at any rate more austere. By way of contrast the following lines from 'The Green Helmet' addressed 'To a Poet, who would have me praise certain bad poets, Imitators of his and mine,' may serve:—

> "You say, as I have often given tongue
> In praise of what another's said or sung,
> 'Twere politic to do the like by these;
> But have you known a dog to praise his fleas?"

At the end of 'Responsibilities' (1916) he seems to take leave of Celtic mythology in 'A Coat':—

> "I made my song a coat
> Covered with embroideries
> Out of old mythologies

From heel to throat;
But the fools caught it,
Wore it in the world's eye
As though they'd wrought it.
Song, let them take it
For there's more enterprise
In walking naked."

A song of farewell to Major Robert Gregory, Lionel
Johnson, Synge and other Irish friends, published in the
August number (1918) of 'The New Review,' illustrates
what T. Sturge Moore in the same issue says of Yeats's
most recent style of versification:

"Mr. Yeats has of late years set the fashion of skating across ever
thinner ice until it seems almost miraculous that verse is not prose.
You watch the skater as the surface warps under his swift passage,
and expect that another minute he will be in it, floundering like any
Walt Whitman, but this does not happen. Rhyme is not discarded,
but strained; rhythms are not free, but licentious."

JOHN MILLINGTON SYNGE (1871-1909)

Even in his early publications, Yeats had shown some
inclination towards the dramatic form, though his
"dramatic" poems of the eighties are in reality lyric.
'The Countess Cathleen,' in the form in which it was
originally published in 1892, falls into the same category,
and two years later W. P. Ryan could say without offence:
—"As the Irish revival expands in new directions, will
not some one take heart and attempt something for Irish
dramatic literature? The real Irish drama is a thing
unknown." Yeats's short lyric drama 'The Land of
Heart's Desire' was produced at the Avenue Theatre in
London the same year (1894) and had no great success,
but he did not relinquish his dream of an Irish literary

theatre, and in 1898, in talk with Lady Gregory, the project took definite shape. Their first plans were simple and modest—the performance by English actors of Yeats's 'The Countess Cathleen' and of Edward Martyn's 'The Heather Field' at the Antient Concert Rooms, Dublin, on May 8 and 9, 1899. George Moore, who had looked after the rehearsals in England, has given in 'Ave' an amusing account of the performance of 'The Countess Cathleen,' which met with a hostile reception on account of supposed heretical implications, but the success of the venture was sufficient to secure the repetition of the experiment in February, 1900, when 'The Bending of the Bough' by George Moore, 'The Last Feast of the Fianna' by Alice Milligan, and 'Maeve' by Edward Martyn were given, and in October, 1901, when 'Diarmuid and Grania' by W. B. Yeats and George Moore was presented by English actors, and 'The Twisting of the Rope' by Douglas Hyde in Gaelic by an Irish company. It was during the rehearsals of the Gaelic play that the brothers Fay conceived the idea of an Irish amateur company for plays in English, encouraged thereto by the enterprise of Ole Bull at the Norwegian National Theatre. Accordingly, in April, 1902, the Irish National Dramatic Company produced 'Deirdre' by "A. E." and 'Cathleen ni Houlihan,' a short play symbolic of Irish patriotism, by W. B. Yeats. Other plays followed, and in 1903 under the presidency of W. B. Yeats the Irish National Theatre Society was formed. The production of 'In the Shadow of the Glen' on October 8th, 1903, marks the accession of a new creative force, J. M. Synge, who had been discovered by Yeats at Paris in 1899, and sent to the Aran Islands in search of native material and a native style. Ernest A. Boyd in his 'Ireland's Literary Renaissance' well says that the great "event" in the history of the Irish theatre was "the discovery and universal recognition of the genius of J. M. Synge." The timely help of Miss Horniman, who restored and endowed the Abbey Theatre for the Company, secured the necessary material opportunity, but what really won the attention of the English-speaking world on both sides of the Atlantic was the dramatic power of Synge's plays, aided no doubt by the simplicity and naturalness of the gestures and speech of the actors, and the quiet appropriateness of costumes and scenery. When Yeats, with Lady Gregory's help, had projected the Irish Literary Theatre in 1899, he had called for plays "that will make the theatre a place of intellectual excitement," and had added:—"Such plays will require, both in writers and audiences, a stronger feeling for beautiful and appropriate language than one finds in the ordinary theatre." Synge's plays satisfied both demands, but not in the way that Yeats expected, for it is evident that what the latter had in mind was lyric drama, though his one permanently successful play on the stage, 'Cathleen ni Houlihan,' is in prose. Synge found the heroes and fairies of Old Irish legend "too far away from life to appease his mood," as Yeats puts it, and he forsook "sweet Angus, Maeve and Fand" for the poachers and topers of the countryside. The plot of 'In the Shadow of the Glen' Synge took from a story he picked up during his wanderings in Aran from old "Pat Dirane," just as he took the story of 'The Tinker's Wedding' from a herd he met at a Wicklow fair. Whence did he gain the "beautiful and appropriate" language, which

Yeats prescribed, and which forms one of the great charms of Synge's plays?   The discovery of the Anglo-Irish idiom is rightly ascribed to Douglas Hyde, with whose 'Love Songs of Connacht' Synge was well acquainted; indeed he borrows from it a phrase or two.   Synge also acknowledges indebtedness to Lady Gregory's 'Cuchulain of Muirthemne,' a rendering of Irish legends in the Anglo-Irish of Kiltartan, which was published the year before his first play was produced, and which he had doubtless seen before it was printed.   But both Dr. Hyde and Lady Gregory drew from a common source—the spoken language of the Irish peasant—with which Synge himself was in direct contact.   He says in the preface to 'The Playboy of the Western World' that in all his plays he used only one or two words he had not heard among the country people of Ireland.

"When I was writing 'The Shadow of the Glen,' some years ago, I got more aid than any learning could have given me, from a chink in the floor of the old Wicklow house where I was staying, that let me hear what was being said by the servant girls in the kitchen.   This matter, I think, is of importance, for in countries where the imagination of the people, and the language they use, is rich and living, it is possible for a writer to be rich and copious in his words, and at the same time to give the reality, which is the root of all poetry, in a comprehensive and natural form."

In another passage Synge speaks of his achievement of striking and beautiful phrases as a collaboration with the Irish peasantry; and so no doubt it was, but it was a collaboration in which his genius was predominant.   In Dr. Hyde or Lady Gregory one gets an occasional poetic phrase or alluring turn of Gaelicized syntax; but no one except Synge (and besides these two predecessors he has had numerous followers) has been able to use the Anglo-

Irish idiom so that (to use his own phrase) "every speech should be as fully flavoured as a nut or apple." The discovery of the idiom was no doubt a lucky chance for Synge, who was acquainted not only with Anglo-Irish but with Gaelic; but the power to use it was his own, partly natural gift, but cultivated by his long studies of French literature and his years of residence in Paris. He came of an old Anglo-Irish family and was educated at Trinity College, but it was neither from Protestant nor from Catholic Ireland, but from modern France that he won his attitude of ironical detachment, which was so alien to Irish sentiment that his plays repeatedly aroused violent protest in Dublin and elsewhere. In 'The Shadow of the Glen,' Synge cancels the ending of the old folk tale in which the faithless wife and her lover meet condign punishment, and allows his heroine to go off by her own choice with the tramp, while her husband sits down to drink with the man who a few minutes before was ready to fill his shoes. The Catholic Church, which has so strong a hold on the affections of the Irish peasantry, furnishes Synge with dramatic machinery, as in 'The Well of the Saints,' or with opportunity for frank ridicule, as in 'The Tinker's Wedding.' As to the latter play, Synge said:—

"In the greater part of Ireland the whole people, from the tinkers to the clergy, have still a life, and view of life, that are rich and genial and humorous. I do not think that these country people, who have so much humour themselves, will mind being laughed at without malice, as the people in every country have been laughed at in their own comedies."

So far as 'The Tinker's Wedding' is concerned, the directors of the Abbey Theatre have not ventured to put

Synge's high estimate of the tolerant humour of the Irish public to the test, and in view of the stormy reception given to 'The Playboy of the Western World,' they were well-advised in not running the risk. Except in that gem of sheer pathos, 'The Riders to the Sea,' it must be confessed that Synge's picture of the Irish peasantry is neither complimentary nor sympathetic. It has humour; it answers Synge's own test of giving "the nourishment, not very easy to define, on which our imaginations live"; his "drama, like the symphony, does not teach or prove anything." It appeals, not to any sense of nationality, but to our sense of humanity and our sense of beauty. If it is regarded from a narrower point of view, the judgment passed on it in a recently recorded conversation between two Irishmen is not wholly unjustified:—

"'They do be putting quare plays on in Dublin nowadays!'
I replied, 'Ah!' with encouraging intimation.
'Yes!' he continued, 'very queer plays. They do be putting on plays where a boy from the country kills his da!'
'That seems wrong.'
'Yes. And they make us out to be nothing but cut-throats, and murderers, and dijinirates.'
'What on earth do they mean by doing that?'
'They calls it—ART.'"

It is art, and art of a very rare and fine quality; but whether one may reasonably expect the Irish peasantry to be proud to be the vehicle of it, is an open question. It seems a good deal to expect from them a higher degree of tolerant intelligence than the townspeople of Tarascon gave to Daudet, or the inhabitants of the Five Towns to Arnold Bennett.

Whether or no the Irish peasant should be grateful to Synge, Synge's literary reputation is under deep indebtedness to the Irish peasant, who gave him not merely an idiom he could turn to beauty, but a way of thinking he could turn to dramatic effect. The idiom proved much less effective in 'Deirdre,' and the way of thinking, which remains much the same, seems less suited to an age of primitive romance, far removed in time, than to the primitive moderns, sufficiently removed in space to allow the imagination play, but endowed with actuality by Synge's realistic genius. Whether he would have succeeded with the Dublin slum drama he was meditating at his untimely death, can only be conjectured. His Irish peasant drama remains a unique achievement, for though there are other plays written for the Abbey Theatre which have literary interest or achieved popular success, no others seem likely to win for themselves the abiding place in literary history to which Synge's work is clearly entitled.

GEORGE MOORE (1852–   )

George Moore was in the Irish movement, but he was never really of it. Born in County Mayo in 1852, he had passed most of his youth and early manhood in Paris and London, and before the Movement really began, he had established his place in literature by his book on 'Modern Painting' and his realistic novel 'Esther Waters.' It was when he was engaged on these works in 1894 that Edward Martyn said to him:—"I wish I knew enough Irish to write my plays in Irish," and he replied, "I thought nobody did anything in Irish except bring turf from the bog and say prayers." Then he learnt that a new literature was springing up in Irish, and he thought what a wonderful thing it would be to write a book in a new language or in an old language revived and sharpened to literary usage for the first time. Five years later, Yeats and Martyn came to Moore to interest him in the project of an Irish Literary Theatre in Dublin, and going to Ireland at their invitation he yielded to the fatal charms of Cathleen ni Houlihan. This, at least, is one of the explanations he gives, for there are many to choose from. "The Englishman that was in me (he that wrote 'Esther Waters'), had been overtaken and captured by the Irishman." After the Boer war, he turned from England in horror; "it became so beastly." Also there was "Stella," who, after receiving two telegrams asking her to come, two telling her not to come, and the last one just in time, met him on the boat. At Lady Gregory's house he undertook to write 'Diarmuid and Grania' with Yeats, who took him aback to begin with by remarking that "the first act of every good play is horizontal, the second perpendicular." "And the third, I suppose, circular?" Moore retorted, and Yeats agreed. He agreed also with Moore's casual suggestion that he preferred to write the play in French rather than in Yeats's vocabulary. "Lady Gregory will translate your text into English. Taidgh O'Donohue will translate the English text into Irish, and Lady Gregory will translate the Irish text back into English." Moore gives us in 'Ave' the French text of the first scene of the second act as the only way of convincing the reader "that two such literary lunatics as Yeats and myself existed, contemporaneously, and in Ireland, too, a country not distinguished for its love of letters." Moore left Ireland for France, as a French atmosphere was necessary for French composition, and returned home to England, but a divine revelation convinced him that "the Messiah Ireland was waiting for was in me and not in another." He had some difficulty in convincing "A. E.," who was experienced in such matters, of the genuineness of the vision, but he stuck to it, and made the acquaintance of all the leading figures in the Irish Movement. Familiarity brought him to the conclusion that the Irish Renaissance was "but a bubble," but he had a second revelation—"that no Catholic had written a book worth reading since the Reformation." Born into a Catholic family and still an agnostic, he determined to become a Protestant, to the no small embarrassment of the Church of Ireland clergy. "My belief never faltered that I was an instrument in the hands of the gods, and that their mighty purpose was the liberation of my country from priestcraft." He knew he was not a preacher, and strove to fashion first a story, then a play, but "the artist in me could not be suborned." Davitt came with a project for a newspaper, but he died. Moore was beginning to lose hope when the form which the book should take was revealed to him—an autobiography—an unusual form for a sacred book he reflected, until the example of St. Paul occurred to him.

This is Moore's own account of 'Hail and Farewell'— the three volumes in which he said 'Ave,' 'Salve,' and 'Vale' to Ireland and the Irish Movement. The Renaissance was well provided with fairies of the serious sort, but had no knavish elves, and Moore took upon himself the part of Puck in the disguise of a literary historian. It is the most entertaining account of the Irish Renaissance, and would be the most authoritative if one could only believe half of what is told. But when **Moore** ascribes to Edward Martyn the remark to himself: "I never believed that your life is anything but pure; it is only your mind that is indecent," we detect invention, as in the definition put in the mouth of "A. E.":—"A literary movement consists of five or six people, who live in the same town and hate each other cordially." It was a good thing that Moore said "Farewell" to Ireland in the last volume, for he could certainly not have returned to it, and it is a wonder that the British Isles remained large enough to contain himself and the victims of his malicious wit. 'Hail and Farewell' is and is likely to be a unique literary achievement, for the combination of impish skill and thorough-going disregard of the feelings of one's most intimate literary associates and friends is fortunately rare.

BIBLIOGRAPHY

WILLIAM BUTLER YEATS

POEMS

1886 'Mosada.' A Dramatic Poem.
1889 'The Wanderings of Oisin, and other Poems.'
1895 'Poems' (including Lyrics published with 'The Countess Cathleen' (1892).
1899 'The Wind among the Reeds.'
1906 'Poems, 1899–1905.'
1914 'Responsibilities.'
1917 'The Wild Swans at Coole, other Verses and a Play in Verse' ('At the Hawk's Well,' a "Noh" play, performed privately in 1916 by the Japanese dancer Ito and others).

PLAYS

1892 'The Countess Cathleen' (acted 1899).
1894 'The Land of Heart's Desire.'
1900 'The Shadowy Waters' (acted 1904).
1902 'Cathleen ni Houlihan.'
1903 'The Hour Glass.'
     'On Baile's Strand' (acted 1904).
1904 'The King's Threshold' (acted 1903).
     'The Pot of Broth' (acted 1902).
1907 'Deirdre' (acted 1906).
1910 'The Green Helmet.'
1911 'Plays for an Irish Theatre,' containing all the above except the first two.
1921 'Four Plays for Dancers' (including the "Noh" play mentioned above).

PROSE

1893 'The Celtic Twilight.'
1897 'The Secret Rose.'
1903 'Ideas of Good and Evil.'
1907 'Discoveries; A Volume of Essays.'
1912 'The Cutting of an Agate.'
1915 'Reveries over Childhood and Youth.'
1918 'Per Amica Silentia Lunae.'
1921 'Four Years' (1887–1891).
1922 'The Trembling of the Veil.'

"A. E." (GEORGE W. RUSSELL)

1894   'Homeward Songs by the Way.'
1897   'The Earth Breath.'
1906   'By Still Waters.'
1907   'Deirdre.'
1913   'Collected Poems.'
1915   'Gods of War and other Poems.'
       'Imaginations and Reveries.'
1917   'Salutation; a Poem on the Irish Rebellion of 1916.'
1918   'The Candle of Vision.'

JOHN MILLINGTON SYNGE

1905   'In the Shadow of the Glen' (acted 1903).
       'Riders to the Sea' (acted 1904).
1907   'The Well of the Saints.'
       'The Playboy of the Western World.'
       'The Tinker's Wedding.'
1910   'Deirdre of the Sorrows.'
    The four volumes of Synge's Works (1911) included 'The Aran
Islands' (1907) and 'Poems and Translations' (1909), in addition
to the dramas listed above, which are collected also in the one volume
edition of his 'Dramatic Works' (1915).

GEORGE MOORE

1878   'Flowers of Passion.'
1881   'Pagan Poems.'
1883   'A Modern Lover.'
1885   'A Mummer's Wife.'
1886   'A Drama in Muslin.'
1888   'Confessions of a Young Man.'
1893   'Modern Painting.'
1894   'Esther Waters.'
1898   'Evelyn Innes.'
1900   'The Bending of the Bough.'
1901   'Sister Teresa.'
1903   'The Untilled Field.'
1911   'Ave.'
1912   'Salve.'

1914 'Vale.'
1916 'The Brook Kerith.'
1919 'Avowals.'
1921 'Héloïse and Abelard.'
  Bibliography by Iolo A. Williams (1921).

BIOGRAPHICAL, CRITICAL AND HISTORICAL

Francis Bickley, 'John Millington Synge and the Irish Dramatic Movement,' 1912.

Jethro Bithell, 'W. B. Yeats,' Paris, 1913.

Maurice Bourgeois, 'J. M. Synge and the Irish Theatre,' 1913.

Ernest A. Boyd, 'Ireland's Literary Renaissance,' 1916, 1922.

Ernest A. Boyd, 'The Contemporary Drama of Ireland,' 1917.

Stopford Brooke, 'The Need and Use of Getting Irish Literature into the English Tongue,' 1893.

Oliver Elton, 'The Irish Literary Movement' in 'Modern Studies,' 1907.

Darrell Figgis, 'A. E.,' 1915.

Lady Gregory (Ed.), 'Ideals in Ireland,' 1901.

Lady Gregory, 'Our Irish Theatre,' 1914.

Patty Gurd, 'The Early Poetry of William Butler Yeats,' Lancaster, Pa., 1916.

J. M. Hone, 'W. B. Yeats,' 1916.

P. P. Howe, 'J. M. Synge, A Critical Study,' 1912.

Douglas Hyde, 'Beside the Fire,' 1890.

Douglas Hyde, 'The Necessity of De-Anglicising the Irish Nation,' Lecture at the Dublin National Literary Society, Nov. 25, 1892.

Douglas Hyde, 'Love Songs of Connacht,' 1893.

Douglas Hyde, 'A Literary History of Ireland,' 1899.

"John Eglinton," W. B. Yeats, "A. E." and W. Larminie, 'Literary Ideals in Ireland,' 1899.

Horatio Sheafe Krans, 'Wm. Butler Yeats and the Irish Literary Revival,' 1904.

John Masefield, 'Recollections of J. M. Synge,' 1915.

Susan L. Mitchell, 'George Moore,' 1916.

David James O'Donohue, 'The Poets of Ireland, A Biographical and Bibliographical Dictionary,' 1912.

Forrest Reid, 'W. B. Yeats, A Critical Study,' 1915.

William P. Ryan, 'The Irish Literary Revival; its History, Pioneers, and Possibilities,' 1894.
Cornelius Weygandt, 'Irish Plays and Playwrights,' 1913.
C. L. Wrenn, 'W. B. Yeats, A Literary Study,' 1920.
W. B. Yeats, 'The Celtic Twilight,' 1893.
W. B. Yeats, 'Synge and the Ireland of his Time,' 1911.

CHAPTER XV

THE NEW POETS

The new generation which learned to scoff at the Victorians produced no poet, who either by the quality or the mass of his work claimed comparison with any one of the great trinity of the later nineteenth century—Tennyson, Browning and Swinburne. William Archer, in the introduction to his survey of the 'Poets of the Younger Generation' (1902), remarked a "general tendency among cultivated people, to assume that English poetry has of late entered on a temporary or permanent period of decadence," and he was so far from denying this assumption that all he claimed for the thirty odd writers included in his review was that they were all "true poets, however small may be the bulk of their work, however unequal its merit." Whether they were major or minor poets he left to the judgment of posterity; and posterity so far has not ventured to promote any one of the 33 to first poetic rank, though (among those who have died since) the work of John Davidson (1857–1909) and Francis Thompson (1859–1907) has stood the test of time. The fact that the lives of both were made miserable by poverty as well as ill-health indicates a lack of appreciation by the contemporary public, which did not find either Davidson's scientific materialism or Thompson's imaginative mysticism to its taste; but the former's 'Fleet Street Eclogues' (1893 and 1896) and 'Ballads' (1894, 1897, and 1899) were in their own way as genuine additions to English poetry as Thompson's 'The Hound of Heaven' (1893), 'Sister Songs' (1895) and 'New Poems' (1897), which had their own little band of convinced and enthusiastic admirers.

But it was not until the new century was well-advanced that a more hopeful and appreciative spirit was to be remarked. When the little collection entitled 'Georgian Poetry 1911–12' was issued in the latter year, it was "in the belief that English poetry is now once again putting on a new strength and beauty, and that we are at the beginning of another 'Georgian period' which may take rank in due time with the several great poetic ages of the past."   The modest enterprise met with a cordial reception from the public, and was followed by two other volumes, 'Georgian Poetry 1913–15' and 'Georgian Poetry 1916–17,' not perhaps quite equal to the first endeavour, either in merit or in the impression made on the public, but going far to sustain the spirit of hopefulness the first volume had engendered.   Professor Gilbert Murray, in the preface to a similar collection, 'Oxford Poetry 1910–13' (which also had annual successors) spoke (in September, 1913) of the "feeling of vivid expectancy which the Georgian volume raised in many lovers of English verse."   This feeling was wide-spread, and it received further encouragement from 'New Numbers' (1914) by Wilfrid Wilson Gibson, Rupert Brooke, Lascelles Abercrombie, and John Drinkwater, the first of a series of collections of verse intended to be published quarterly; but across this brilliant dawn there fell the black shadow of the Great War.

What Sir Gilbert Murray says of the first Oxford

volume is true of its more ambitious predecessor and successors:—"Each writer has his own special quality and
character, and hardly any two of them are much alike.
There is no remotest sign of a school, a clique, or a coterie.
These writers are not Futurists, nor Unanimists, nor
Paroxysts, nor Asphyxiasts, nor members of any other
rising doctrinal body.   They have written as suited them
best, and their work has been judged for its poetry, not
for its tendency."   This being so, it seems wisest to deal
individually with such of the "Georgians" as seem to
have "poetical sinews in them" and to have done work
likely to endure.

JOHN MASEFIELD (1874–   )

Masefield's name has been coupled with that of Kipling, who obviously influenced his earlier verse, but the
younger man, being a much subtler metrist, soon worked
out his own independent and freer style.   His wander-
ing, adventurous youth suggested comparison with
Joseph Conrad, with whom his chief link is a passion for
the sea; but Masefield is profoundly English and his
first volume of poems showed a native grip on English
lower-class life and diction; his love of the sea comes from
within, and not from any literary influence or tradition.
He might have said with his hero Dauber:—

> "It's not been done, the sea, not yet been done,
> From the inside by one who really knows."

He did it from the inside in 'Salt Water Ballads,' and
though his life was enriched by experiences in London,
Rome, and New York, his sea poems remain his most
remarkable achievement.   He reproduces the tang, look,

and movement of the sea; in the unspeakable beauty of
ships he found his first inspiration:—

> "When I saw
> Her masts across the river rising queenly,
> Built out of so much chaos brought to law,
> I learned the power of knowing how to draw,
> Of beating thought into the perfect line,
> I vowed to make that power of beauty mine."

Beyond and above all this, Masefield has realized and
rendered the life of sea-faring men—not merely their
wild romantic adventures on sea and shore—yarns "of
ships and mermaids, of topsail sheets and slings," but the
hard everyday experiences of the common sailor—it was
only here that he found "life and life's romance":—

> "The sailor, the stoker of steamers, the man with the clout,
> The chantyman bent at the halyards putting a tune to the shout,
> The drowsy man at the wheel and the tired look-out.

> "Others may sing of the wine and the wealth and the mirth,
> The portly presence of potentates goodly in girth;
> Mine be the dirt and the dross, the dust and scum of the earth!

> "Theirs be the music, the colour, the glory, the gold;
> Mine be a handful of ashes, a mouthful of mould.
> Of the maimed, of the halt and the blind in the rain and the cold—
> Of these shall my songs be fashioned, my tales be told."

He could write of these because he had himself known
their experiences—not merely "wild days in a pampero
off the Plate" with surf-swimming between rollers, but

> "Days of labour also, loading, hauling;
> Long days at winch or capstan, heaving, pawling;
> The days with oxen, dragging stone from blasting,
> And dusty days in mills, and hot days masting."

These are the things, he tells us in his 'Biography,' that made him:—

> "Not alone the ships
> But men hard-palmed from tallying-on to whips,
> The two close friends of nearly twenty years
> Sea-followers both, sea-wrestlers and sea-peers,
> Whose feet with mine wore many a bolthead bright
> Treading the decks beneath the riding light."

To a keen human sympathy with the humble and oppressed, Masefield added, even in his earlier poems, a delicate sense of beauty and a questioning mind. His "Seekers" are looking for "the City of God and the haunt where beauty dwells," and in spite of the "Waste" of human life, he is confident that "Death brings another April to the soul." His love poems, 'Her Heart,' 'Being Her Friend' and 'Born for Nought Else,' have the right simple charm and music, and so has 'Beauty':—

> "I have heard the song of the blossoms and the old chant of the sea,
> And seen strange lands from under the arched white sails of ships;
> But the loveliest things of beauty God ever has showed to me,
> Are her voice, and her hair, and eyes, and the dear red curve of her lips."

Masefield might well have been content with the reputation won by his sea poems and ballads; but in 'The Everlasting Mercy' he attempted an entirely new style. It is the story of a drunken poacher's conversion as told by himself. A single stanza will give some idea of the effects attempted:—

> "'You closhy put'—
> 'You bloody liar'—
> 'This is my field.'
> 'This is my wire.'
> 'I'm ruler here.'

> 'You ain't.'
> 'I am.'
> 'I'll fight you for it.'
> 'Right, by damn.'
> 'Not now, though, I've a-sprained my thumb,
> We'll fight after the harvest hum.
> And Silas Jones, that bookie wide,
> Will make a purse five pounds a side.'
> Those were the words, that was the place
> By which God brought me into grace."

This, and the description of the prize fight that follows shows a great deal of metrical versatility and literary skill, but at times one hardly knows whether the poet is aiming at a burlesque effect, thus:—

> "Jack chucked her chin, and Jim accost her
> With bits out of the 'Maid of Gloster.'
> And fifteen arms went round her waist.
> (And then men ask, Are Barmaids chaste?)"

The last line may be attributed to the hero of the story (though it is not altogether in character), but the poet must take the responsibility for such rhymes as "is and was—Caiaphas," "honest schism—pauperism," "knows his—disposes," "offence—Testaments," which would only be excusable if the poacher were the author of the poem.

'The Widow in the Bye Street,' like the two long poems that followed it, is in Chaucerian stanza, which Masefield manages with great skill, though he occasionally slips into grotesqueness, rhyming "bastard—lasted," and "Susan's—nuisance" and ending one stanza thus:—

> "And then swept out repeating one sweet name
> 'Anna, O Anna,' to the evening star.
> Anna was sipping whiskey in the bar."

And again:—

> "She sighed, to hint that pleasure's grave was dug,
> And smiled within to see him such a mug."

The tale of Jimmy's love for the faithless Anna and his slaying of her paramour is told with no sparing of plain words, but the attempt to regard this story of murder and sensuality *sub specie eternitatis* is unsuccessful. Like Chaucer, Masefield moralises upon destiny:—

> "So the four souls are ranged, the chessboard set,
> The dark, invisible hand of secret Fate
> Brought it to come to being that they met
> After so many years of lying in wait.
> While we least think it he prepares his Mate.
> Mate, and the King's pawn played, it never ceases
> Though all the earth is dust of taken pieces."

The story fails because its psychology is not deep enough to be interesting; in 'The Everlasting Mercy' the hero tells his own story; here it is the author who narrates, and the loss is hardly made up by the addition of descriptive passages, though some of these are of great beauty:—

> "All through the night the stream ran to the sea,
> The different waters always saying the same,
> Cat-like, and then a tinkle, never glee,
> A lonely little child alone in shame.
> An otter snapped a thorn twig when he came,
> It drifted down, it passed the Hazel Mill,
> It passed the Springs; but Jimmy stayed there still."

'Dauber' gains the interest of a really attractive central character with a touch of romance and above all it gains the interest of the sea, where Masefield is at home and has room for both his narrative and descriptive

powers so that his imagination warms to its task and
gives us some of his best work.

In 'The Daffodil Fields' Masefield reverted to a somewhat melodramatic story of rustic love and jealousy ending in mutual slaughter, but the workmanship is fine,
and the characters clearly drawn. The Chaucerian
stanza is retained, but with the last line an Alexandrine,
which takes it part way over to the Spenserian, but falls
between the two. There are brilliant passages, but as a
whole the poem does not attain the cumulative effect of
'Dauber.'

All four poems attracted a great deal of attention and
there was much discussion, praise and dispraise, alike of
detail and general conception. It was agreed that they
were remarkable, original in their method of treatment
and metrical handling, but most, even of the appreciative
critics, had reservations, and the general impression was
that Masefield could do better work—had indeed done
better work in the poems of the sea. The outbreak of the
War gave him a great occasion and he rose to it easily
and perfectly. 'August, 1914' is not only the best of the
numberless poems the War produced, but it is bound to
take its place as a classic in the long and glorious history
of English poetry. With a few quiet strokes he realized
the beauty of the English landscape, enriched by the
affection of unknown generations, who, "century after
century held these farms" and knew what it meant to
answer the summons of War:—

> "Yet heard the news, and went discouraged home,
>   And brooded by the fire with heavy mind,
> With such dumb loving of the Berkshire loam
>   As breaks the dumb hearts of the English kind.

"Then sadly rose and left the well-loved Downs
And so, by ship to sea, and knew no more
The fields of home, the byres, the market towns,
Nor the dear outline of the English shore.

"But knew the misery of the soaking trench,
The freezing in the rigging, the despair
In the revolting second of the wrench
When the blind soul is flung upon the air.

"And died (uncouthly, most) in foreign lands
For some idea but dimly understood
Of an English city never built by hands,
Which love of England prompted and made good."

The grave elegiac mood of 'August, 1914' prepares the reader for the high philosophy of 'Lollingdon Downs.'

"What is this life which uses living cells
It knows not how nor why, for no known end,
This soul of man upon whose fragile shells
Of blood and brain his very powers depend.
Pour out its little blood or touch its brain,
The thing is helpless, gone, no longer known;
The carrion cells are never man again,
No hand relights the little candle blown."

He finds no answer to his restless questioning of here and hereafter:—

"It may be, that we cease; we cannot tell.
Even if we cease, life is a miracle."

Most of all is he puzzled by man:—

"This atom which contains the whole,
This miracle which needs adjuncts so strange,
This, which imagined God and is the soul."

If its business is not mainly earth, why should it demand such heavy chains to sense?

> "A heavenly thing demands a swifter birth,
> A quicker hand to act intelligence;
> An earthlier thing were better like the rose,
> At peace with clay from which its beauty grows."

"We are neither heaven nor earth, but men," he concludes, and God is of our own making:

> "Let that which is to come be as it may,
> Darkness, extinction, justice, life intense,
> The flies are happy in the summer day,
> Flies will be happy many summers hence.

> "And when the hour has struck, comes death or change,
> Which, whether good or ill, we cannot tell,
> But the blind planet will wander through her range
> Bearing men like us who will serve as well.
> The sun will rise, the winds that ever move
> Will blow our dust that once were men in love."

After the War, Masefield's gift of narrative poetry woke to new life in 'Reynard the Fox.' First comes the description of the meet, with its lively and tender reminiscences of Chaucer, not unworthily introduced, for nothing better of its kind has been written in English since the Prologue to the Canterbury Tales. The verse has vigour of movement and variety of colour, and the strongly individualised characters of the English countryside are presented in a few dashing but powerful strokes. The run, narrated from the point of view of the fox, is magnificently done, and the reader's sympathies, thoroughly awakened by Reynard's craft and pluck, are left glowing by his final escape, another fox being sacrificed to the hounds at the last moment, so that everybody rests content with a happy ending. So stirring a tale in verse has not been seen in English for many a day, and it is very likely to remain Masefield's supreme achievement in narrative.

'Right Royal,' the story of a steeplechase, though good, was not so good, in spite of many excellences in detail. The same is true of 'King Cole,' a narrative poem dealing with the vicissitudes of a travelling circus. In both, especially in the latter, the effect is weakened by the introduction of supernatural elements; and neither poem has the rush and force of 'Reynard.'

Masefield has a wide range and his career is by no means finished. He is a diligent student and a careful editor, a critic of insight and independent judgment, a dramatist of unusual power, an excellent storyteller in prose as well as in verse, and one of the best descriptive writers of the day; but it seems probable that his permanent fame will depend upon his poetry, which unites very varied qualities—a keen instinct for beauty, metrical versatility, skill in swift narrative and vivid description of nature, reasoning powers of a high order, and sympathetic contact with subjects ranging from the wrongs and sorrows of the humblest and most degraded to the philosophic questionings which beset the keenest intellects of our time.

RUPERT BROOKE (1887-1915)

It would be difficult to imagine a more complete contrast to Masefield's early life of struggling vagabondage than the fortune-favoured career of Rupert Brooke. The gods lavished upon him every gift of circumstance and endowment—physical beauty, a brilliant and attractive personality, every educational opportunity (he was a prize-winner at Rugby, and a fellow of King's College, Cambridge), the ease and dignity of academic life, a charming retreat at Grantchester Vicarage, congenial and sympathetic friends, devotion to a great cause, death in service on St. George's Day, and a fitting burial place in the Island of Skyros. His loss was lamented by the leading masters of prose and verse, and the romantic ending of his career at once won public attention. The War, which stunned older writers into silence or stammering inadequacy, gave him a lofty and dignified utterance he had hitherto failed to attain. The coldest literary historian cannot but be impressed by so bright a spirit, suddenly rising to the height of a great opportunity and as suddenly extinguished by death in the service of the cause he celebrated. Whether he could have kept the pitch is a question no one can answer; but the perfect rounding of his achievement offers at least some consolation for his early death.

"I suppose," says his friend and fellow poet John Drinkwater, "no one of his years can ever have had in greater measure the gifts that can be used to make easily swayed admiration gape, or greater temptations so to employ his qualities; and I am sure no man has ever been more wholly indifferent to any such conquests. Humour he had in abundance, but of witty insincerity no trace. Never was a personality more finely balanced. . . . It has been said that he had a strain of self-consciousness about his personal charm and brilliance, that he was a little afraid lest that side of him should claim too much attention. To answer the suggestion would be an impertinence. He was properly glad of his qualities; also, he was properly careless of them. The notion that any such matter ever occupied his mind for a moment can be nothing but ludicrous to those who knew him."

It is interesting to compare with this the personal impression made by Rupert Brooke upon Henry James as a "beautifully producible" specimen of the amenity and energy of the English tradition, of the exquisite civility, the social instincts of the race. He imagines the English as being able to say:—

"Yes, this, with the imperfection of so many of our arrangements, with the persistence of so many of our mistakes, with the waste of so much of our effort and the weight of the many-coloured mantle of time that drags so redundantly about us, this natural accommodation of the English spirit, this frequent extraordinary beauty of the English aspect, this finest saturation of the English intelligence by its most immediate associations, tasting as they mainly do of the long past, this ideal image of English youth, in a word, at once radiant and reflective, are things that appeal to us as delightfully exhibitional beyond a doubt, yet as drawn, to the last fibre, from the very wealth of our conscience and the very force of our own history. We haven't, for such an instance of our genius, to reach out to strange places or across other, and otherwise productive tracts; the exemplary instance himself has well-nigh as a matter of course reached and revelled, for that is exactly our way in proportion as we feel ourselves clear. But the kind of experience so entailed, of contribution so gathered, is just what we wear easiest when we have been least stinted of it, and what our English use of makes perhaps our vividest reference to our thick-growing native determinants."

The generously perfect endowment of Brooke suggested to Henry James the question, "Why *need* he be a poet, why need he so specialize?" Well, the gods had added this gift too. Even in the poems written before he was 21, Brooke shows an almost uncanny power of deft expression. He can versify two Germans in the night train between Bologna and Milan (second class) or a sensual music lover at a Wagner concert:—

> "The music swells. His gross lips quiver
> His little eyes are bright with slime.
> The music swells. The women shiver
> And all the while, in perfect time,
> His pendulous stomach hangs a-shaking."

In technique, in intelligence he was already mature. He imagines the poet as going on a magnificent quest to curse God on His throne of fire, and finding— nothing:—

> "All the great courts were quiet as the sun,
> And full of vacant echoes; moss had grown
> Over the glassy pavement, and begun
> To creep within the dusty council-halls.
> An idle wind blew round an empty throne
> And stirred the heavy curtains on the walls."

Only in emotional experience is he immature, with the assumed maturity of extreme youth. His "heart is sick with memories," and even in the hour of "one last mad embrace" he reminds his love that

> "Each crawling day
> Will pale a little your scarlet lips, each mile
> Dull the dear pain of your remembered face."

Obviously no lover is conscious of such truths in the moment of passion. In Meredith's 'Modern Love' the husband says "Ah, Yes, love dies!" but he adds in recollection "I never thought it less." With Brooke it was a thought he could never get away from. In the fine sonnet included in the poems of 1908–11 'The Hill,' the lovers defy old age and death—

> "And then you suddenly cried, and turned away."

In the poems of this period Brooke has a surer touch, not merely of phrase, but of presentation. His cynicism begins to gain in humour. In 'Menelaus and Helen' he contrasts, effectively enough, the Helen of romance with the repentant wife who

> "Bears
> Child on legitimate child, becomes a scold,
> Haggard with virtue."

'The One before the Last' is also in a lighter vein:—

> "Oh! bitter thoughts I had in plenty
> But here's the worst of it—
> I shall forget, in Nineteen-twenty,
> *You* ever hurt a bit!"

'A Channel Passage' is Brooke's most outrageous example in the presentation of offensive ugliness, and it it necessary to remember that he was still young, with gifts that demanded some price to be paid, if only in the way of temptation to misuse them.

In the summer of 1913 Brooke crossed the American continent and went by way of the Pacific in the autumn to Samoa. Some of the poems suggested by the visit were published in 'New Numbers' for February and August, 1914, but a growing ripeness of thought is more fully shown in 'The Great Lover,' published along with them in the latter month and dated "Mataiea, 1914." The intervening April number contained 'Heaven,' one of his deftest ironical analyses of romance—in this case the romantic anthropomorphism of popular theology:—

> "Fish say, they have their stream and pond,
> But is there anything beyond?
> This life cannot be all, they swear,
> For how unpleasant if it were!
> One may not doubt that, somehow Good
> Shall come of Water and of Mud!"

and so on to the faith in "wetter water, slimier slime":—

> "And under that Almighty Fin,
> The littlest fish may enter in.
> Oh! never fly conceals a hook,
> Fish say, in the Eternal Brook,
> But more than mundane weeds are there,
> And mud, celestially fair;
> Fat caterpillars drift around,
> And paradisal grubs are found;
> Unfading moths, immortal flies,
> And the worm that never dies.
> And in that Heaven of all their wish,
> There shall be no more land, say fish."

Upon this poem it is perhaps well to quote the comment of John Drinkwater:—"When the poet elects to make brief intellectual holiday, so long as he does so in the terms of his own personality, we should do nothing but make holiday gladly with him." 'The Old Vicarage, Grantchester,' which appears to belong to an earlier date, is an altogether charming example of intellectual playfulness; the lightheartedness of 'The Chilterns' suggests that Brooke had at last got the better of the eternal antinomy between love and old age which haunted his early youth:—

> "And I shall find some girl perhaps,
> And a better one than you,
> With eyes as wise, but kindlier,
> And lips as soft, but true.
> And I daresay she will do."

So Rupert Brooke stood at the beginning of the war—the ideal modern Englishman with senses and intelligence all alert, a keen gift of humour, a supreme gift of expression which had hitherto not found its way. He has given us, under a thin veil, his impressions when he first heard of the war:—

"As he thought 'England and Germany,' the word 'England' seemed to flash like a line of foam. . . . He was immensely surprised to perceive that the actual earth of England held for him a quality which he found in A——, and in a friend's honour, and scarcely anywhere else, a quality which, if he'd ever been sentimental enough to use the word, he'd have called 'holiness.' His astonishment grew as the full flood of 'England' swept him on from thought to thought. He felt the triumphant helplessness of a lover."

It was this that gave the sonnet series '1914' its distinguishing note. A fellow poet, Lascelles Abercrombie, has well said:—"Rupert Brooke had a decided advantage over other patriotic poets; when he celebrated the faultless beauty of sacrificing oneself for England, they were his own immediate emotions that he expressed. He knew that beauty of self-sacrifice not by any effort of imagination, but simply because it was the thing that entirely governed his life from the beginning of the war. And in five sonnets he set forth the whole of it, with a beauty of music and imagery perfectly answering to the spiritual beauty."

There is no question that the sonnet series is the crowning glory of Brooke's poetic achievement. He was moved to the depths of his rich nature as he had never been before, and all his gifts of artistic endowment thrilled for use in the supreme offering of himself and his powers to one great object. The sacrifice was consecrated by his death; but even without this added glory, the emotion expressed in these five sonnets would have remained an abiding witness of the power of England to stir the hearts of men to devotion and to beauty.

WILFRID WILSON GIBSON

Wilfrid Gibson's poetic development is interesting in itself, and helps us to understand the kind of work he has come to do. He began to publish in 1902 lyrics which have grace and charm, but are not otherwise distinguished amid much other meritorious work of the type and time. But in 'The Stonefolds' (1907) he turned aside from conventional romance to present the life of the rather grim shepherd folk of his own rugged Northumbrian hills. The form is very simply dramatic—there are only three or four characters in each little scene and the incident is slight, though the characterisation is clear; the metre is

THE NEW POETS 289

blank verse, which combines oddly with the North Country "thou" to give an impression of artificiality. Such a line as the following, coming from a shepherd's wife, strikes cold on the ear:—

> "Is this thy wisdom? Little hast thou learned."

Evidently some different medium was needed, and in 'Daily Bread' (1910) Gibson tried again. He was by this time perfectly clear about what he was trying to do, as the motto of the book shows:—

> "All life moving to one measure—
> Daily bread, daily bread—
> Bread of life, and bread of labour,
> Bread of bitterness and sorrow,
> Hand to mouth, and no to-morrow,
> Dearth for housemate, death for neighbour. . . .
> Yet, when all the babes are fed,
> Love, are there not crumbs to treasure?"

The poet's aim was to catch the gleam of romance in everyday life without ever losing hold of reality. "Free verse" was at this time being much discussed, not only in England but in France and the United States, and it was not surprising that Gibson should try what he could do with it. It seemed to suit the subject he had chosen—the struggle of the labouring poor for daily bread—and to be capable of reproducing the effect of everyday conversation. Take such a passage as this:—

> "And there's small blame to them
> Who drink too much, at whiles.
> There's little else the poor can get too much of,
> And life, at best, is dull enough, God knows.
> Sometimes, it's better to forget. . . .
> And . . . it's a lovely dizziness."

The experiment attracted considerable attention and some praise. Mary C. Sturgeon in her 'Studies of Contemporary Poets' (1916) says of it:—

"The curious structure of the verse is apparent at a glance—the irregular pattern, the extreme variation in the length of the line, the absence of rhyme and the strange metrical effects. It is a new musical instrument, having little outward resemblance to the grace and dignity of regular forms. Its unfamiliarity may displease the eye and ear at first, but it is not long before we perceive the design which controls its apparent waywardness, and recognize its fitness to express the life that the poet has chosen to depict. For it suggests, as no rhyme or regular measure could, the ruggedness of this existence and the characteristic utterance of its people. No symmetrical verse, with its sense of something complete, precise and clear, could convey such an impression as this—of speech struggling against natural reticence to express the turmoil of thought and emotion in an untrained mind. Mr. Gibson has invented a metrical form which admirably produces that effect, without condescending to a crude realism. He has made the worker articulate, supplying just the coherence and lucidity which art demands, but preserving, in this irregular outline, in the plain diction and simple phrasing, an acute sense of reality."

Be this as it may, the poet himself was not entirely satisfied; he probably felt that the rhythm of the new verse was not sufficiently distinguished from prose to give the necessary artistic suggestion to the imagination, and even in his skilful hands the impression of monotony was not always avoided. In his next series of studies of the lives of humble toil—narrative this time—he returned definitely to rhyme. The three little volumes are collectively called 'Fires,' and the charming prelude pictures the poet dreaming by his hearth and seeing fantastic shapes in the embers:—

"Till, dazzled by the drowsy glare,
I shut my eyes to heat and light;
And saw, in sudden night,

> Crouched in the dripping dark,
> With steaming shoulders stark,
> The man who hews the coal to feed my fire."

These sketches give a fuller, richer impression of the life of the poor, with more colour and humour, and the poet, whether speaking in his own name or dramatically, infuses more of his own imagination into the story.   Take for example 'The Hare,' which is told by a lad of seventeen who, after dreaming of taking in his hands a terror-stricken hare, follows one along the roadside and catches the same look of terror in the eyes of a girl he meets by a gipsy camp-fire.   He helps her to escape from the man she is afraid of, and together they tramp the moorland trackways.   One night his dream of the hare comes back to him and he wakes in a fright:—

> "Her place was empty in the straw.   .   .   .
> And then, with quaking heart, I saw
> That she was standing in the night,
> A leveret cuddled to her breast.   .   .   .
>
> I spoke no word; but, as the light
> Through banks of Eastern cloud was breaking,
> She turned, and saw that I was waking.
> And told me how she could not rest;
> And, rising in the night, she'd found
> This baby hare crouched on the ground;
> And she had nursed it quite a while.
> But, now, she'd better let it go.
> Its mother would be fretting so.
> A mother's heart.   .   .   .
>   I saw her smile,
> And look at me with tender eyes;
> And as I looked into their light,
> My foolish, fearful heart grew wise
> And now, I knew that never there
> I'd see again the startled hare,
> Or need to dread the dreams of night."

Some critics objected to the hare episodes as too fanciful and strained, but there is no question that the execution of the poem is as beautiful as the original conception; it is all suffused with delicate imaginative feeling, and the verse is a delight.

Gibson returned to this form in subsequent volumes and practised it with infinite variety of subject and tone. 'The Swing' reproduces a little servant girl's enjoyment of a hard-won holiday:—

> "Yesterday
> She'd hardly thought she'd get away;
> The mistress was that cross, and she
> Had only told her after tea
> That ere she left she must set to
> And turn the parlour out.   She knew,
> Ay, well enough, that it meant more
> Than two hours' work.   And so at four
> She'd risen this morn, and done it all
> Before her mistress went to call
> And batter at her bedroom door
> At six to rouse her.   Such a floor,
> So hard to sweep; and all that brass
> To polish!   Any other lass
> But her would have thrown up the place,
> And told the mistress to her face.   .   .   ."

'Between the Lines' is a war-study, but one in Gibson's characteristic manner.   His soldier had been a draper's assistant (dry goods clerk) and as he lies wounded in a shell-hole he muses:—

> "This was different certainly,
> From selling knots of tape and reels of thread
> And knots of tape and reels of thread and knots
> Of tape and reels of thread and knots of tape,
> Day in, day out, and answering 'Have you got's?'

> And 'Do you keep's?' till there seemed no escape
> From everlasting serving in a shop,
> Inquiring what each customer required,
> Politely talking weather, fit to drop,
> With swollen ankles, tired. . . . "

Only great imaginative sympathy and technical skill could achieve the bringing out of the romance in the shopman's life at the very point at which it seems most prosaic—its monotony. In the same volume, entitled 'Battle,' Gibson perfected a new form of short rhymed poem of which one example will serve better than description or definition, 'The Father':—

> "That was his sort.
> It didn't matter
> What we were at
> But he must chatter
> Of this and that
> His little son
> Had said or done;
> Till, as he told
> The fiftieth time
> Without a change
> How three-year-old
> Prattled a rhyme,
> They got the range
> And cut him short."

The ironical humour of this and of many others of these miniatures is grim enough, but it is never lacking in sympathy, and it is extraordinarily effective. Gibson shows us the weariness, the madness, the cruelty and pain of the trenches as they appear to the common soldier, and clothes them in his own imaginative beauty of phrase and setting.

WILLIAM H. DAVIES (1872–   )

The poems of W. H. Davies need no extrinsic circumstance to commend them, but their interest is certainly enhanced by the extraordinary conditions under which he began his literary career. As he has told the whole story fully and frankly in his 'Autobiography of a Super-Tramp,' there can be no indiscretion in summarizing it here. Born in a Newport (Monmouthshire) public-house, he passed a wayward youth, which brought him at an early age into conflict with the police (he was whipped in goal for heading a youthful gang of thieves), and as soon as he was out of his apprenticeship as a picture frame maker, he crossed the Atlantic. Falling in with a professional tramp at a small town in Connecticut, he beat his way to Chicago, begging victuals from the farmers' wives, and stealing an occasional ride on the railway. He objected to this mode of life because it gave him no chance to enrich his mind, but he kept at it through many wanderings until an attempt in Canada to board a train in motion so as to escape paying his fare deprived him of a foot. He then returned to England, and, as he had fallen in for a legacy which brought him in a few shillings a week, he decided to devote himself to literature. He read widely in free libraries and wrote a tragedy in blank verse, which, to his astonishment, was returned by one publisher after another. English tramping expeditions, combined with collecting the pennies for a one-legged "gridler" (street-singer), enabled him to save enough money to get his first poems printed, but the periodicals to which they were sent for review paid no attention to them. After vainly seeking the help of sundry charitable organizations, he took the matter into his own hands. Personal appeals (accompanied by copies of the poems) not merely brought in money but secured reviews in the leading papers, and his literary position was established forthwith. Within ten years he had published two or three considerable volumes of prose and eight little books of verse, immediately re-issued as 'Collected Poems.'

It was a most astonishing, almost an incredible achievement, and the most remarkable thing about it was that the poems made their own way when their author's romantic story was forgotten. Once well-started on his literary career, Davies made no attempt to exploit his sensational past or to find in it materials for such realistic studies of low life as were winning fame and fortune for contemporary poets. A pure lyrist, he continued to sing the graceful songs of love and nature with which he had first won the ear of the public, although such early poems as 'In a Lodging House,' 'Saints and Lodgers,' and 'The Lodging House Fire' proved that he was not unaware of the opportunity or incapable of taking advantage of it. A small Government pension (£50 a year) "in recognition of his poetical work" suffices for his simple wants:—

> "No maid is near,
>   I have no wife;
> But here's my pipe
>   And, on my life;
> With it to smoke,
>   And woo the Muse,
> To be a king
>   I would not choose."

Davies's contempt for the ordinary luxuries and comforts of life is genuine. What he sought in the life of a tramp was freedom, and he did not find it. He quotes himself as saying to a fellow-tramp from whom he wished to part:—"Your life is not mine. We often go for days without reading matter, and we know not what the world is saying; nor what the world is doing. The beauty of nature is for ever before my eyes, but I am certainly not enriching my mind, for who can contemplate Nature with any profit in the presence of others? I have no leisure to make notes in hopes of future use and I am so overpacking my memory with all these scenes, that when their time comes for use, they will not then take definite shape. I must go to work for some months, so that I may live sparingly on my savings in some large city, where I can cultivate my mind."

What Davies wanted was leisure, and having gained it after a hard and painful struggle, he has used it to some purpose. He has the genuine poet soul, born in a strange time and in stranger surroundings, but speaking the unmistakably authentic accent of sincerity:—

> "Let me be free to wear my dreams
>   Like weeds in some mad maiden's hair,
>   When she believes the earth has not
>   Another maid so rich and fair;
>   And proudly smiles on rich and poor,
>   The queen of all fair women then;
>   So I, dressed in my idle dreams,
>   Will think myself the king of men."

WALTER JOHN DE LA MARE (1873–   )

Davies has some charming poems about children, but the children's poet of the period is Walter de la Mare. His 'Songs of Childhood' continued in delicate verse the well-established tradition of ogres and witches, gnomes and elves, and 'Peacock Pie' has a wealth of fanciful rhymes arranged under headings such as 'Up and Down,' 'Boys and Girls,' 'Places and People,' 'Witches and Fairies,' 'Earth and Air.' But besides dainty rhymes for children, he writes more profound fancies for older readers and some that would do for both. Perhaps we should put in the latter class the poem in 'The Listeners' which tells how on a summer afternoon a little girl found her mother asleep in a chair:—

> "Even her hands upon her lap
> Seemed saturate with sleep.
> And as Ann peeped, a cloudlike dread
> Stole over her, and then,
> On stealthy, mouselike feet she trod,
> And tiptoed out again."

No less charmingly effective—though perhaps only for grown ups—is the poem in the same volume entitled 'Miss Loo,'—an absent-minded maiden lady whom the poet re-embodies from the recollections of his childhood:—

> "And I am sitting, dull and shy,
> And she with gaze of vacancy,
> And large hands folded on the tray,
> Musing the afternoon away;
> Her satin bosom heaving slow
> With sighs that softly ebb and flow,
> And her plain face in such dismay,
> It seems unkind to look her way.
> Until all cheerful back will come
> Her cheerful gleaming spirit home.
> And one would think that poor Miss Loo
> Asked nothing else, if she had you."

Less successful is a similar sketch in 'Motley' (1918) of 'Mrs. Grundy,' who has

"Called me, 'dear Nephew,' on each of those chairs,
Has gloated in righteousness, heard my prayers.
High-coifed, broad-browed, aged, suave yet grim,
A large flat face, eyes keenly dim,
Staring at nothing—that's me!—and yet,
With a hate one could never, no, never forget."

This lacks the innocence which is the chief charm of
childhood, and is so far less effective on that account, but
the little picture is clearly drawn. Perhaps under the
weight and stress of the War, de la Mare has been drifting
away from the simplicity of his earlier Muse into something like mysticism. Thus, 'The Scribe' imagines himself drawing on for ever with the ink of some tarn in the
hills the wonders of God he sees about him:—

"Still would remain
My wit to try—
My worn reeds broken,
The dark tarn dry,
All words forgotten—
Thou, Lord, and I."

LASCELLES ABERCROMBIE (1881–   )

Lascelles Abercrombie has none of the various qualities which have given the poets already discussed, for
one reason or another, some popular appeal. His massive
and acute intellect finds freer play in criticism and meta-
physics than in poetry, and his verse is almost devoid of
sensuous attraction of any kind. Severe alike in subject
and in treatment, it appeals only to the intelligence.
His first volume treats dramatically in blank verse without a touch of romance two mediæval legends, along with
other subjects, all regarded on the intellectual side, and
contains also a dialogue between the Body and the Soul,

and an Ode to Indignation. Two more mediæval
legends, 'Mary and the Bramble' and 'The Sale of St.
Thomas,' followed, and were published by the author
privately. A brief extract from the latter poem may give
a hint of the poet's method and style. St. Thomas, bidden to take ship for the conversion of India, hesitates on
the quay, not from cowardice but from prudence, until
his Lord appears and sells him as a slave to the sea-
captain:—

> "Now, Thomas, know thy sin. It was not fear;
> Easily may a man crouch down for fear,
> And yet rise up on firmer knees, and face
> The hailing storm of the world with graver courage.
> But prudence, prudence is the deadly sin,
> And one that groweth deep into a life,
> With hardening roots that clutch about the breast,
> For this refuses faith in the unknown powers
> Within man's nature.".

In 'Emblems of Love' the subject treated is still more
abstruse and difficult. A 'prelude of discovery and
prophecy' reveals first two warriors at the dawn of civilization; one cherishes women as the breeder of more
warriors against the wolves, the other as the source of
beauty and pleasure. In 'Vashti' we move a step onward
in the distinction she puts to Ahasuerus:—

> "Lovest thou me, or dost thou rather love
> The pleasure thou hast in me?"

She refuses herself to Ahasuerus and is driven out of
the palace, but as she goes the Goddess Ishtar appears to
her and reveals the future:—

> "There shall be
> Of man desiring, and of woman desired,
> A single ectasy divinely formed,

> Two souls knowing themselves in one amazement.
> All that thou hatest to arouse in man
> Prepareth him for this; and thou thyself
> Art by thy very hate prepared."

Part II shows us in three dramatic episodes love in imperfection; Part III, 'Virginity and Perfection,' dramatizes the story of Judith, who is taken as an emblem of the power of the spiritual against the material. We have next a dialogue 'The Eternal Wedding,' a 'Marriage Song,' and finally an 'Epilogue,' all rendered in the same high intellectual strain. There is no question of the keenness of the intelligence at work or of the excellence of the verse; but it is a cold arid region of the mind where few can long breathe the rarified air. Abercrombie is highly esteemed, especially by his fellow poets; but that he will ever win any large number of readers seems very improbable.

BIBLIOGRAPHY

JOHN MASEFIELD

POEMS

1902 'Salt-Water Ballads.'
1903 'Ballads.'
1910 'Ballads and Poems.'
1912 'The Everlasting Mercy' ('English Review,' Oct., 1911).
      'The Widow in the Bye Street' ('English Review,' Feb.)
1913 'Dauber' ('English Review,' Oct., 1912).
      'The Daffodil Fields' ('English Review,' Feb.).
1916 'Sonnets and Poems.'
1917 'Lollingdon Downs and other Poems.'
1919 'Reynard the Fox, or the Ghost Heath Run.'
1920 'Enslaved and other Poems.'
      'Right Royal.'
1921 'King Cole.'
      'The Dream.'

PLAYS

1907 'The Campden Wonder.'
1909 'The Tragedy of Nan.'
1910 'The Tragedy of Pompey the Great.'
1914 'Philip the King.'
1915 'The Faithful.'
1916 'Good Friday' ('Fortnightly Review,' Dec., 1915).
      'The Locked Chest.'
      'The Sweeps of '98.'
1922 'Esther' (trans. from Racine).
      'Berenice' (adapted and partially translated from Racine).
      'Melloney Holtspur.'

TALES AND NOVELS

1905 'A Mainsail Haul.'
1907 'A Tarpaulin Muster.'
1908 'Captain Margaret.'
1909 'Multitude and Solitude.'

1910 'Lost Endeavour.'
1911 'The Street of To-day.'

PROSE

1911 'William Shakespeare.'
1916 'Gallipoli.'

BIOGRAPHICAL AND CRITICAL

W. H. Hamilton, 'John Masefield, A Critical Study,' 1922.
Bibliography by Iolo A. Williams (1921).

RUPERT BROOKE

1911 'Poems.'
1915 '1914 and other Poems.'
      'The Collected Poems of Rupert Brooke' (New York).
1916 'Letters from America,' with a preface by Henry James.
1918 'The Collected Poems of Rupert Brooke' (London).

There are short essays on Rupert Brooke in 'Studies of Contemporary Poets' by Mary C. Sturgeon (1916) and in 'Prose Papers' by John Drinkwater (1917).   Walter de la Mare's lecture on 'Rupert Brooke and the Intellectual Imagination' was published in New York in 1921.

WILFRID WILSON GIBSON

1907 'Stonefolds.'
1910 'Akra the Slave.'
      'Daily Bread.'
1912 'Fires.'
1914 'Thoroughfares.'
      'Borderlands.'
1915 'Battle.'
1916 'Friends.'
1917 'Livelihood.'
1918 'Whin.'
1920 'Neighbours.'
1922 'Collected Verse.'
      'Krindlesyke.'

WILLIAM H. DAVIES
Poems

1906 'The Soul's Destroyer.'
1907 'New Poems.'
1908 'Nature Poems.'
1910 'Farewell to Poesy.'
1911 'Songs of Joy.'
1913 'Foliage.'
1914 'The Birds of Paradise.'
1916 'Child Lovers.'
1920 'The Song of Life.'
      'The Hour of Magic and other Poems.'

Prose

1907 'The Autobiography of a Super-Tramp.'
1916 'A Pilgrim in Wales.'
1918 'A Poet's Pilgrimage.'

WALTER DE LA MARE

1902 'Songs of Childhood.'
1904 'Henry Brocken,' a romance.
1906 'Poems.'
1910 'The Return,' a novel.
1912 'The Listeners, and other Poems.'
1913 'Peacock Pie.'
1918 'Motley and other Poems.'
1921 'Memoirs of a Midget.'

LASCELLES ABERCROMBIE

1908 'Interludes and Poems.'
1910 'St. Mary and the Bramble.'
1911 'The Sale of St. Thomas.'
1912 'Emblems of Love.'
      'Thomas Hardy; a critical study.'
1913 'Deborah, A Play in three acts.'
      'Speculative Dialogues.'
1922 'Four Short Plays.'

CHAPTER XVI

THE NEW NOVELISTS

The English novel, rich as it is in great names and superb achievement, cannot be said to be altogether fortunate in its artistic tradition. George Moore, himself a competent practitioner, said of it in an interview with John Lloyd Balderston published in the 'Fortnightly Review' for October, 1917:—

> "The English novel remains as it was in the beginning—a drawing-room entertainment addressed chiefly to ladies. Men are not expected to put their best thoughts into novels, but into poetry and into essays, and, as man is a creature of habit, the novel remains the weakest part of English literature. The ambition of the English story-teller of the eighteenth century was to amuse the drawing-room, and I do not think the ambition of any story-teller since has been different."

After making very considerable allowance for Moore's habitual tendency to hyperbole, one must admit that there is a germ of truth in what he says. The great masters, from Fielding to Dickens, were negligent not merely of style but of structure, and the nineteenth century added to the lax artistic traditions of the eighteenth the limitations of Victorian prudishness. The attempts of George Eliot, Meredith, Galsworthy and Wells to enrich the social and intellectual content of the novel left it still somewhat indeterminate and amorphous as a type. The efforts of the younger men continued to be directed, not so much to perfecting the form of the novel

as to enlarging its scope. The evasions and reserves of
the great Victorians as to sexual passion gave place to
increasing freedom and frankness, until illicit love came
into the foreground of the picture and was portrayed,
in some cases, to the exclusion of almost every other
interest. Yet, in 'A Novelist on Novels' (1918), W. L.
George assures us that the British novelist has not yet
attained complete freedom in dealing with matters of
sex, which still play a much larger part in life than they
do in fiction. One would have thought that the dispro-
portion at present was the other way, and that the
novelists had rather overdone sex psychology in comparison with some of the other interests in life—such as
war and earning a livelihood—but it is an issue on which
everyone must form his own conclusion. Galsworthy's
'The Dark Flower' and 'Beyond' are almost entirely
taken up with the analysis of sexual attraction, and there
is hardly a novel of his into which this element does not
enter to a very large extent. Wells deals with it largely
and frankly, in some novels almost exclusively. Arnold
Bennett takes one aspect of it for the main theme of
'The Pretty Lady.' W. L. George himself has made it
in one phase or another the exclusive subject of 'A Bed
of Roses' and 'The Second Blooming.' With D. H.
Lawrence it is almost an obsession, and the brutal frankness of 'The Rainbow' surely reached the limits of the
permissible. Gilbert Cannan usually puts sex interests,
in one form or another, in the foreground, and in the
work of Compton Mackenzie they are hardly less prominent. 'The Early Life and Adventures of Sylvia Scarlett' prefaces the account of the amatory escapades of the
heroine with a review of those of her mother and her

grandmother, and though in nearly 500 pages her own course is pursued through marriage, divorce, promiscuity, and association with all manner of vileness, at the end we are promised another volume in which Sylvia will be "off with the raggle-taggle gipsies in deadly earnest,"— a promise fulfilled in 'Sylvia and Michael.' Henry James, in an essay on 'The New Novel' (1914) which has already become a classic, commends the new novelists for their courage in hugging the shore of the real in this regard instead of flying to the open sea of sentiment at the least sign of difficulty. Varying his metaphor, he applauds also their possession of and saturation in their material:—

"The act of squeezing out to the utmost the plump and more or less juicy orange of a particular acquainted state and letting this affirmation of energy, however directed or undirected, constitute for them the 'treatment' of a theme—*that* is what we remark them as mainly engaged in. . . . Nothing is further from our thought than to undervalue saturation and possession, the fact of the particular experience, the state and degree of acquaintance incurred, however such a consciousness may have been determined; for these things represent on the part of the novelist, as on the part of any painter of things seen, felt or imagined, just one half of his authority —the other half being represented of course by the application he is inspired to make of them. Therefore that fine secured half is so much gained at the start, and the fact of its brightly being there may really by itself project upon the course so much colour and form as to make us on occasion, under the genial force, almost not miss the answer to the question of application."

The question of application, however, cannot be avoided, for even on the "slice of life" theory the principle of selection is involved. There can be no such thing as an amorphous slice; it has been *born* of naught else but measured excision. Reasons have been the fairies waiting on its cradle:—

"How can a slice of life be anything but illustrational of the loaf, and how can illustration not immediately bristle with every sign of the extracted and related state? The relation is at once to what the thing comes from and to what it waits upon—which last is our act of recognition. We accordingly appreciate it in proportion as it so accounts for itself; the quantity and the intensity of its reference are the measure of our knowledge of it."

What then Henry James finds missing in the new novelists is treatment, composition, structure, fusion, a centre of interest, and he ascribes this to the pernicious influence of Tolstoy, "the great illustrative master-hand on all this ground of the disconnection of method from matter."

In an incisive article in the London 'Nation' published soon after Henry James's essay, his judgment of the facts is admitted, but a different explanation is suggested. The new novels are "social documents, imaginative history, crusades, reactions, biology, or natural science," but they are not works of art; they lack style, and they lack form. Their accumulation of material circumstance is "the inevitable result of the autobiographical obsession obtruding upon the critical, the measuring, the selective faculty. The energy of an unconscious self-expression is too much for them."

This is an interesting theory, and it would not be difficult to cite particular novels or parts of novels which lend it support, but it is hardly tenable in view of the variety of the work of the new novelists, or even the variety of the work of any one of them. Every novelist reproduces more or less indirectly his own experience and observation. De Maupassant, one of the most objective of writers of fiction, says:—

"We can only vary our characters by altering the age, the sex, the social position and all the circumstances of life of that *ego* which nature has in fact enclosed in an unsurmountable barrier of organs of sense. Skill consists in not betraying this *ego* to the reader, under the various masks which we employ to cover it."

Here and there in the work of the new novelists, one may discern (as in the work of their predecessors) auto-biography more or less assimilated to the artistic purpose they have in view; but the charge of unassimilated auto-biography cannot be brought with justice against their work as a whole, or, indeed against that of any particular author. The characteristic of the new novels of which both Henry James and the 'Nation' critic complain may have still another explanation. What Henry James condemns as a disregard of the essential principles of art and what the alternative view holds to be unconscious self-absorption may be really a deliberate effort to pro-duce the effect of the variety—even the haphazard con-fusion—of life. The grouping of character and circum-stance round a central theme may be an aim they have not merely not endeavoured to attain, but have con-sciously striven to avoid, and to criticize them for not reaching it is simply to disapprove of the theory of art they have taken over, either from the older English novelists or from the Russians. Fortunately we have, in Hugh Walpole's little book about Joseph Conrad, a statement (by one of themselves) of the aims and models the new novelists had in view. He says:—

"The influence of the French novel, which was at its strongest between the years of 1885 and 1895, was towards Realism, and the influence of the Russian novel, which has certainly been very strongly marked in England during the last years, is all towards Romantic-Realism. If we wished to know exactly what is meant by Romantic-

Realism, such a novel as 'The Brothers Karamazov,' such a play as 'The Cherry Orchard' are there before us, as the best possible examples. We might say, in a word, that 'Karamazov' has, in the England of 1915, taken the place that was occupied, in 1890, by 'Madame Bovary.' "

Now 'Madame Bovary' is exactly the treatment of "a case" according to the method Henry James, in theory and practice, approved; the looser structure of the Russian authors Walpole mentions—if indeed it can be called structure at all—is that adopted ,by the younger English school. That Henry James should find them lacking in this respect is not surprising; but his criticism goes back to a discussion of the fundamental principles of the art of fiction to which there is no end. We may regret that the new novelists were apparently so little interested in the form of their work, or, if one agrees with Henry James, that they were influenced by the evil example of the Russians, but obviously we must take them for what they are, since it is fruitless to condemn them for what they are not. There will certainly be those who will contend that in spite of the apparent lack of a central interest, there is a subtler unity to be discerned, and that this more delicate and fluid creation represents a higher artistic standard than the more obvious and artificial construction of the older French school. The apparent formlessness which the older English novelists enjoyed in the innocence of childhood may be adopted by the latest exponents of the art not from thoughtlessness, or lack of skill, or unconscious self-absorption, but from deliberate design.

HUGH WALPOLE (1884–   )

Walpole's father became Bishop of Edinburgh in 1910, after holding the incumbency of St. Mary's Pro-Cathedral, Auckland, New Zealand, 1882–9, and the professorship of dogmatic theology in the General Theological Seminary, New York, 1889–96. Hugh Seymour Walpole (to give him his full name) is presumably the "Hugh Seymour" of 'The Golden Scarecrow,' who "was sent from Ceylon, where his parents lived, to be educated in England. His relations having, for the most part, settled in foreign countries, he spent his holidays as a minute and pale-faced 'paying guest' in various houses where other children were of more importance than he, or where children as a race were of no importance at all."

"Hugh Seymour" is described by his creator (or biographer) as a short-sighted, sensitive child who did not care very greatly for reading but told himself long stories of "trains of elephants, ropes and ropes of pearls, towers of ivory, peacocks, and strange meals of saffron buns, roast chicken, and gingerbread. He was bullied at school until his appointment as his dormitory's story-teller gave him a certain status."

Cornwall is dimly suggested as the scene of this story of childhood, and Cornwall was certainly the scene of the three "studies in place" (as he afterwards called them) with which Walpole began his literary career. His most successful novel, 'The Duchess of Wrexe,' was written at Polperro in that county, August 1912–January 1914, and the author's fondness for its romantic coast may be connected with family friendships formed by his father as tutor at the Chancellor's School at Truro 1877–82. But this was before Hugh Walpole was born, and one

may be very sure that it was neither this school nor
King's School, Canterbury, at which he himself was
educated, that stood for model for the third and most
remarkable of his "studies of place"—'Mr. Perrin and
Mr. Traill.' "Moffatt's" is a second rate boarding
school for middle-class boys, presented from the point of
view of the staff, one of whom thus describes the type:—

"There are thousands of them all over the country—places where
the men are underpaid, with no prospects, herded together, all of
them hating each other, wanting, perhaps, towards the end of term,
to cut each other's throats. You must not be friends with the Head,
because then we shall think that you are spying on us. You must
not be friends with us, because then the Head will hear of it, and will
immediately hate you because he will think that you are conspiring
against him. You must not be friends with the boys, because then
we shall all hate you and they will despise you. You will be quite
alone. . . .

"Here we are—fifteen men—all hating each other, loathing everything that the other man does—the way he eats, the way he moves,
the way he teaches. We sleep next door to each other, we eat together, we meet all day until late at night—hating each other."

The situation is, one hopes, not typical—the speaker
is a disappointed and embittered man—but it is a possible
one where a small number of overworked, nervous and
uncongenial teachers are cooped up together under an
unsympathetic or selfseeking Headmaster. It is worked
out in the story, perhaps with an undue indulgence in
physical violence, but with undoubted power. The life
of the teaching staff is presented skilfully and forcefully,
their petty cares, squabbles, and resentments, and the
most guilty of them (always omitting the unspeakable
Headmaster who looms in the background as the evil
genius of the scene) is represented as a victim of under-
pay, over work, and overstrained nerves. Conditions

have improved in schools of this type since the story was written, but the lot of the secondary school teacher is still far from what it should be, either for his own sake or for those under his care, and Walpole did a public service in drawing attention to it so effectively.

Walpole's story of university life, 'The Prelude to Adventure,' owes merely its external machinery to the fact that he was at Emmanuel College, Cambridge. It is classed by him as a 'prologue'—to what, is not clear. It is the story of the murder of one undergraduate by another—a murder inexplicably committed, inexplicably undiscovered, inexplicably confessed, and inexplicably condoned. Even as a study of the external conditions of university life it has very slight value.

The other prologue, 'Fortitude'—though again one does not see to what, unless Walpole had in mind the writing of a continuation—is a very much firmer and stronger piece of work. The scene is mainly in Cornwall or in London, and there is a wealth of well-conceived characters. The theme of the story is set forth in the opening sentence:—" 'Tisn't life that matters! 'Tis the courage you bring to it," and the plot follows the vicissitudes of the hero, Peter Westcott, from boyhood to manhood, in his conflicts with various antagonists, without and within. We leave him almost vanquished, baffled but triumphant, for he is still fighting, and the work as a whole attains the effect aimed at, in addition to many excellent strokes in detail.

'The Duchess of Wrexe' had also an ambitious theme. The Duchess herself is an excellent character study, but beyond this Walpole aimed at the portrayal of a disappearing class—the Autocrats.

"You *must* have your quarterings, and you must look down on those who haven't. But, more than that, everything must be preserved, and continual ceremonies, dignities, chastities, restraints, pomps and circumstances. Above all, no one must be admitted within the company who is not of the noblest, the stupidest, the narrowest."

The Duchess is beaten, and at the end of the story we are given a glimpse of the rising city of the new age— "instead of this old house, the hooded furniture, the anger at all freedom of thought, the jealousy of all enterprise, the slander and the malice, an age of a universal Brotherhood, of unselfishness, restraint, charity, tolerance"— but upon this prospect descended the curtain of the War, and Walpole went off to Russia to serve with the Russian Red Cross, 1914–16. The outcome was 'The Dark Forest'—a romantic treatment of his experiences on the Russian front, done in the Russian manner. It was greatly admired, perhaps most of all by those who took on hearsay the great Russian models which it was supposed to follow and which in fact it followed more in form than in spirit, as is generally the case with deliberate imitations.

'The Green Mirror,' which resumed the series of 'The Rising City,' was again a study of London life, with a tyrannical mother, entrenched in family tradition and, like the Duchess, ultimately defeated, as its central figure. It is remarkable as an analysis of a small section of the upper middle class in England, but suffered somewhat in interest from the restriction of the field and the lack of vitality of all but the principal character.

Walpole's production since the War has been promising rather than significant. 'The Secret City' is a further outcome of his Russian experiences, but the Rus-

sian situation had changed so astonishingly during the
time he was engaged on the novel as to rob it of all but
temporary interest. 'Jeremy' and 'Jeremy and Hamlet'
are clever and amusing tales of boyhood. 'The Captives'
is a careful study of one of those obscure religious communities which are still a feature of English life in its
back-eddies. 'The Young Enchanted' is a definite effort
to deal with post-war England and the point of view of the
younger generation; incidentally Walpole brings back his
old hero, Peter Westcott, and leaves him with the promise
of a happy ending to all his troubles. In both the novels
last mentioned, Walpole shows an increasing tendency to
romance in characterization and incident.

'The Cathedral' is a greater work, both in achievement
and in promise. In it Walpole reveals to us the life of
"the Close" with a sympathetic and critical insight that
need not fear comparison with Anthony Trollope. "Pol-
chester" reminds one at times of Durham or Truro or
Canterbury, though it is none of these; it is a city devised
by the novelist's imagination to make clear and real to us
the inner workings of English ecclesiastical society. The
novel is something more than "a study in place," to use
the phrase by which the author described some of his
earlier work; it has a centre of spiritual interest, and its
"treatment" would have delighted the heart of Henry
James. Without ever forgetting that the novelist's first
duty is to tell a story and to make his characters live,
Walpole implicitly suggests the gravest danger of ecclesiastical institutionalism—the danger that the Cathedral may
become an end in itself instead of a means, something that
comes between the worshipper and God, even to the very
clergy who serve in it an obstacle instead of a help to the

life of the spirit. The subtlety and charm with which this idea is worked out give hope of similar and even stronger work in the future—possibly in the same *milieu*.

GILBERT CANNAN (1884–   )

Gilbert Cannan was educated at the University of Manchester and King's College, Cambridge, read for the Bar, and served a brief apprenticeship to the writer's craft as dramatic critic for the London 'Star,' 1909–10. He was also engaged in the translation (1910–13) of 'Jean Christophe' by Romain Rolland, who, along with Samuel Butler, of whom Cannan published a critical study in 1915, had considerable influence upon his original novels. In the critical study of Butler he sets forth his own ideas of what the English novel should be:—

"Irony is one of the essential ingredients of your true novel, which is a special species distinct from the romance, and begins with the application in 'Don Quixote' of irony to romance. A novel is an epic with its wings clipped, that is, with its action and characters viewed ironically. The modern story in which action and characters are viewed sentimentally is not, properly speaking, a novel at all. . . As for the story in which action and characters are regarded only in relation to political and sociological considerations, that is a fearful wild-fowl, wingless, featherless, strange and indecent."

As to form, he says more specifically elsewhere:—

"The happy, leisurely technique of Fielding is unsuited to the purposes of the modern novel. The French technique is too rigorous, the Russian too large for our insular temper. Besides, as we are insisting upon our character and striving to retrieve it, all that we learn or borrow must be assimilated to it. Easy imitation lends itself too readily to our deplorable sentimentality, and adds to our enormous pile of too-easily-written books. . . . Our own writers are either too near their emotions or too near their facts. They cannot arrange both in due proportion in their fable, yet they labour with such astonishing zest and hopefulness that it is not unreasonable to be sanguine as to the creation of a form and a technique which will make it possible for a whole generation to produce richly."

Cannan tried the Butler manner in 'Little Brother,' 'Old Mole' and 'Old Mole's Novel,' without any great success, for he had not Butler's stock of original ideas or his quizzical humour, but in 'Round the Corner,' although it has an obvious relation to 'The Way of all Flesh,' he achieved a more independent and original piece of work, conscientious, if not inspired. He was much more successful in 'Mendel,' though here again there is an unconcealed indebtedness to 'Jean Christophe,' which is more than once referred to in the course of the book.   But in this instance Cannan surpassed his model, avoiding the *longueurs* of the French original and keeping the talk about art within much severer bounds than Jean Christophe's interminable divagations about music.   Cannan's young Jewish painter is also a more original conception than Romain Rolland's hero, and his father, mother and brothers are all admirably realized.   The arrival of this family of Polish Jews in London and their settlement in Whitechapel is wonderfully described, and their attitude to the London life they touch only at a few points (chiefly of pain and discomfort) is consistently maintained throughout.   They are weird people, according to English notions, and yet Cannan has made them entirely comprehensible, and even likeable, especially the absolutely Jewish father and mother.   The half Jewish children become less sympathetic; the hero's character is very carefully worked out, with its oriental passion only veneered by the manners and ideas he acquires from the English people he meets in his artistic career, but in

vitality and solidity the figure of the mother, with her
strong affection, limited ideas, and shrewd observations,
is the masterpiece of the book. The English painters,
art-students and models are much thinner and more
shadowy figures, and they are not made any more real by
a constant insistence on their fondness for sensual indulgence or their dislike of it. This element of the novel
seems to be developed out of all proportion to other interests. The physical attraction exercised by Nelly Oliver
for Logan is laboured to an extent and to a degree of detail hardly justified either by the conflict between this
narrow and degrading passion and the wider interest of
his friendship for Mendel, or by the contrast between this
fleshly bond and the higher spiritual relation between
Greta Morrison and the hero. It is an excellent moral,
but it does not seem worth while to go through so much
slime for the sake of so little. The Hetty Finch episode,
though more closely connected with the fortunes of the
hero and commendably shorter, is hardly significant
enough to save it from becoming wearisome. But when
all deductions are made, 'Mendel' is a powerful novel and
exhibits with vivid reality, both in the scenes in the
Mendel home and in those of the studios and the artists'
cafés, sides of life little known to English fiction.

'Pugs and Peacocks' is the first of a series (continued
in 'Sembal') dealing with the distracted state of English
society during and after the War "not from any political
or sociological point of view, but to discover the light
thrown upon human nature by abnormal events and
conditions." The first novel of the series, in spite of its
fantastic title, is an ambitious and serious study of a
group of conscientious objectors, whose idiosyncracies are

set forth with underlying sympathy, but not without a good deal of pungent humour. The hero is a Trinity College (Cambridge) don, a distinguished mathematician, of aristocratic connections, who goes to prison for a technical breach of the law against correspondence with Germany. The parallel with a well-known Cambridge philosopher is uncomfortably close, and no doubt other identifications of the "Liberty Defence" Association could be made; in any case these "queer" characters, with their strange mixture of sincerity and the desire to advertise themselves at other people's expense, are strongly realised. The hero's love affair has a look of being dragged into an atmosphere where it does not belong, but this element is slight and may be disregarded. The novel is better thought out and more clearly written than anything the author had done since 'Mendel,' in spite of the intellectual and spiritual heights on which some of the characters habitually move.

COMPTON MACKENZIE (1883–   )

Compton Mackenzie, whose parents were well known and highly esteemed under their stage names of Edmund Compton and Virginia Bateman, showed early signs of literary versatility. He had become an editor (of the 'Oxford Point of View') before he left Magdalen College in 1904, and within a few years after had produced a comedy, published a volume of poems, and written an Alhambra revue. After his marriage he retired to Cornwall, and from this rustic seclusion sent his first novel, 'The Passionate Elopement,' to one publisher after another until it was accepted in 1911 and scored an immediate success. It is "an eighteenth century exercise in concentration and flexibility," and gives little hint of the very different style and manner he adopted in 'Carnival.' This is a realistic study of the life and character, especially in her childhood and youth, of a London ballet girl, conducted with admirable skill and verve until the author whisks her away from the glare of the footlights to meet an untimely death by the Cornish sea. There seems no call or excuse for this hurried ending, as the character might just as well have been taken over, as some of the others were, into the author's subsequent work. His plan of detailed realistic incident demands extensive space, and though it is difficult to bring a novel written on this scale to a satisfactory conclusion, sudden death is not a solution of the problem. The story really breaks into two parts, and the second part is out of proportion and out of tone with the first.

In 'Sinister Street' the novelist took a much larger canvas and found himself more at ease. The two parts relate with abundant detail the childhood and youth, school days and love-affairs of Michael and Stella Fane, the offspring of an irregular union in the English upper class. The development of the characters of the two children under their peculiar social conditions is wonderfully done, and the conflict in Michael's nature between the sensualist and the ascetic is movingly presented. 'Guy and Pauline' is a detached idyll arising out of Michael's life at Oxford, but even at the end of this third novel the young people, after rich and varied experiences, are left still at the beginning of their careers. The author's task was twice interrupted, in 1913 by a physical breakdown, which drove him to Capri for a rest, and in 1915 by volunteering for the ill-fated expedition to the

Dardanelles. In 'Sylvia Scarlett' he made a fresh start,
with an entirely new set of characters, but about halfway
through the book the old ones begin to come back again,
and by the end it is evident that the real crisis in the lives
of Michael Fane and Sylvia Scarlett is still to come. It does
come in 'Sylvia and Michael,' which rounds out the series,
with the help of a minor appendix in 'The Vanity Girl.'

The detailed method adopted by Compton Mackenzie
has obvious dangers, and he does not altogether escape
them. He has inexhaustible inventiveness of incident,
but his versatility betrays him at times into the irrelevant
and the insignificant—not the loose, easy-going scheme
of the Russians, which is not at all motiveless, but the
merely episodical manner of Smollett, the multiplica-
tion of incident for its own sake. Take for instance the
battle royal between two of Sylvia's early lovers, in the
course of which Danny Lewis knocks Jay Cohen into a
slop-pail:—

"Danny kicked off the slop-pail, and invited Cohen to stand up to
him; but when he did get on his feet, he ran to the door and reached
the stairs just as Mrs. Gonner was wearily ascending to find out what
was happening. He tried to stop himself by clutching the knob of
the baluster, which broke; the result was that he dragged Mrs. Gonner with him in a glissade which ended behind the counter. The con-
fusion in the shop became general: Mr. Gonner cut his thumb, and
the sight of the blood caused a woman who was eating a sausage to
choke; another customer took advantage of the row to snatch a side
of bacon and try to escape, but another customer with a finer moral
sense prevented him; a dog, who was sniffing in the entrance, saw the
bacon on the floor and tried to seize it, but getting his tail trodden
upon by somebody, he took fright and bit a small boy, who was
waiting to change a shilling into coppers."

In the midst of the hubbub, Sylvia makes her escape,
but one fails to see what all this has to do with the devel-

opment of her character or what influence it has on her future career. It may excite the laughter of the groundlings, but it makes the judicious grieve, for the author had shown himself capable of better things. 'Sinister Street' is a very solid and remarkable accomplishment for a novelist of Compton Mackenzie's years and experience, and it seems a pity for so fine a talent to waste itself on such mere *tours de force* as 'Poor Relations' and 'Rich Relatives.'

In 'The Altar Steps,' Compton Mackenzie started on a new tack which gave promise of work not unworthy of his abilities. It is a study of the Anglo-Catholic movement in the Church of England, centred in the life-history of a boy, who, at the age of fifteen, vows himself to the priesthood, and on his seventeenth birthday is vouchsafed what the author describes as "the miracle of St. Mary Magdalene's intervention" in the summary taking-off, by the fall of her image, of the blasphemous and too ardent lover of a girl the young hero admires. Up to the point of this crudely melodramatic episode, Mark Lidderdale's boyhood is charmingly recounted, with many delightful touches of humour, and the novelist holds the scales fairly even between the Anglo-Catholic party and its opponents, though his sympathies are obviously on the side of his hero's faith. But about midway through the book the author abandons all appearance of artistic impartiality. He tells us, twice in the same words, that "the first episcopal act of the Bishop of Silchester drove many poor souls away from God." Now whatever may be thought of the Bishop's action in disallowing prayers for the dead at an altar of which he disapproved, the spiritual result of that action is obviously a matter of opinion on which it is not wise for the novelist to obtrude his own religious views. From this point on, though the author does not blink the human frailties of those characters in the book on his side of the controversy, his attitude is one of avowed partisanship. The interest diminishes accordingly, and the author's besetting fault of exaggerated detail produces pages of hard and even dull reading. Few readers, for instance, will care to know exactly what occupation the Rule of the Order of St. George prescribed to the Brothers for each hour of the day from 6 a. m. to 9 p. m., nor does the recital seem of any moment either for the development of the story or of the hero's character. It is the latter element that really holds the attention of the admirers of this novel, for the accumulated incidents of the author's preceding books find no place in the comparatively uneventful career of the young and enthusiastic Anglo-Catholic on his way to become a priest. The character of Mark Lidderdale is carefully and sympathetically developed, and as this first volume is described as a prelude, dealing with the hero's spiritual adventures up to the time of his admission to deacon's orders, one looks forward with interest to the further unfolding of his inner life and struggles with the world in 'The Parson's Progress.'

D. H. LAWRENCE (1887–   )

In the introduction to 'The Widowing of Mrs. Holroyd,' Edwin Björkman gives some interesting particulars of Lawrence's early struggles towards authorship. He was born in a coalminer's cottage on the borders of Nottinghamshire and Derbyshire—the scene in which all his best work is cast. His mother was a woman of character and refinement and some education, and encouraged the boy to win a scholarship at Nottingham High School, which he left at sixteen to become a pupil-teacher in an elementary school, receiving instruction from the headmaster before and after the day's work. From twenty-one to twenty-three he was a student at the Nottingham Day Training College, and he taught school for a while in London until he got his first two novels published.

'The White Peacock,' Lawrence's first novel, is a work of promise rather than of performance. He writes well—in descriptive passages, such as this:—

"I was born in September, and love it best of all the months. There is no heat, no hurry, no thirst and weariness in corn harvest as there is in the hay. If the season is late, as is usual with us, then mid-September sees the corn still standing in stook. The mornings come slowly. The earth is like a woman married and fading; she does not leap up with a laugh for the first fresh kiss of dawn, but slowly, quietly, unexpectantly lies watching the waking of each new day. The blue mist, like memory in the eyes of a neglected wife, never goes from the wooded hill, and only at noon creeps from the near hedges. There is no bird to put a song in the throat of morning; only the crow's voice speaks during the day. Perhaps there is the regular breathing hush of the scythe—even the fretful jar of the mowing machine. But next day, in the morning, all is still again. The lying corn is wet, and when you have bound it, and lift the heavy sheaf to make the stook, the tresses of oats wreathe round each other and droop mournfully."

But in this first book he has no command of dialogue or perhaps not enough knowledge of how educated people talk. The teller of the story reports himself as saying to a girl about her eyes:—"To have such soft, vulnerable eyes as you used makes one feel nervous and irascible. But you have clothed over the sensitiveness of yours, haven't you?—like naked life, naked defenceless protoplasm they were, is it not so?" This is a conversation between two young people in a Nottinghamshire public house parlour, and after this we are not surprised that they "drifted into a discussion of Strauss and Débussy"— whom the novelist (or his proof reader) did not yet know well enough to spell the name correctly. In the same chapter the servant makes the hero think of "the girl in Tchekoff's story," and an old woman lying in a bed suggests Guy de Maupassant's 'Toine.' Lawrence had been doing a lot of reading in London and he had not yet digested it.

His second novel, 'The Trespasser,' is written in an easier style, but is an ordinary story of an irregular love affair ending in suicide. It was only in his third novel, 'Sons and Lovers,' that he struck back to the memories of his childhood and the speech of his youth. His mother had died just before his first novel was published—the great disappointment of his life—and it was no doubt her memory that inspired the central figure of Mrs. Morel, who is, perhaps unnecessarily (for the purposes of the story), enriched with an education unusual in a collier's cottage. But once this little improbability is overcome, the fortunes of the Morel family are unrolled with uncommon skill and power. The father—drunken, sometimes violent—is not without features that make him human and natural; the mother is magnificently realised. The dialogue, now chiefly dialect, reproduces with astonishing verve and colour the forthright, picturesque colloquialism of the collier folk. Miriam, the farmer's daughter who discusses Michael Angelo and reads Baudelaire and Verlaine, is less real; and Clara, who plays profane love to Miriam's spirituality, is a fleshly woman —nothing more—but the children of the Morel household are astonishingly real and vivid. One is a little disappointed that the eldest, William, should be so suddenly cut off after winning our intense interest, but his brother Paul takes his place in the reader's as well as in his mother's heart. Her consuming affection for him, her jealousy of other women, her absolute devotion masking itself under ordinary sayings and doings, is a triumph of feeling and expression, and in the last crisis of her death the novelist finds for the stricken son the words of utter simplicity and sincerity—the cry of the heart.

'The Rainbow,' also cast in the Nottinghamshire border, this time among the farmers, has nothing like the grip the novelist had shown of the more familiar material in the colliery village; and it developed to excess the physical aspect of passion which had been dealt with, though only as an episode, in the greater novel. Lawrence's poetry shows that this is a part of his genius, and he uses it for artistic purposes; the effect is often unpleasant, but it is probably only in England that it would bring an author within the jurisdiction of the police court. 'The Rainbow' was destroyed by magisterial order.

The blow stopped for five years Lawrence's output of fiction. But in 1920 he came back with 'The Lost Girl,' which returns to a Nottinghamshire mining town, and begins with what Gissing called "stark realism in the sphere of the ignobly decent." The misfortunes of the heroine's father, who is an unsuccessful shopkeeper, are followed painstakingly for a hundred pages, and the general effect, if not, as Gissing said it would be, "intolerably tedious," is at least mildly dull. The author himself says on p. 95:—

"Now so far the story of Alvina is commonplace enough. It is more or less the story of thousands of girls. They all find work. It is the ordinary solution of everything. And if we were dealing with an ordinary girl we should have to continue mildly and dully down the long years of employment; or, at the best, marriage with some dull school-teacher or office-clerk."

But the author goes on to say:—

"There have been enough stories about ordinary people. . . . We detest ordinary people. We are in peril of our lives from them: and in peril of our souls too, for they would damn us one and all to the ordinary. Every individual should, by nature, have his extraordinary points."

Now the extraordinary point about Alvina is a smothered flame of passion, which breaks out to compel her to reject her commonplace suitors and to surrender herself before marriage to an Italian variety artiste, who takes her off to his native hills in the Abruzzi. Both the passionate and the picturesque sides of this theme are congenial to Lawrence, and he treats them with characteristic distinction, leaving Alvina at the end of the story alone in the wilds (her husband being called off to the War), and expecting the birth of her first child. It is a finely-told story, especially in the last hundred pages; in the centre of the book, the transition from the girl of English middle-class traditions to the woman who abandons herself to passion is difficult to manage, but when she has made up her mind to the man as her mate, the story moves more easily. There are few pages to distress the readers who dislike the intensity of Lawrence's concern with sex, and apart from these the novel has much to commend it to those likely to be attracted by the less exceptional phases of his genius.

'Women in Love' carries on the theme and some of the characters of 'The Rainbow'; it is chiefly of interest as a transition to the author's more philosophical view of sex, considered in relation to individuality. "Love," says the chief spokesman, "is one of the emotions like all the others . . . just part of human relationship, no more." But the philosophy is not closely interwoven with the story, and this makes the book hard reading. The principal characters are all excessively neurotic, over-sexed, and over-strained, and their continual analysis, conveyed mainly by dialogue, of their desires and impulses produces an impression of artificiality. The lover who says at a picnic to the lady he shortly afterwards marries, "When the stream of synthetic creation lapses, we find ourselves part of the inverse process, the blood of destructive creation," philosophizes too much and inopportunely, and most readers will take him for a bore as well as a prig. Lawrence had seized his new idea, but he had not yet succeeded in embodying it in the appropriate form of narrative fiction.

'Aaron's Rod,' the last of Lawrence's novels published at the time of writing, shows a very distinct growth in thought and style; the author has completely assimilated his material, and manages his dialogue easily and naturally, though it ranges from the humblest themes to the highest. The story begins in the familiar Midland mining district, where the hero is a check-weighman, and secretary to the Miners' Union for his colliery; but he is a man of very exceptional taste and talent for music and philosophy, exceptional not only in his position in life, but in any position. The opening chapters are still in the manner of Gissing, but after the hero has been emancipated from his family and his surroundings by his flight, first to London and then to Florence, the book is continued according to the prescription of Meredith, that the novel should be "fortified by philosophy"; Lawrence, however, imitates no predecessor, but is an independent artist, with a style and manner of his own. His theme is still sex, but sex as conceived in a very curious relation to individual character and society. For the author's new point of view, which has an obvious relation to his studies in psychological analysis, the hero is naturally the main exponent and example. Aaron deserted his wife, not because he was in love with another woman, or because he was not in love with his wife, but because at home his soul was not free. "Love was a battle in which each party strove for the mastery of the other's soul," and neither would give way. The author thus analyses and interprets his hero's impulse to flight in a passage introduced about midway in the book:—

"Born in him was a spirit which could not worship women: no, and would not. Could not and would not. It was not in him. In early days, he tried to pretend it was in him. But through his plaintive and homage-rendering love of a young husband was always, for the woman, discernible the arrogance of self-unyielding male. He never yielded himself: never. All his mad loving was only an effort. Afterwards, he was as devilishly unyielded as ever. And it was an instinct in her, that her man must yield to her, so that she should envelop him, yielding, in her all-beneficent love. She was quite sure that her love was all-beneficent. Of this no shadow of doubt. She was quite sure that the highest her man could ever know or ever reach was to be perfectly enveloped in her all-beneficent love. This was her idea of marriage. She held it not as an idea, but as a profound impulse and instinct: an instinct developed in her by the age in which she lived. All that was deepest and most sacred in her feeling centred in this belief."

The whole novel is a plea for the freeing of men from the dominance of woman exercised in and through love. Aaron realised as he meditates further on his own position and experience that "love, even in its intensest, was only an attribute of the human soul: one of its incomprehensible gestures. And to fling down the whole soul in one gesture of finality in love was as much a criminal suicide as to jump off a church tower or a mountain peak. Let a man give himself as much as he liked in love, to seven thousand extremities, he must never give himself *away*."

Lilly, the argumentative exponent of the individualistic side of this theory, says in the course of a long summing-up at the end of the book:—

"You *are* yourself and so be yourself. Stick to it and abide by it. Passion or no passion, ecstasy or no ecstasy, urge or no urge, there's no goal outside you, where you can consummate like an eagle flying into the sun, or a moth into a candle. There's no goal outside you—and there's no God outside you. No God, whom you can get to and rest in. None . . .

"There is only one thing, your own very self. So you'd better stick to it. You can't be any bigger than just yourself, so you needn't drag God in. You've got one job, and no more. There inside you lies your own very self, like a germinating egg, your precious Easter egg of your own soul. There it is, developing bit by bit, from one single egg-cell which you were at your conception in your mother's womb, on and on to the strange and peculiar complication in unity which never stops till you die—if then."

Naturally, Lilly, who is a journalistic vagabond, and Aaron, who wanders about Europe as an irresponsible flute-player, give no clue as to the way in which this remarkable theory of stark individualism is to be adjusted to the demands of life and of society. Much of the talk goes on among sophisticated, neurotic exiles in after-war

Florence, among whom, a reviewer observes, "very nearly all the women are as devoid of chastity as the men are of honour." The sensual pages in the book are few, but it is not one for callow youth or for the general reader, who will be bored with it long before he is shocked. But for the mature and detached mind there are pages of thrilling intellectual interest, which give hope that Lawrence, having freed himself from obsession with the physical side of sex, will develop into the great novelist we have been so long waiting for.

BIBLIOGRAPHY

HUGH WALPOLE

1909 'The Wooden Horse.'
1910 'Marmaduke at Forty.'
1911 'Mr. Perrin and Mr. Traill.'
1912 'The Prelude to Adventure.'
1913 'Fortitude.'
1914 'The Duchess of Wrexe.'
1915 'The Golden Scarecrow.'
1916 'The Dark Forest.'
1918 'The Green Mirror.'
1919 'The Secret City.'
     'Jeremy.'
1920 'The Captives.'
1921 'The Young Enchanted.'
1922 'Jeremy and Hamlet.'
     'The Cathedral.'

GILBERT CANNAN

1909 'Peter Homunculus.'
1910 'Devious Ways.'
1910–13 'John Christopher.' (Translation.)
1912 'Little Brother.'
1913 'Round the Corner.'
1914 'Old Mole.'
     'Old Mole's Novel.'
1915 'Young Earnest.'
1916 'Mendel.'
1917 'The Stucco House.'
1918 'Mummery.'
1919 'Pink Roses.'
1920 'Time and Eternity.'
     'Pugs and Peacocks.'
1922 'Sembal.'

331

COMPTON MACKENZIE

1907 'Poems.'
1911 'The Passionate Elopement.'
1912 'Carnival.'
1913 'Sinister Street,' Vol. 1.
1914 'Sinister Street,' Vol. 2.
1915 'Guy and Pauline.'
1918 'Sylvia Scarlett.'
      'Sylvia and Michael.'
1919 'Poor Relations.'
1920 'The Vanity Girl.'
      'Rich Relatives.'
1922 'The Altar Steps.'

D. H. LAWRENCE

1911 'The White Peacock.'
1912 'The Trespasser.'
1913 'Sons and Lovers.'
1914 'The Widowing of Mrs. Holroyd, a drama in three acts.'
      'The Prussian Officer and other stories.'
1915 'The Rainbow.'
1916 'Amores; Poems.'
      'Twilight in Italy' (Sketches of travel).
1920 'The Lost Girl.'
      'Touch and Go, A Play in Three Acts.'
1921 'Women in Love.'
      'Psychoanalysis and the Unconscious.'
      'Sea and Sardinia' (Sketches of travel).
1922 'Tortoises' (Poems).
      'Aaron's Rod.'
      'England, My England' (Short Stories and Sketches).

BOOKS OF GENERAL REFERENCE

William Archer, 'Poets of the Younger Generation,' 1902.

F. W. Chandler, 'Aspects of Modern Drama,' 1914.

W. L. Courtney, 'The Feminine Note in Fiction,' 1904.

T. H. Dickinson, 'The Contemporary Drama of England,' 1920.

Ashley Dukes, 'Modern Dramatists,' 1912.

John Freeman, 'The Moderns,' 1916.

Walter Lionel George, 'A Novelist on Novels,' 1918.

Douglas Goldring, 'Reputations. Essays in Criticism,' 1920.

E. E. Hale, 'Dramatists of To-day,' 1911.

Archibald Henderson, 'The Changing Drama,' 1914.

P. P. Howe, 'Dramatic Portraits,' 1913.

James Huneker, 'Iconoclasts: a Book of Dramatists,' 1905.

Holbrook Jackson, 'The Eighteen Nineties,' 1913.

Henry James, 'Notes on Novelists,' 1914.

Lionel Johnson, 'Reviews and Critical Papers,' 1921.

R. Brimley Johnson, 'Some Contemporary Novelists (Women),' 1920.

R. Brimley Johnson, 'Some Contemporary Novelists (Men),' 1922.

John McFarland Kennedy, 'English Literature 1880–1905,' 1912.

Ludwig Lewisohn, 'The Modern Drama,' 1915.

Percy Lubbock (Ed.), 'The Letters of Henry James,' 1920.

Percy Lubbock, 'The Craft of Fiction,' 1922.

G. H. Mair, 'Modern English Literature,' 1914.

J. M. Manly and Edith Rickert, 'Contemporary British Literature,' 1921.

Harold Monro, 'Some Contemporary Poets,' 1920.

C. E. Montague, 'Dramatic Values,' 1911.

B. Muddiman, 'The Men of the Nineties,' 1920.

J. Middleton Murry, 'Aspects of Literature,' 1920.

William Lyon Phelps, 'The Advance of the English Novel,' 1916.

William Lyon Phelps, 'The Advance of English Poetry in the Twentieth Century,' 1918.

William Lyon Phelps, 'The Twentieth Century Theatre,' 1918.

William Lyon Phelps, 'Essays on Modern Dramatists,' 1919.

Firmin Roz, 'Le Roman Anglais Contemporain,' 1912.

Dixon Scott, 'Men of Letters,' 1916.

R. A. Scott-James, 'Modernism and Romance,' 1908.

R. A. Scott-James, 'Personality in Literature,' 1913.

Edwin E. Slosson, 'Major Prophets of To-Day,' Boston, 1914.

Edwin E. Slosson, 'Six Major Prophets,' Boston, 1917.

Mary C. Sturgeon, 'Studies of Contemporary Poets,' 1916; revised edition, 1920.

A. B. Walkley, 'Drama and Life,' 1908.

Arthur Waugh, 'Tradition and Change,' 1919.

Harold Williams, 'Modern English Writers,' 1918.

Harold Williams, 'Outlines of Modern English Literature, 1890–1914,' 1920.

INDEX

Titles of Works are in single quotation marks.